The Politics of the Earth

The Politics of the Earth

Environmental Discourses

John S. Dryzek

OXFORD UNIVERSITY PRESS
1997

Oxford University Press, Great Clarendon Street, Oxford OX2 6DP

Oxford New York

Athens Auckland Bangkok Bogota Bombay
Buenos Aires Calcutta Cape Town Dar es Salaam
Delhi Florence Hong Kong Istanbul Karachi
Kuala Lumpur Madras Madrid Melbourne
Mexico City Nairobi Paris Singapore
Taipei Tokyo Toronto

and associated companies in
Berlin Ibadan

Oxford is a trade mark of Oxford University Press

Published in the United States
by Oxford University Press Inc., New York

British Library Cataloguing in Publication Data
Data available

Library of Congress Cataloging in Publication Data
Dryzek, John S., 1953–
The politics of the earth: environmental discourses / John Dryzek.
Includes bibliographical references and index.
1. Environmentalism.   2. Green movement.   3. Environmental policy.
I. Title.
GE195.D79   1997   363.7—dc21   97-7366
ISBN 0–19–878160–1
ISBN 0–19–878159–8 (Pbk.)

10 9 8 7 6 5 4 3 2 1

Typeset by Hope Services (Abingdon) Ltd.
Printed in Great Britain
on acid-free paper by
Bookcraft (Bath) Ltd
Midsomer Norton, Somerset

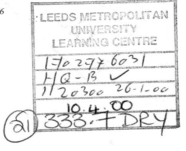

To Margaret

Preface

A lot has happened in the last three decades or so of environmental affairs. Environmental crisis arrived in the late 1960s, along with dire warnings about global shortages and ecological collapse. Since then, the Earth's population has increased by over 50 per cent. There have been spectacular nuclear accidents at Three Mile Island and Chernobyl, spectacular non-nuclear accidents at Bhopal in India and Prince William Sound in Alaska. Green parties have emerged as a significant electoral force in many countries. Mainstream environmental groups have developed massive memberships. Populist backlashes against environmentalism have flared. Global environmental issues relating to climate change and ozone layer depletion have come to the fore. We have had Earth Summits, Earth Days, environmental presidents, ecological sabotage, civil disobedience, legislation and regulation by the bookful, and movements for environmental justice, animal liberation, sustainable development, deep ecology, and "wise use."

The idea of this book is to make sense of all these developments. I do so by deploying the notion of environmental discourses. A discourse is a shared way of looking at the world. Its adherents will therefore use a particular kind of language when talking about events, which in turn rests on some common definitions, judgments, assumptions, and contentions. There turns out to be rather little in common between (say) partisans of a discourse believing in the unproblematical nature of uncontrolled economic growth and a radical green discourse seeking renewed harmony among humans and between humans and nature. The history of environmental affairs is largely a matter of the history of the discourses I survey, their rise and fall, their interactions and impacts. As it turns out, all these discourses are still with us, and none has fallen by the wayside (which itself says a lot about the increasing complexity of environmental affairs). I will recount their history, and assess their impact, strengths, and weaknesses as ways of dealing with environmental issues.

I have tried to approach these questions from a position of critical detachment, but at the end of the day I do have some strong positions of my own. I have left an explicit statement of these to the conclusion, under the heading of ecological democracy, though they do put in occasional earlier appearances.

This book began life on the 9th of September, 1994 at 12.45 pm, when Tim Barton of Oxford University Press suggested I write it, and since then he has proven himself a prince among editors. The deeper life of this project exists in years of environmental discourse with students, scholars, and activists. In eight years in Oregon I learned much from Joseph Boland, David Carruthers, Irene Diamond, Dan Goldrich, Jeff Land, Gerry Mackie, Michael McGinnis, Ronald Mitchell, Alan Moore, David Schlosberg, Stuart Shulman, Paul Thiers, and Michael Welsh. Australia has a lively community of ecopolitical and ecophilosophical folk, and it has been a pleasure getting to know them in the last year or two: notably, Tim Bonyhady, Mark Carden, Peter Christoff, David Downes, Robyn Eckersley, Nicholas Low, Freya Mathews, Val Plumwood, Cassandra Star, Richard Sylvan, Janna Thompson, and Ken Walker. Elsewhere, correspondents and conversationalists have included Terence Ball, Robert Bartlett, Gary Bryner, Margaret Clark, Tim Clark, Andrew Dobson, Frank Fischer, Robert Goodin, Adolf Gundersen, Bronwyn Hayward, Tim Hayward, Hans-Kristian Hernes, Susan Hunter, Michael Jacobs, William Lafferty, James Lester, Tim Luke, James Meadowcroft, Soon-Hong Moon, Arne Naess, Richard Norgaard, James O'Connor, Claus Offe, Robert Paehlke, Thomas Princen, Craig Rimmerman, Paul Wapner, Albert Weale, Douglas Wilson, Edward Woodhouse, Iris Young, and Oran Young. If I have left anyone out, the fault lies in my powers of recall. The particular shape taken by this book depends a lot on advice from Douglas Torgerson and Maarten Hajer. Thanks to people such as these, the environmental field is today alive, growing, and the site of some of the most interesting thinking in social science, philosophy, public policy, and practical politics, making a book like this so much easier to write.

In the preface to his classic *Risk Society*, Ulrich Beck says that he wrote most of it overlooking a picturesque lake, and that readers should imagine a lake in the background. I wrote most of this book overlooking a garbage dump; one day soon it will be a park.

J.S.D.

Northcote, Victoria, November, 1996

Contents

Detailed Contents

List of Boxes and Figures

Boxes

Figures

PART I
INTRODUCTION

1

Making Sense of Earth's Politics: A Discourse Approach

The Changing Terms of Environmental Politics

In the last four decades, the politics of the Earth has featured a large and growing range of issues. The initial concerns were with pollution, wilderness preservation, population growth, and depletion of natural resources. Over time, these concerns have been supplemented by worries about energy supply, animal rights, species extinction, global climate change, depletion of the ozone layer in the upper atmosphere, toxic wastes, the protection of whole ecosystems, and environmental justice (the distribution of environmental damage across ethnic groups and social classes). All these issues are interlaced with a whole range of moral and aesthetic questions about human livelihood, human attitudes, and our proper relation to other entities on the planet (occasionally even off it). Thus the whole environmental area is home to some heated debates and disputes, ranging from the details of the implementation of policy choices in particular localities, to the arguments of philosophers debating the appropriate ethical position to apply to environmental affairs in general.

The terms of these debates have changed substantially over time. Consider the following illustrations:

- Once areas of marshy land were called swamps. The only sensible thing to do with swamps was to drain them, so the land could be put to some useful purpose. Governments subsidized landowners to drain swamps. Today, we call these same areas wetlands, and governments have enacted legislation to protect their recognized value in providing habitat for wildlife, stabilization of ecosystems, and absorption of pollutants.

- In the nineteenth century, European colonization moved gradually westwards in North America. The United States government provided all kinds of incentives to tame the frontier. In the late twentieth century, the land at the edge of European settlement, which used to be called frontier and was there only to be subdued is now called wilderness, to be treasured and protected.

- Meanwhile, in Australia and New Zealand, European colonization was followed by the establishment of "Acclimatisation Societies" to introduce European flora and fauna to the Antipodes. These societies approached their task in a spirit of altruism and concern for the public good. Today, governments and citizens in these two countries devote massive effort to the protection of native plants, animals, and ecosystems, and to the extermination of exotic imported species that threaten these ecosystems—imports that were once cultivated so lovingly by the Acclimatisation Societies.

- What is a whale? Once whales were regarded as sources of food and other useful products such as oil and baleen. The idea that whales were sentient creatures with a right to exist and flourish free from human interference would have been laughable. Yet this view is now widely held, and indeed dominates the policies of many nations on the whaling issue.

- What are people? The idea that there is such a thing as "population" is a development no more than 200 years old. Population as an aggregate is something to be controlled and managed: that is, it is more than just "people." Given that once there was no such thing as population, the idea of population as a problem, still less population explosion, could not be conceptualized. The Pope, Islamic fundamentalists, and contemporary anti-environmentalists in the United States still resist conceptualizing population in these terms.

- What is the environment? The environment did not exist as a concept in politics and policy making in any country until the 1960s (though concern with particular aspects of what we now call the environment, such as open spaces, resource shortages, and pollution do of course pre-date the 1960s). Today, all countries have environmental legislation and government departments with environmental missions, and environmental problems are at the forefront of public attention.

- What is nature? Some radical environmentalists believe that any area modified by human activity is no longer worth caring about. In Edward Abbey's novel *The Monkey Wrench Gang*, one of the environmental heroes measures road distances in terms of six packs of beer, and having finished a can throws it out of the window. The litter is irrelevant, as it ends up in places that have already been destroyed by the construction of a road. Such attitudes horrify more tender-minded environmentalists.

- What, then, is wilderness? One widely held definition is that wilderness consists of land that remains untouched by human extractive activity. But what about the indigenous peoples who have long populated such areas, and in many cases shaped the landscape? And can there be such a thing as wilderness restoration in lands damaged by industrial and agricultural activity?

- What is the Earth? We have long known that it is a planet, but the idea that it might be a finite planet with limited capacities to support human life has only really received widespread attention since the late 1960s. Not coincidentally, this was when the Earth was first photographed from space. Since the early 1980s, there has also been a sustained attack on the idea that the Earth is in any sense finite, especially in the United States.

The moral of these examples is that the way we think about basic concepts concerning the environment can change quite dramatically over time, and this has consequences for the politics and policies that occur in regard to environmental issues. The most basic consequence (to which the last example of the finite Earth points) is that we now have a politics of the Earth, whereas once we did not. If the environment itself were not conceptualized—and it was not, prior to the 1960s—then a book about environmental politics could not be written. Today, of course, we not only have an environment, but most of the important things that happen to it are the subject matter of politics, and occasionally the target of public policy.

Some of the examples I have adduced might seem to suggest that we have a clear trajectory pointing in the direction of environmental enlightenment; it is just a matter of humanity becoming more sensitive or aware as time goes on, and escaping from past misconceptions and ignorance. Now, I happen to believe in progress (which, sadly, sets me apart from many of my colleagues in the social sciences and humanities in contemporary universities). Still, it would be a mistake to think of the history of environmental affairs in these terms. What we see instead is that these matters are subject to continuing dispute between people who think about environmental affairs in sharply different ways. Some people deny that environmental issues matter at all (how else could President Ronald Reagan have once said that "ninety per cent of pollution is caused by trees"?). Consider the following examples of environmental conflicts:

- Cairo in 1994 played host to the United Nations Conference on Population and Development. The basic numbers on global human population are clear enough and not in dispute: human numbers are increasing at a rapid rate. Whether or not these numbers mean anything is in sharp dispute. To some present, the whole reason for such a conference is to explore ways to control populations in order to prevent the environmental collapse that excessive human pressure on the earth's ecosystems will cause, and in many cases is already causing. To others present, such as representatives of the Vatican, Islamic countries, ecofeminists, and US conservatives, matters look very different. To the Catholics and Islamists, population control means only birth control and is therefore intrinsically evil. To ecofeminists, population control means only the control of women's fertility by the male power structure. To some US conservatives, especially those with fond memories of the Reagan years, population growth is a good thing, as more people means more human problem-solvers, producing more benefits for humanity in many ways; population control looks like socialism. How can all these individuals look at the world in such different ways? Who is right? In the light of these competing viewpoints, how should we approach global population issues?

- The initial growth of the nuclear industry in the 1950s and 1960s took place in secret, away from public scrutiny and concern. By the 1980s, proposals for new nuclear installations were typically the subject of extensive public inquiries, at least in the developed liberal democracies. In Austria, Sweden, and the Netherlands broad national discussions took place in the late 1970s about the whole future of nuclear power, and the kind of society it helped construct. In Britain, inquiries presided over by judges used legalistic rules concerning the admissibility of evidence and argument. Inquiries were focused narrowly on safety issues. It was assumed that the economic benefits of any proposal were positive. Objectors were not allowed to introduce economic evidence against the proposal, still less arguments about whether nuclear power belongs in a free society, or is consistent with environmental values. The most notorious British nuclear plant is at Windscale/Sellafield on the Irish Sea. A pipeline carries nuclear waste material into the Irish Sea. In 1990 a team of Greenpeace divers placed a symbolic plug in the end of the pipeline. Greenpeace was fined £50,000, and admonished by the judge for being so arrogant as to put their special interests above the law. Why does Britain, in contrast to more progressive European countries, put "the law" on a pedestal above ecological concerns, rather than trying to integrate ecological principles into the law? Why does "the law" in Britain consistently serve the interests of the nuclear-industrial complex, and fail to accommodate the kinds of ecological concerns that motivate a group like Greenpeace?

- In the United States and Canada the last decade or more has seen intense conflict over the logging of remnant old growth forests, especially in the Pacific Northwest. In the United States, logging has been impeded, but by no means halted, by the presence of the spotted owl, an endangered species whose only habitat is the old growth forest. Why is there legislation to protect a species such as the spotted owl (the Endangered Species Act), but no legislation to protect ecosystems such as the forest itself? The conflict between companies and logging communities on the one hand and environmentalists on the other is intense and intractable. Attempts to solve the conflict through the courts, through legislation, and through consensus-seeking exercises (such as the "timber summit" sponsored by and attended by President Clinton in 1993) have all failed. Why is the conflict so intractable? Why do timber workers support logging of old growth to exhaustion by the timber companies instead of sustainable forestry, which would guarantee their jobs and their incomes in the longer term? Can the simultaneous pursuit of environmental and economic values which sustainable forestry connotes actually be achieved in practice? Would this pursuit be secured, as some economists have suggested, by dividing the National Forests into chunks of land and selling each chunk to the highest bidder? Why are such proposals, even when their economic logic seems faultless, resisted so strenuously by both environmentalists and loggers?

In all these conflicts, the different sides seem to interpret the issues at hand in very different ways. At any particular time, the way the issue is dealt with depends largely (though not completely) on the balance of these competing perspectives. In this book I intend making sense of the last thirty years or so of environmental concern by mapping these perspectives. But why do these different perspectives exist? Why do debates between partisans of different perspectives sometimes seem so intractable, as some of the examples I have discussed indicate?

A Discourse Approach

Environmental issues do not present themselves to us in well-defined boxes labelled radiation, national park, pandas, coral reefs, rainforest, heavy metal pollution, and the like. Instead, they are interconnected in all kinds of ways. For example, issues of global climate change due to buildup of carbon dioxide in the atmosphere from burning fossil fuels relate to air pollution in more local contexts, and so to issues of transportation policy.[1] These issues also

[1] For example, in my own city of Melbourne, the main obstacle to the construction of a freeway network proposed by the state government was the possibility that the Australian federal government would invoke its obligations resulting from signing international agreements relating to the control of greenhouse gases in order to require an environmental impact statement for the project.

relate to destruction of the ecosystems (such as tropical forests) which act as carbon sinks, absorbing carbon dioxide from the atmosphere; and to issues of fossil fuel reliance and exhaustion; and so to problems related to alternative sources of energy such as nuclear power. Thus environmental problems tend to be interconnected and multi-dimensional; they are, in a word, complex. Complexity refers to the number and variety of elements and interactions in the environment of a decision system. When human decision systems (be they individuals, or collective bodies such as governments) confront environmental problems, they are confronted with two orders of complexity. Ecosystems are complex, and our knowledge of them is limited, as the biological scientists who study them are the first to admit. Human social systems are complex too, which is why there is so much work for the ever-growing number of social scientists who study them. Environmental problems by definition are found at the intersection of ecosystems and human social systems, so one should expect them to be doubly complex.

The more complex a situation, the larger is the number of plausible perspectives upon it—because the harder it is to prove any one of them wrong in any simple terms. Thus the proliferation of perspectives on environmental problems that has accompanied the development and diversification of environmental concern since the 1960s should come as no surprise. It is my intention here to make sense of this proliferation. I shall do so be deploying the notion of "discourse."

A discourse is a shared way of apprehending the world. Embedded in language, it enables those who subscribe to it to interpret bits of information and put them together into coherent stories or accounts. Each discourse rests on assumptions, judgments, and contentions that provide the basic terms for analysis, debates, agreements, and disagreements, in the environmental area no less than elsewhere. Indeed, if such shared terms did not exist, it would be hard to imagine problem-solving in this area at all, as we would have to return to first principles continually. The way a discourse views the world is not always easily comprehended by those who subscribe to other discourses. However, as I will show, complete rupture or discontinuity across discourses is rare, such that interchange across discourse boundaries can occur, however difficult it may sometimes prove.

Now, trying to make sense of the Earth's politics through reference to discourses is not the only way of going about the task. Other analysts' treatments are organized differently. Some look at the institutions (markets, government bureaucracies, legal systems, etc.) that have been developed for handling environmental issues.[2] Some look at the policies that governments

---

[2] For my own contribution to this genre, see Dryzek, 1987.

have pursued. Some care little about the details of real-world practices, focusing instead on the political philosophies that can be applied in environmental affairs. Some look only at particular case studies of environmental issues. In fact, I shall have plenty to say about institutions, policies, political philosophies, and case studies, for all owe much to the discourses in their vicinity.

This inquiry rests on the contention that language matters, that the way we construct, interpret, discuss, and analyze environmental problems has all kinds of consequences. My intent is to lay out the basic structure of the discourses that have dominated recent environmental politics, and present their history, conflicts, and transformations. I intend to produce something more than just an account of environmentalism. Environmental discourse is broader than that, extending to those who do not consider themselves environmentalists, but either choose or find themselves in positions where they are handling environmental issues, be it as politicians, bureaucrats, corporate executives, lawyers, journalists, or citizens. Environmental discourse even extends to those who consider themselves hostile to environmentalism. My geographic coverage for the most part encompasses Europe, North America, Australasia, and the global arena; though sometimes it is appropriate to look elsewhere.

Some recent studies in this idiom examine discourse carefully in the context of a particular issue. That such an approach is productive is demonstrated in recent studies by Maarten Hajer of transformations in discourse on acid rain in Britain and the Netherlands in the late 1980s and early 1990s (Hajer, 1995), and by Karen Litfin of changing international discourse about global ozone layer depletion in the 1980s (Litfin, 1994). However, there is room for breadth as well as depth in analysing environmental discourse, for looking at the big picture rather than the details. My own accounts will lack the richness of Hajer and Litfin inasmuch as I cannot always say exactly who said what and why behind which closed doors to whom else about a particular point, and how the other responded.

In offering a view of a much bigger territory, I will be guided by some analytical devices and distinctions (to be introduced shortly) that give me some confidence in taking very large cuts at large and complex discursive terrain. I seek vindication only in the plausibility of the stories I tell. These stories are backed by my own twenty years of working and teaching in the environmental field, but others might still carve up the territory somewhat differently. For example, Andrew Dobson (1990) makes a threefold distinction between old-fashioned conservationism, reform environmentalism, and radical ecologism. Robyn Eckersley (1992) thinks that the key difference is between anthropocentric (human-centered) and ecocentric perspectives.

Relatedly, in histories of US environmentalism, it is standard practice to distinguish between two traditions, heirs respectively to the anthropocentric rational resource management advocated by the US Forest Service's first chief forester Gifford Pinchot and the deeper respect for nature propounded by Sierra Club founder John Muir (see, for example, Taylor, 1992). To Martin Lewis (1992), the only distinction that makes sense is between moderates and extremists, or "Promethean" and "Arcadian" environmentalists as he styles them (I will use the term "Promethean" somewhat differently than Lewis). Less worthy of serious attention, former US Secretary of the Interior James Watt distinguished between environmentalists and Americans. I have already noted that environmental issues are complex, and so afford plenty of scope for alternative perspectives on them.

Discourse is important, and conditions the way we define, interpret, and address environmental affairs. This should not be taken to mean that there is only discourse when it comes to environmental problems. Many postmodernists might believe that. Indeed, the idea that people look at the world in fragmented and radically different ways pretty much defines postmodernism. Certainly it is fashionable in these circles to point to the arbitrary and specific ways we apprehend the world (for an application to environmental affairs, see Bennett and Chaloupka, 1993). Yet just because something is socially interpreted does not mean it is unreal. Pollution does cause illness, species do become extinct, ecosystems cannot absorb stress indefinitely, tropical forests are disappearing. But people can make very different things of these phenomena and—especially—their interconnections, providing plenty of grist for political dispute. Sometimes particular constructions can be exposed as thoroughly misguided—as, for example, when automobile company executives in the 1950s dismissed the possibility of smog in cities such as Los Angeles by claiming that car exhaust emissions were simply "absorbed" by the atmosphere. More often, it is hard to prove these constructions right or wrong in any straightforward way. But one might say the same about scientific worldviews, political ideologies, or governmental constitutions. In the analysis of environmental discourse no less than in these other cases, it is still possible to engage in rational, critical, comparative judgment, to apply evidence and argument, and to hope that in so doing we can correct some errors, and so move toward a better overall understanding of environmental issues and problems.[3]

Aside from the reality of ecological problems, there is another dimension which a one-sided emphasis on discourse can miss: this is the dimension of

[3] As Litfin puts it, it is possible to subscribe to both a hermeneutic epistemology (i.e. an interpretive philosophy of inquiry) and a realist ontology (i.e. a commitment to the actual existence of problems) (1994: 26–7, 50).

interest and power. Again, discourse is not all that matters, and powerful actors who see established or emerging discourses as threatening their vital interests can attempt to override developments at the level of discourse. For example, Hajer (1995) argues that in the Netherlands, the discourse of ecological modernization achieved dominance in the late 1980s. The basic idea of ecological modernization is that environmental conservation is good for business profitability; I will discuss it at length in Chapter 8. However, the ascendancy of ecological modernization was not always easily translated into Dutch policy practice, in part because established state and corporate actors resisted. These actors may have conceded at the level of discourse, but their particular interests subsequently led them to stick to more established policy practices.

Perhaps more often than simply resisting environmental values, recalcitrant actors will try to cloak themselves in the language of environmentalism. The public relations departments of multinational corporations are especially good at this. According to *O'Dwyers PR Services*, a major public relations journal, the environment is "the life and death PR battle of the 1990s" (*The Guardian*, London, 18 Sept. 1996). In the United States, the Weyerhauser Corporation advertises itself as "the tree growing company." At one level this is true enough: Weyerhauser plants and grows a lot of trees. But the trees it plants are in the form of single-species plantations, managed with the use of herbicides and pesticides. Many of the trees it cuts down are in complex, multi-species old growth forests, which take hundreds of years to mature. Corporate front groups often have names that connote environmental concern. But the real intent of the Global Climate Coalition, for example, is to put a spin on climate issues that is conducive to the short-term interests of oil companies (see Rowell, 1996).

Alternatively, such recalcitrant actors can sponsor other discourses of environmental concern more conducive to their own interests. Perhaps this is why so many of them find the idea of "sustainable development" and its potential commitment to continued economic growth so attractive (as we will see in Chapter 7). Discourse and power can be interconnected in all kinds of ways, which I will attempt to bring out.[4]

Beyond the simple exercise of political power by interested parties, another constraint acts to limit the influence of discourse. Governments in capitalist economies have to perform a number of basic functions whether they want to or not, irrespective of any discourses which may have captivated government officials (see Dryzek, 1992a). These imperatives include, first

---

[4] Michel Foucault, among others, would deny that this distinction between power and discourse makes sense, on the grounds that discourse *is* the operation of power. See, for example, Foucault (1980).

and foremost, ensuring continued economic growth. If governments pursue environmental policies that corporations do not like, then corporations can stop investing. The increasing mobility of capital and finance across national boundaries intensifies this pressure, because businesses can easily threaten to transfer their operations to other countries with less stringent environmental policies and practices. Just South of the United States–Mexico border is a zone of *maquiladora* industries, producing for US markets, but without having to worry about US anti-pollution laws, still less about Mexican laws that look good on paper but are never enforced. Thus the first task of governments, in environmental policy and everything else, is to keep actual and potential corporate investors happy. If governments make investors unhappy—for example, through enacting tough anti-pollution policy—then they are punished by disinvestment, which in turn means recession, unpopularity in the eyes of voters, and falling tax revenues. Again, the relative influence of discourse and this kind of economic constraint on government policies merits investigation in particular cases.

Classifying the Main Environmental Discourses

Environmental discourse begins in industrial society, and so has to position itself in the context of the long-dominant discourse of industrial society, which we can call industrialism. Industrialism may be characterized in terms of its overarching commitment to growth in the quantity of goods and services produced and to the material well-being which that growth brings. Industrial societies have of course featured many competing ideologies, such as liberalism, conservatism, socialism, Marxism, and fascism. But whatever their differences, all these ideologies are committed to industrialism. Indeed, from an environmental perspective they can all look like variations on the theme of industrialism. This commonality might surprise their adherents, who are far more conscious of their ideological differences than of their industrialist commonalities. But all these ideologies long ignored or suppressed environmental concern. If what we now call environmental issues were thought about at all, it was often in terms of inputs to industrial processes. For example, rational use of such inputs was the main concern of the Conservation Movement founded at the beginning of the twentieth century in the United States, whose key figure was Gifford Pinchot.[5] This movement did not want to preserve the environment for aesthetic reasons, or for

---

[5] True, a few romantics such as John Muir extolled wilderness—but they did so in rejection of industrial society.

the sake of human health. Instead, the Conservation Movement sought only to ensure that resources such as minerals, timber, and fish were used wisely and not squandered, so that there would always be plenty of them to support a growing industrial economy.

Environmental discourse cannot therefore simply take the terms of industrialism as given, but must depart from these terms. This departure can be reformist or it can be radical; and this distinction forms one dimension for categorizing environmental discourses.

A second dimension would take note of the fact that departures from industrialism can be either prosaic or imaginative. Prosaic departures take the political-economic chessboard set by industrial society as pretty much given. On that chessboard, environmental problems are seen mainly in terms of troubles encountered by the established industrial political economy. They require action, but they do not point to a new kind of society. The action in question can be quite dramatic and radical. As we will see, there are those who believe that economic growth must be reined in, if not brought to a halt entirely, in order to respond effectively to environmental problems. But the measures endorsed or proposed by these people are essentially those which have been defined by and in industrialism. For example, those who would curb economic growth normally propose that this be done by strong central administration informed by scientific expertise—a quintessentially industrialist instrument.

In contrast, imaginative departures seek to redefine the chessboard. Notably, environmental problems are seen as opportunities rather than troubles. Imaginative redefinition of the chessboard may dissolve old dilemmas, treating environmental concerns not in opposition to economic ones, but potentially in harmony. The environment is brought into the heart of society and its cultural, moral, and economic systems, rather than being seen as a source of difficulties standing outside these systems. The thinking is imaginative, but the degree of change sought can be small and reformist, or large and radical. As we shall see, imaginative reformist ways of rendering the basic political-economic structure bequeathed by industrial society capable of coping with environmental issues may be found. On the other hand, imaginative radical changes can also be envisaged, requiring wholesale transformation of this political-economic structure. Combining these two dimensions—reformist versus radical and prosaic versus imaginative—produces four cells, as indicated in Box 1.1.

Environmental Problem Solving is defined by taking the political-economic *status quo* as given but in need of adjustment to cope with environmental problems, especially via public policy. Such adjustment might take the form of extension of the pragmatic problem-solving capacities of liberal

BOX 1.1. CLASSIFYING ENVIRONMENTAL DISCOURSES		
	Reformist	Radical
Prosaic	Problem Solving	Survivalism
Imaginative	Sustainability	Green Radicalism

democratic governments by facilitating a variety of environmentalist inputs to them; or of markets, by putting price tags on environmental harms and benefits; or of the administrative state, by institutionalizing environmental concern and expertise in its operating procedures. Within the overall discourse of environmental problem solving there may be substantial disagreement as to which of these forms is appropriate. So, for example, a debate between proponents of administrative regulation and market-type incentive mechanisms for pollution control has been under way since the 1970s, and shows few signs of letting up.

Survivalism is the discourse popularized in the early 1970s by the efforts of the Club of Rome (which I will discuss in the next chapter) and others, still retaining many believers. The basic idea is that continued economic and population growth will eventually hit limits set by the Earth's stock of natural resources and the capacity of its ecosystems to support human agricultural and industrial activity. The limits discourse is radical because it seeks a wholesale redistribution of power within the industrial political economy, and a wholesale reorientation away from perpetual economic growth. It is prosaic because it can see solutions only in terms of the options set by industrialism, notably, greater control of existing systems by administrators, scientists, and other responsible élites.

Sustainability begins in earnest in the 1980s, and is defined by imaginative attempts to dissolve the conflicts between environmental and economic values that energize the discourses of problem solving and limits. The concepts of growth and development are redefined in ways which render obsolete the simple projections of the limits discourse. There is still no consensus on the exact meaning of sustainability; but sustainability is the axis around which discussion occurs, and limits are nowhere to be seen. Without the imagery of apocalypse that defines the limits discourse, there is no inbuilt radicalism to the discourse. The era of sustainability begins in earnest with the publication of the Brundtland Report in 1987 (World Commission on Environment and Development, 1987). More recently, ideas about ecological modernization, seeing economic growth and environmental protection as essentially complementary, have arisen in Europe.

Green Radicalism is both radical and imaginative. Its adherents reject the basic structure of industrial society and the way the environment is conceptualized therein in favor of a variety of quite different alternative interpretations of humans, their society, and their place in the world. Given its radicalism and imagination, it is not surprising that green radicalism features deep intramural divisions—to which I shall attend. In the United States, social ecologists with a pastoral vision and a concern for social justice debate with deep ecologists, who prefer landscapes without humans. In Germany, Green *Fundis* eventually lost a struggle with Green *Realos* over tactical questions about action in the streets versus action in parliament. Everywhere, green romantics disagree with green rationalists, proponents of the rights of individual creatures disagree with more holistic thinkers, and advocates of green lifestyles disagree with those who prefer to stress green politics. These debates are lively and persistent; but the disputants have far more in common with each other in terms of basic dispositions, assumptions, and capabilities than they do with either industrialism or with the three competing discourses of environmental concern just introduced.

These, then, are the four basic environmental discourses, and I will organize the chapters that follow according to how they fit with these four categories. All four reject industrialism; but all four engage with the discourse of industrialism—if only to distance themselves from it. And this is why their engagement with industrialism and its defenders is often more pronounced than their engagement with each other.

Questions to Ask about Discourses

So far I have identified the four basic discourses in fairly general terms. But in order to see why and how these discourses have developed, and to what effect, it is necessary to pin down their content more precisely. This I shall do in the chapters that follow. To this end, let me now develop a set of questions for the analysis of discourses.[6]

Discourses enable stories to be told; in fact, the title of a discourse can be an abbreviated story line (the concept of environmental story lines is employed by Hajer, 1995). To refer back to the four discourses just enumerated, limits or survivalism connotes a story about the need to curb ever-

[6] This checklist extends and modifies a scheme I developed in Dryzek (1988) in a non-environmental context.

growing human demands on the life-support capacities of natural systems. Problem solving connotes a different story—indeed, can subsume a number of different stories—about the unpleasant side-effects of particular economic activities requiring piecemeal remedies. Each discourse constructs stories from the following elements:

1. Basic Entities Whose Existence is Recognized or Constructed

Technically, this is what is meant by the "ontology" of a discourse. Different discourses see different things in the world. Some discourses recognize the existence of ecosystems, others have no concept of natural systems at all, seeing nature only in terms of brute matter. At least one other entertains the idea that the global ecosystem is a self-correcting entity with something like intelligence. This is the idea of Gaia, which I will address in my analysis of Green radicalism. Some discourses organize their analyses around rational, egoistic human beings; others deal with a variety of human motivations; others still recognize human beings only in their aggregates such as states and populations. Most believe it is fruitful to deal with "humans" as a category, a few that it is necessary to break down on the basis of gender. Some assume governments and their actions matter; others believe it is the human spirit that is crucial.

2. Assumptions about Natural Relationships

All discourses embody notions of what is natural in the relationships between different entities. Some see competition, be it between human beings in markets or between creatures locked in Darwinian struggle, as natural. Others see cooperation as the essence of both human social systems and natural systems. Hierarchies based on gender, expertise, political power, species, ecological sensibility, intellect, legal status, race, and wealth are variously assumed in different discourses; as are their corresponding equalities.

3. Agents and their Motives

Story lines require actors, or agents. These actors can be individuals or collectivities. They are mostly human, but can be nonhuman. In one discourse we may find benign and public-spirited expert administrators. Another discourse might portray the same people as selfish bureaucrats. Still others might ignore the presence of government officials altogether. Many other kinds of agents and motives put in appearances. They include enlightened élites, rational consumers, ignorant and short-sighted populations, virtuous ordinary citizens, a Gaia that may be tough and forgiving or fragile and punishing, among others.

4. KEY METAPHORS AND OTHER RHETORICAL DEVICES

Most story lines, in the environmental arena no less than elsewhere, depend crucially on metaphor. Key metaphors that have figured in environmental discourse include:

- spaceships (the idea of "spaceship earth");
- the grazing commons of a medieval village ("the tragedy of the commons");
- machines (nature is like a machine that can be reassembled to better meet human needs);
- organisms (nature is a complex organism that grows and develops);
- human intelligence (ascribed to non-human entities such as ecosystems);
- war (against nature);
- goddesses (treating nature in benign female form, and not just as Mother Nature).

Metaphors are rhetorical devices, deployed to convince listeners or readers by putting a situation in a particular light. Many other devices are available to perform the same tasks. These include appeal to widely accepted practices or institutions, such as established rights, freedoms, constitutions, and cultural traditions. For example, the rights of species, animals, or natural objects can be justified through reference to the long-established array of individual human rights in liberal societies. Appeals can be made to deeper pasts, such as pastoral or even primeval idylls, as a way to criticize the industrial present. The negative and discredited can be accentuated as well as the positive and treasured. For example, it is possible to collect horror stories about government mistakes on environmental issues, and sprinkle these horror stories into arguments. On the other hand, some discourses collect and accentuate success stories.

This completes my checklist of items for the scrutiny and analysis of discourses. The items are summarized in Box 1.2. If my discussion of each element has been brief, matters should become clearer when I deploy this checklist in subsequent chapters in order to capture the various discourses

Box 1.2. **CHECKLIST OF ELEMENTS FOR THE ANALYSIS OF DISCOURSES**

1. Basic entities recognized or constructed
2. Assumptions about natural relationships
3. Agents and their motives
4. Key metaphors and other rhetorical devices

more precisely. Beyond capturing the essence of the various discourses and their subdivisions, it is of course important to determine what difference each of them makes. I have already asserted that the language we use in addressing environmental affairs does make a difference, but this needs to be demonstrated for particular discourses, rather than just asserted as a general point.

The Differences that Discourses Make

With this need to demonstrate the implications of different discourses in mind, I will take a look at the history as well as the content of each discourse. As I noted earlier, this history can generally be traced back to some aspect of industrialism—if only as a rejection of that aspect. With time, environmental discourses develop, crystallize, bifurcate, and (perhaps someday) dissolve. A crucial part of this history consists of the kind of politics surrounding, shaping, and shaped by the discourse. In some cases the politics might be that of a social movement or political party; in other cases, that of governmental commissions and intergovernmental negotiations; in others, that of administrative control; in others, élite bargaining; in others, rationalistic policy design. Sometimes there will be little in the way of politics at all, as, for example, in the case of "lifestyle" greens. Sometimes the politics may be local, sometimes national, sometimes transnational, sometimes global.

The impact of a discourse can often be felt in the policies of governments or intergovernmental bodies, and in institutional structure. For example, the flurry of environmental legislation enacted in many industrialized countries around 1970 mostly reflected a discourse of administrative rationalism (a sub-category of what I have defined as problem solving). Since 1970, problem-solving discourse has also been embodied in a number of institutional innovations that extend the openness and reach of liberal democratic control of environmental affairs (in the form of devices such as public inquiries and various procedures for consensual dispute resolution). Beyond affecting institutions, discourses can become embodied in institutions. When this happens, discourses constitute the informal understandings that provide the context for social interaction, on a par with formal institutional rules. Or to put it slightly differently, discourses can constitute institutional software while formal rules constitute institutional hardware. Sometimes, though, discourses do not have direct effects on the policies or institutions of governments, but take effect elsewhere. For example, green radicalism has helped some individuals and communities to distance themselves from both government and corporate capitalism in putative attempts to create an alternative political economy relying on self-sufficiency.

To assess more fully the worth and impact of a discourse requires attention to its critics as well as its adherents. Sometimes adherents of different discourses will ignore and dismiss rather than engage one another. Nevertheless, some dispute does indeed occur across the boundaries of different discourses. Most frequently, this occurs between the environmental discourse in question and the older discourse of industrialism. Given that each of the four categories of discourse I have identified has its roots in either modification or conscious rejection of industrialism, this is not too surprising. Occasionally, debate is engaged between the problem solving, limits, sustainability, and green radical discourses. If such engagement is infrequent, that is mostly a matter of these four discourses viewing issues and problems in such different ways that little interchange across their boundaries can occur. One goal of this book is to promote such interchange.

Attention to the arguments of critics will facilitate identification of flaws in the discourse. Such identification will also be helped by attention to experience of the practical implications of the discourse, in politics, policies, institutions, and beyond. The tools of discourse analysis which I have enumerated enable further critical analysis of the promise and peril attached to each discourse in its contribution to environmental debate, analysis, and action. It may even turn out that there are some complementarities between different discourses, rather than simple rivalry.

The set of questions I will ask in order to assess the impact, plausibility, and attractiveness of each discourse is summarized in Box 1.3.

Box 1.3. **Checklist of Items for Assessing the Effects of Discourses**

---

1. Politics associated with the discourse
2. Effect on policies of governments
3. Effect on institutions
4. Arguments of critics
5. Flaws revealed by evidence and argument

The Uses of Discourse Analysis

As should be clear by now, my intent is to advance analysis in environmental affairs by promoting critical comparative scrutiny of competing discourses of environmental concern. This intent distances me from some others who have developed and deployed discourse analysis.

The concept of discourse in the sense I am using it owes much to the efforts of Michel Foucault (for example, 1980), who revealed the content and history of discourses about illness, sex, madness, criminality, government, and so forth. Foucauldians are generally committed to the idea that individuals are for the most part subject to the discourses in which they move, and so seldom able to step back and make comparative assessments and choices across different discourses. It should be evident that I disagree. Discourses are powerful, but they are not impenetrable (as Foucault and his readers have themselves inadvertently demonstrated in their own exposé of the history of various discourses; they at least have escaped from the prison of particular discourses!). Foucault and his followers also often portray discourses in hegemonic terms, meaning that one single discourse is typically dominant in any time and place, conditioning not just agreement but also the terms of dispute. In contrast, I believe that variety is as likely as hegemony. The environmental arena reveals that for long the discourse of industrialism was indeed hegemonic, to the extent that "the environment" was hardly conceptualized prior to the 1960s. However, this hegemony eventually began to disintegrate, yielding the range of environmental discourses now observable. While in its totality environmentalism does challenge industrialism, it does not constitute a unified counter discourse to industrialism. Rather, environmentalism is composed of a variety of discourses, sometimes complementing one another, but often competing. With the necessary preliminaries over, it is to a mapping of these discourses and their consequences that I now turn.

Part II

Global Limits and their Denial

Environmental issues can be as local as the dog droppings on the grass in front of my house, or as global as the greenhouse effect. When environmental issues made their first dramatic leap to the top of the political agenda in so many countries in the late 1960s, it was the global issue which really captured the public attention. Not coincidentally, this was also the first time the Earth was photographed from space, and a beautiful, fragile place it looked. For the first time in human history the Earth could be conceptualized readily as a finite planet, and for the first time a true politics of planet Earth became conceivable. Environmental problems were soon cast in terms of threats to the capacity of this planet to support life—especially human life.

The threats in question involved degradation of the global environment through pollution, and exhaustion of the Earth's natural resources (fossil fuels, minerals, fisheries, forests, and croplands). Urgency came from population explosion and economic growth. Exponential growth in both human numbers and their level of economic activity meant that there was no time to lose, for humanity seemed to be heading for the limits at an ever-increasing pace. Hitting these limits would mean global environmental disaster, accompanied by a crash in human populations.

This discourse of limits and survival was given a major boost by the Club of Rome, an international organization composed of industrialists, politicians, and academics. The Club's most famous product was a set of computer-generated projections of the global future published in 1972 in the international best seller *The Limits to Growth*. These projections showed in quite precise graphical terms that if humanity continued on its profligate course then it had at the very most a century before disaster would strike on a scale unparalleled in human history. Not surprisingly, there were many calls for radical action to stop this headlong rush to destruction; though the survivalists' political repertoire turned out to consist mainly of some tried-and-tested practices, especially strong governmental control.

Survivalism met with an immediate counterattack from defenders of the established industrial economy, whose taken-for-granted order of things survivalism had challenged. These defenders argued that humans are characterized by unlimited ingenuity, symbolized in Greek mythology by the progress made possible by the theft of fire from the gods by Prometheus. Six Prometheans asserted that the Earth was in truth unlimited; that as soon as one resource threatened to run out, ingenious people would develop a substitute. This had always happened in the past, and it would continue to happen in the future. The Promethean reaction gathered speed in the 1980s, for it fit quite well with the ideological climate of the Reagan years in the United States.

The dispute between the two camps continues, and neither shows any side of conceding. Yet it matters crucially which side is right. If the Second Prometheans are correct, then not only is survivalism wrong, but environmentalism of any kind simply loses its urgency. So: who is right?

2

Looming Tragedy: Survivalism

The Origins of Survivalism

Population biologists and ecologists have long deployed the concept of "carrying capacity"—essentially, the maximum population of a given species that an ecosystem can support in perpetuity. According to the population biologist and survivalist Garrett Hardin, the ecologist's Eleventh Commandment is "Though shalt not transgress the carrying capacity" (1993: 207). When the population of a species grows to the point where carrying capacity is exceeded, then the ecosystem is degraded, the population crashes, recovering only if and when natural processes restore the ecosystem to its previous capacity to support the species. Such crashes are readily observable in relatively simple ecosystems, for example when large herbivores such as deer are introduced to environments with no predators. Their populations soon explode to the point where the food supply is exhausted.

When population biologists turn to human affairs they see identical possibilities (see especially Catton, 1980). Historical examples of human transgression of carrying capacity are readily observable in once-fertile deserts in North Africa and the Middle East and in the denuded landscapes of the Mediterranean littoral. The concept of carrying capacity has to be adjusted downward inasmuch as quality rather than quantity of human lives becomes an issue—obviously an ecosystem can support more humans at subsistence level than it can with any greater quality of human life. The waters are muddied still further when it comes to contemporary human populations, because trade and aid mean that human societies can escape the constraints imposed by the carrying capacities of geographically bounded ecosystems. For example, biologists note that the carrying capacity of East African ecosystems for human beings has been exceeded; but that continued food aid from overseas means that population does not crash.

This sort of analysis is, needless to say, controversial, as it calls into question some basic humanitarian (population biologists would say soft-headed) impulses on the part of donors, not to mention some radical analyses of international political economy; but those critiques can wait.

Given trade and aid, it now only really makes sense to talk in terms of the human carrying capacity of the global ecosystem. Analyses at regional, national, or local levels soon get into all kinds of conceptual tangles. It really matters little that Singapore, New York City, London, and Los Angeles have vastly exceeded the carrying capacity of their local ecosystems, so long as they can exploit distant resources and sinks for their pollutants in order to support large and sometimes growing human populations.

The other complicating factor when it comes to applying population biology to human societies is the possibility of economic growth. Unique among animals, the ecological burdens imposed by each human are not roughly constant—indeed, they can seem virtually unbounded. Think, for example, of the conspicuous consumption of a Malcolm Forbes (magazine proprietor and thrower of the world's biggest-ever birthday bash), Michael Jackson, or Sarah Ferguson, Duchess of York. So if the number of humans is growing (and it is) and the amount consumed per human is growing (and it is), the ecological news is not good. Now, there are those who argue that economic growth is good for the environment because it allows some of the financial fruits of growth to be diverted to conservation; but such arguments belong in a different discourse, and will be dealt with in the next chapter. Let me stick for the moment to the discourse of those who stress ecological limits on human activity.

This sort of analysis, which anticipates misery, starvation, and death resulting from unconstrained human procreation and consumption, and which sees the main political challenge in terms of ensuring some level of human survival at an adequate level of amenity, is not new. It goes back to William Forster Lloyd (1794–1852) and, more famously, Thomas Malthus (1766–1834). Malthus, though, was widely reviled as a reactionary, the dismal parson who could not accept the possibility and benefits of human progress. Free-market liberal economists dismissed him because he cast doubt on cherished Victorian notions of material progress and wealth accumulation leading to social improvement more generally. Marxists and other socialists were more scornful still, as he cast doubt on their postulate of material plenty in a free and equal post-capitalist society, where individuals defined their own needs and the means for their satisfaction. And ultimately Malthus's argument was falsified by two hundred years of population growth combined not with misery, but with plenty, with rising living standards (at least in what is now the developed world). Or so it would seem.

In 1968 Garrett Hardin published his enormously influential essay on "The Tragedy of the Commons." Despite his own self-image as a taboo-breaker and iconoclast, Hardin's analysis quickly became part of the toolkit for anyone engaged in the analysis of environmental problems. Hardin's analytics had in fact been a staple of resource economics for some time (see for example Gordon, 1954). Hardin himself seemed unaware of this, even as he payed homage to his more distant precursor, William Forster Lloyd.[1] Unlike the economists, Hardin had the good sense to give the analysis a catchy name, publish it in the large-circulation journal *Science*, refrain from using graphs and algebra, and put it out just as the widespread perception of environmental crisis hit for the first time throughout the developed world.

Hardin's logic of the commons is quite straightforward. When it comes to a decision about whether or not to put an extra cow on the village commons, each rational self-interested peasant will recognize that the benefits of the extra cow accrue to himself alone, whereas the costs (in terms of stress upon the commons) are shared with the other villagers. Thus all villagers will quickly put more cows on the commons, which will in turn be quickly destroyed. Obviously, Hardin was using the commons of a medieval village as a metaphor for all kinds of environmental resources (never mind that the process he described never actually happened in any medieval village, to our knowledge). So each decision maker deciding whether or not to catch an additional netful of fish, or dump an additional ton of sewage into a lake, or cut down a tree, or drive an extra mile in Los Angeles, or get that malfunctioning catalytic converter fixed, is facing essentially the same decision: private benefit and the public interest always point in opposite directions. Hardin himself, in the original essay and subsequent writings, made the connection to childbearing decisions: if the world is a commons, each additional child adds stress to the commons, even though calculations of private interest determine that the child should be conceived, born, and raised.

Of course, all this is only tragic if the commons is finite—that is, if there are limits. If there are no limits, then we can populate, grow, and consume at will. For several centuries it had seemed that unconstrained economic growth was the natural order of things, and so social survival in finite systems was simply not conceptualized (save by the odd individual not even worth noting widely as a crank). But come 1970 everything changed in a hurry. The world looked as though it was being hit by what Paul Ehrlich (1968) sensationalized as a population bomb, more powerful than nuclear bombs. Combined with economic growth, population explosion was shortly going to exhaust stocks of energy, cropland, clean water, minerals,

---

[1] Moreover, as some observers noted, his analysis was formally identical to the account of the 17th-century political philosopher Thomas Hobbes of the "war of each against all."

and the assimilative capacity of the atmosphere and the oceans. Matters were dramatized further by the energy crisis which arrived suddenly in 1973 with the oil embargo organized by the Organization for Petroleum Exporting Countries, designed to exert pressure on the industrial world to take an anti-Israel line in the Middle East conflict.

To the Limits—and Beyond

Now, this discourse of limits and survival was not all there was to environmentalism circa 1970. Many concerns were more local, more aesthetic, more concerned with quality of life than its mere perpetuation. But survivalism did set the apocalyptic horizon of environmentalism, giving the basic reason why care and concern about the environment were not just desirable, but also necessary. This is no less true in the 1990s than in the late 1960s. In the early 1970s, though, survivalism did more than set these horizons. One of the most visible and heated debates in the history of environmental concern was occasioned in 1972 by the appearance of a book called *The Limits to Growth* (Meadows, Meadows, Behrens, and Randers, 1972), which within four years had sold four million copies.

This famous study was sponsored by the Club of Rome, founded in 1968 as a front for a group of well-heeled industrialists and sympathetic academics concerned with what they styled the "predicament of mankind."[2] Curiously, these industrialists were keen to show that industrialism itself, at least inasmuch as it features economic growth, is unsustainable. The Massachusetts Institute of Technology team commissioned by the Club of Rome to undertake the study were not population biologists who knew about carrying capacity, or economists who might know a bit about economic growth, but systems modellers (with business school backgrounds looming large). Systems dynamics was a relatively new technology rendered useful by the development and availability of computers. The MIT team of systems modellers was in a sense, as one of their critics would aver, "Malthus with a computer" (Freeman, 1973), though unlike Malthus they believed the predicament of mankind had more causes than the single one of population growth. The whole exercise was legitimated by its use of computers—for both analysis and salvation. As Torgerson (1995: 9) notes, the film version of *The Limits to Growth* portrays a dramatic contrast between the chaos and

---

[2] The Club's founder and president, Aurelio Peccei, eventually published his own survivalist tract, *One Hundred Pages for the Future* (Peccei, 1981). This book is actually 187 pages long, at least in the edition I have, surely a case of growth beyond the limit.

misery of a world seemingly hell-bent on using resources to exhaustion, polluting till it choked, with population exploding into misery, on the one hand, and the calm authority symbolized by a computer and the experts who could run it on the other. These days were of course well before the appearance of user-friendly personal computers and anarchistic hackers, in the days when computers were large, slow, and complicated.

The computer runs themselves were essentially simulations stretched out over a hundred years or more into the future of predicted pathways of several key aggregates, which interacted with one another through a host of interrelated variables. The key aggregates were resources, population, industrial output, food supply, and pollution. (Critics were quick to point out the absence of technology and prices.) All variables were measured at the global level. The predictions varied somewhat depending on the assumptions that were built into different computer runs, but given postulated limits to resource availability, agricultural productivity, and the capacity of the ecosphere to assimilate pollution, some limit was generally hit within a hundred years, leading to a collapse of industrial society and its population. The policy prescription was obvious: humanity needed to change its profligate ways if it were to survive, or, more precisely, to avoid the apocalypse of overshoot and collapse. Meadows and colleagues envisaged a "stationary state" economy as an alternative; this would be a global economy operating at a fixed level of throughput of resources, with a stable world population. As they note, such a stationary state had been envisaged more than a hundred years earlier by the political economist John Stuart Mill (p. 175). Within these constraints, economic change and growth is not ruled out. Quite how humanity could move to this steady state was less clear, though as we shall see others quickly supplied the political prescriptions.

In a sense, the elaborate computer simulations carried out under the auspices of the Club of Rome did little more than state the obvious: that exponential growth cannot go on forever in a finite system. Exponential growth is growth at a constant percentage rate. This produces a growth curve over time of the sort depicted in Figure 2.1. With this sort of curve, it matters little whether a limit such as the global supply of natural resources is doubled, tripled, or quadrupled; a little more time may be bought, but the limit is hit soon enough (see Figure 2.2). Nor should we expect much advance warning that the limit is about to be hit, for under exponential growth the limit will (by definition) be approached at an absolute speed unprecedented in human history.

Foresight is, then, essential. Lester Brown (1978) deploys the metaphor alluded to in the title of his book *The Twenty-Ninth Day* to ask on what day a pond will be half-covered with lilies if the coverage doubles every day, and

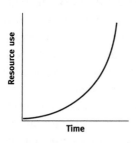

Figure 2.1. Exponential Growth

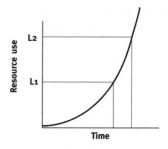

Figure 2.2. Exponential Growth with Limits

Note: Doubling the available supply of resources from L1 to L2 buys very little time.

will cover the whole pond on the thirtieth day. The answer is, of course, the twenty-ninth day. It would be very easy to look at the pond on the twenty-ninth day and conclude there is plenty of clear water. The challenge is to figure out how to build a capacity for foresight into collective decision making, before any evidence of global collapse is apparent. Currently, decision making in government and business is almost entirely geared to the short term. As will be seen, no feasible solution to this challenge has yet been established by survivalists.

With or without systems dynamics, global modelling continued throughout the 1970s under the auspices of the Club of Rome, the United Nations, and the United States government, among others. Under President Jimmy Carter, the US government's various global modelling enterprises were brought a step closer to integration in the *Global 2000 Report to the President*, a gloomy report for a gloomy presidency. As its title implies, *Global 2000* did not look as far ahead as *The Limits to Growth*, but only to the year 2000. Its major findings are summarized in the opening paragraph of its Volume 1:

If present trends continue, the world in 2000 will be more crowded, more polluted, less stable ecologically, and more vulnerable to disruption than the world we live in now. Serious stresses involving population, resources, and environment are clearly visible ahead. Despite greater material output, the world's people will be poorer in many ways than they are today.

With exquisitely bad timing, *Global 2000* was released in 1980, just in time for the arrival in Washington DC of Ronald Reagan, with an entourage and a world view that could not fathom such pessimism. Still, the Reagan presidency and the exuberant era it symbolized did not completely silence the survivalist discourse, even in the United States, even in its capital.

In Washington, a focus on the parlous state of key global aggregates was kept alive by the strenuous efforts of the Worldwatch Institute, under the leadership of Lester Brown. With its annual *State of the World* reports, beginning in 1984, the Institute keeps reminding us that all the indicators of environmental quality and resource availability point in the wrong direction, and that disaster is just around every corner. Though its view of the world is more sophisticated and nuanced than that of the *Limits to Growth* modellers, the emphasis remains on monitoring systems and aggregates at the global level. The main systems monitored are forests, grasslands, fisheries, and croplands. The overall limit identified by the Worldwatchers is the photosynthetic energy these systems can make available for human use. Humans currently appropriate a large and growing proportion of this energy, wasting much of it. The challenge is to devise ways to make use of photosynthetic energy more efficiently.

In 1992 the US National Academy of Sciences combined with the British Royal Society to produce a report which concluded that the pace of growth in consumption and population meant that "the future of our planet is in the balance" (Press and Atiyah, 1992). The same year, twenty years of survivalism was celebrated by the publication of an updated *Limits to Growth* entitled *Beyond the Limits* (Meadows, Meadows, and Randers, 1992), whose major theme was that little had changed except the passage of these twenty wasted years, making it harder than ever to move humanity back from beyond the limits.

Authors such as Paul Ehrlich, Lester Brown, Norman Myers, and Garrett Hardin continued to contribute to the survivalist discourse in the 1990s. More surprisingly, in 1995 a few leading economists broke ranks with their colleagues to announce that economic growth sooner or later must encounter limits imposed by the environment's carrying capacity (see Arrow *et al.*, 1995). Remarkably, these economists endorsed the basic survivalist tenet that the Earth's resource base is finite, and called for institutional redesign to reduce stress on the resilience of natural systems. Clearly, something new and noteworthy is afoot in the discipline of economics, once near-unanimous in its condemnation of survivalism. That something is ecological economics.

The first thing to be said about ecological economics is that it should not be confused with environmental economics. Environmental economics is the handmaiden of economic rationalism, discussed at length in Chapter 6. Ecological economics, in contrast, treats the environment not as an adjunct to the human economy, nor as a mere medium through which some human actions harm or benefit other humans. Instead, ecosystems are conceptualized as the fundamental entities within which human economic systems are embedded. Thus environmental problems are to be thought of in terms of shortfalls in the capacity of ecological systems and economic systems acting in conjunction to sustain the conditions to support human—and possibly nonhuman—life. Ecological economics, unlike environmental economics, takes a systems view of economic phenomena; the field can be defined as the study of interdependent natural and economic systems. Ecological economics treats natural systems as finite, and so the scale of human economic activity which they can support becomes an issue (this limit is ignored by economic rationalists). The main challenge is to figure out how economic systems might be made sustainable within these constraints. Ecological economics is quite open-ended in the way we might respond to this challenge.

While still meeting resistance (or indifference) within the mainstream discipline of economics, ecological economics is gradually acquiring the trappings of academic respectability, through the International Society for Ecological Economics and its journal *Ecological Economics*, both founded in 1989.

The pioneers of ecological economics include Nicholas Georgescu-Roegen (1971) and Herman Daly (1977). Georgescu-Roegen explored the economic implications of the second law of thermodynamics, which specifies that any closed system will over time deteriorate in the direction of sameness or disorder in the absence of any external input of energy. The fact that there is only a limited supply of low entropy or order on this planet has all kinds of economic implications. Low entropy is really the ultimate form of scarcity. It exists in mineral structures, concentrated fossil fuels, in ecosystems; but human economic activity seems to be inexorably running down this supply of low entropy.

Herman Daly, for his part, was the first person to work out some principles of steady state economics. Conventional economics is committed to perpetual economic growth, and indeed sees economic health and normality in terms of the presence of growth. Daly rose to the challenge presented by the survivalist denial of unlimited growth, describing how an economy could indeed be run on steady-state lines, without requiring ever-increasing environmental and natural resource inputs.

The basic idea that there are global limits is shared by many if not most green radicals. Their critic Martin Lewis (1992: 9–10) credits survivalism with being the mainspring of green radicalism—as he puts it, "green extremism is rooted in a single, powerful conviction that continued economic growth is absolutely impossible, given the limits of a finite planet." Lewis is wrong about survivalism being the core of green radicalism, but right to note that green radicalism recognizes and stresses limits. However, the politics of green radicalism prove very different from survivalism.

The Political Philosophy of Survivalism

Many of the more prominent figures who have furthered the discourse of limits and survival have a background in biology. Others, such as the global modellers sponsored by the Club of Rome, have a background in systems dynamics, and are most at home in business schools. These figures do develop policy prescriptions, whose severity can obliquely commit their authors to particular kinds of political structure. For example, Ehrlich (1968) countenances compulsory sterilization in countries such as India, which could hardly be effective without a more authoritarian political structure than India possessed then or now.[3] Missing in the analyses of such figures, and so in the public debates in which they have been central, is more sustained attention to the politics, economics, and—crucially—political economy of survival. Where such analysis should be, one often finds wishful thinking. For example, in *Beyond the Limits* Meadows, Meadows and Randers (1992: 222–36) conclude with prescriptions for visioning, networking, truth-telling, learning, and loving as the keys to achievement of a sustainable global society. Quite how these all might play out in the real-world political economy is less clear. In fairness to Meadows and colleagues they do address the deficiencies of the market, noting that it is "blind in the long term and pays no attention to ultimate sources and sinks until it is too late" (1992: 184; see also, much earlier, Meadows, 1976). Given the stress that critics of their earlier work had laid upon the market as the location of solutions to the problems they identified, they really had no choice but to say something about it. But this is about as far as their political-economic analysis goes. They do not tell exactly what we might do about the market.

Other authors, however, have produced much more in the way of detailed, bold, and striking political-economic analyses, and this is where survivalism as a political program gets into full swing. Especially in the 1970s, and in some cases continuing to the present, survivalist political prescriptions have been centralized and authoritarian. Garrett Hardin stands out among the limits biologists in his willingness to tackle questions of political-economic organization very explicitly. If, as he avers in his classic essay, "freedom in the commons brings ruin to all" (1968), then obviously freedom, including the

---

[3] Countries such as the United States, in contrast, require relatively restrained policies, such as heavy taxes on diapers and toys to discourage people from having children. Later, Paul and Anne Ehrlich (1974) give up on the possibility of any government doing much right, and propose only that individuals prepare to protect themselves in the coming crunch by laying in stores of food and practising self-sufficiency. With this suggestion, the Ehrlichs find common ground with the right-wing, gun-toting survivalists in the United States. But such aggressive individualism is very much a peripheral theme in the environmental discourse of limits and survival.

freedom to breed, needs to be curtailed. The solution to the tragedy of the commons in situations characterized by limits is "mutual coercion mutually agreed upon," and this is true whether the commons in question is a local fishery or the global atmosphere. In his later writings, Hardin (for example, 1977) expresses skepticism about effective central authority above the level of the nation-state, in which case protection of the commons can only be achieved effectively at the national level. Taking survivalism quite literally, Hardin recommends that the more developed countries abandon the underdeveloped world if governments in the latter wish to continue policies that promote population explosion and ecological devastation. Developed nations would then constitute "lifeboats" afloat in a world otherwise drowning in misery. (Hardin's argument here downplays the fact that it is the developed nations, not the poor ones, that impose the greater stresses on the world's ecosystems. It is Americans, not Bangladeshis, who drive expensive cars, live in huge houses, and eat massive quantities of animal products.)

Other survivalists are less obviously callous than Hardin, though in basic agreement with him that abuse of the commons, resource exhaustion, and environmental despoliation are largely (though not necessarily totally) a matter of individuals and other actors pursuing their material interests in decentralized systems. Decentralized systems have no cohesive leadership directing them: examples include markets, liberal democratic political systems, and the international system. In such systems there is no incentive to care about collective goods like environmental quality or long-term human wellbeing. Thus Robert Heilbroner in 1974 concluded that the only hope for humanity lies in the establishment of monastic government combining "religious orientation with a military discipline" (Heilbroner, 1991: 176–7) in order to cure humanity's profligate ways. Such totalitarian government will control economic transactions as well as the political sphere. Obviously, authoritarian governments committed to industrialism rather than environmental conservation are no help, as the disastrous environmental records of the former Soviet bloc countries and military dictatorships around the world testify.

The need to control access to the commons is just one prop for authoritarian government in the limits discourse. A second prop comes with the fact that the discourse of limits and survival places great emphasis on expertise, be it that of systems modellers, population biologists, or ecologists. Such expertise is not, of course, evenly distributed in society. It some cases, the relevant knowledge is quite hard to master: ecology does, of course, deal in very complex systems. This sort of recognition leads William Ophuls, in the most comprehensive and sophisticated analysis of the political ramifications of ecological crisis to appear in the 1970s, to recommend establishment of a class of "ecological mandarins," which would govern by applying ecological principles (Ophuls, 1977: 163). The expertise in question is "on top" rather than "on tap," because ecology's claim to primacy means that there is no room for tradeoff against competing values of the sort that ordinary politicians routinely seek in liberal democratic political systems. Ophuls also echoes the arguments of Hardin to the effect that management of the commons needs strong central authority.[4]

Later survivalists would soften this authoritarianism. For example, contemporary ecological economists mainly seek only intelligent and creative use of some well-understood policy instruments. Thus Michael Jacobs (1991) details how sustainability planning can work through government creation and enforcement of environmental quality standards. These standards might refer to air quality, biodiversity, or the wellbeing of the ozone layer. Using models of the impact of particular economic activities on these indicators, governments would be in a position to enact policies that limit the damage. Any number of policy instruments could be used here. Daly (1992) is quite keen on the tradeable pollution permit approach developed by economic rationalists (see Chapter 6), on the grounds that governments can specify the overall amount of pollution allowed within, say, a watershed based on ecological principles, but then let the market operate to determine who should pollute how much within this overall limit.

Some survivalists have even become positively enthusiastic about democracy and citizen action. So Richard Barnet (1980) catalogued a host of limits, but proposed democratic mobilization, not authoritarianism, to confront them. Norman Myers, carrying the limits torch prominently and ably into the 1990s, issued a clarion call for citizen action to confront limits (in his contribution to Myers and Simon, 1994). Lester Brown has consistently placed greater faith in localized citizen action than in national leadership (Brown, 1981; Brown, Flavin, and Postel, 1992: 180), though this faith sits uneasily with a plea for a stronger United Nations to "do for all people what national governments cannot" (Brown, Flavin, and Postel, 1992: 179). Such calls to citizen action are far indeed from the imagery of technocrats in white coats operating computers associated with the limits discourse in the early 1970s, and the oligarchy proposed by survivalist political theorists in the same decade. These theorists did, though, remain unrepentant in the 1990s (see Hardin, 1993; Heilbroner, 1991; Ophuls and Boyan, 1992).

---

[4] Later, Ophuls protests that he raises the specter of authoritarianism simply as a warning of what might have to happen unless humanity gets its political-ecological house in order through less draconian means (Ophuls and Boyan, 1992: 312). And in addition to this authoritarian model, his book also contains, in uneasy juxtaposition, a model of a decentralized, Jeffersonian political economy of self-reliant small-scale communities.

To see why broad-based citizen action can only fit uneasily into the discourse of limits and survival, a closer examination is in order, using the tools of discourse analysis introduced in Chapter 1.

Discourse Analysis of Survivalism

The basic story line of survivalism is clear enough: human demands on the carrying capacity of ecosystems threaten to explode out of control, and draconian action needs to be taken in order to curb these demands. This story line is in turn constructed from the following basic entities, metaphors, other rhetorical devices, assumptions about natural relationships, agents, and motives.

1. Basic Entities whose Existence is Recognized or Constructed

Survivalism recognizes and emphasizes the resources upon which human beings depend for their existence. These in turn include stocks of non-renewable resources, such as oil, gas, coal, metallic ores, and cropland. Ecosystems are recognized in the basic survivalist ontology, but only in limited fashion: as sources of renewable resources such as firewood, timber, soil, and fish, or as sinks for the absorption of pollution.[5] Crucially, stocks of non-renewable resources and the capacity of ecosystems to produce renewable resources and assimilate wastes are treated as finite (though hard to measure with any precision). The discourse also recognizes and emphasizes human population as an aggregate entity (i.e., it is something other than just "people"), whose size and growth has all kinds of implications for human destiny. Finally, élites—especially those associated with governments, and especially those with pertinent expertise, be it in systems modelling, ecology, or population biology—play a central role in the discourse.

Finite stocks of resources, ecosystems as founts of renewable resources and sinks for pollutants, population, and élites—all these might sound unremarkable, and just what one would expect to find in talk about environmental affairs. In fact, these items together constitute a highly selective and, as I will show later in this chapter, a deeply problematical set. For the moment, though, it should be noted that this basic ontology is not exhaustive (ontologies never are). Missing, for example, are individual problem solvers, human beings as social creatures capable of devising cooperative

---

[5] Different notions of ecosystems appear in other discourses.

arrangements, markets (except to be dismissed in passing), social movements, genders, resilient ecosystems, states, and interest groups.

2. ASSUMPTIONS ABOUT NATURAL RELATIONSHIPS

The relationship assumed by survivalists to be the most natural in human affairs is, in a word, hierarchy. Often this is taken for granted to the extent that it needs no discussion or justification; it is simply assumed that there are elites who are responsible for the world. In contrast, the survivalists I have discussed who actually analyze alternative forms of political-economic organization, such as Hardin, Heilbroner, and Ophuls, reason their way toward hierarchy rather than take it for granted. The basis for hierarchy can be expertise, or virtue, or both. Certainly human beings conceptualized *en masse* as "population" do not have the required virtue to control their appetites or their procreation. Garrett Hardin, for one, argues at length that conscience is self-eliminating, for those without a conscience will have more children (1968). (This argument relies on the premise that desired number of children is a hereditary trait, which flies in the face of all the evidence.) I have noted that survivalists such as Lester Brown and Norman Myers have by now softened this hierarchical commitment to include pleas for widespread citizen action. But these pleas notwithstanding, the survivalist discourse deals ultimately in aggregates such as population, resource stocks, global pollution levels—and, crucially, monitoring and control of these aggregates. Such control is hard to envisage on anything other than a hierarchical basis. The hierarchy in question does not need to be the tight, authoritarian style of government proposed by some survivalists; but it does require coordinated action on the part of élite groups.

3. AGENTS AND THEIR MOTIVES

It is, then, elites who have agency, the capacity to act. Their motivations are up for grabs. Élites can choose to operate national political economies according to established principles of maximizing economic growth, leavened by a touch of social justice, and the need to placate special interests; or they can choose to oversee the transition to a stationary state through coordinated global action. "Populations," be they national, global, or class-specific, have no agency; they are only acted upon, as aggregates to be monitored through statistics and controlled by government policy. At most their component individuals can only follow their short-sighted desires (though they are allowed to be quite rational in this blinkered sense). Populations are basically objects to be managed.

4. Key Metaphors and other Rhetorical Devices

Survivalism is rich in metaphors. These include, first and foremost, the notion of overshoot and collapse, drawn of course from models of simple ecosystems where one species breeds to excess and then experiences a crash. The tragedy of the commons is rooted in metaphor: note that Garrett Hardin made his original argument in the context not of any resource currently threatened with exhaustion, but rather in the context of the common land of a medieval village. Another favorite metaphor is the spaceship, introduced by Kenneth Boulding (1966). If the life-support systems of the spaceship are not maintained, the crew dies. "Spaceship earth" became a credible notion as real spaceships left the earth with humans aboard for the first time and—crucially—these humans photographed the earth from space. This image gave a most powerful impetus to thinking about the earth as a whole system—and a finite, fragile one at that. Indeed, a photograph of the earth from space graces the cover of around half the books on my "environmental" shelf (will my publisher conclude that this book merits one too?). Other metaphors attempt to capture the nature of exponential growth: I have already mentioned the lily pond whose surface covered by lilies doubles every day, and the population bomb, or population explosion. Cancer as a metaphor has occasionally been raised. So Peccei refers to "the cancerous growth of population" (1981: 29; see also Gregg, 1955). The obvious inference is that we human beings are the cancer cells upon the body of the earth. While this is perhaps not a metaphor calculated to have broad appeal, Paul Ehrlich did once draw the further inference that "the cancer itself must be cut out" (Ehrlich, 1968: xi).

A key rhetorical device in the early days of the limits discourse in the 1970s was the computer. Ostensibly, the computer was used to carry out complex calculations about the interaction of a host of variables; in fact, as I have noted, these computer models did nothing more than state the obvious, that exponential growth cannot proceed indefinitely in a finite environment. In the late 1990s computers are far less mysterious to ordinary people and political actors than they were in the 1970s, which is why the computer has lost its rhetorical power in the survivalist discourse.

If the computer represented the rationalistic, calculating side of survivalist discourse, it co-exists uneasily with quasi-religious images of doom and redemption. The earthly paradise of a stationary state is attainable—but only if we recognize our sin, and change our ways quite thoroughly.

Box 2.1. **DISCOURSE ANALYSIS OF SURVIVALISM**

---

1. **Basic Entities Recognized or Constructed**

   - Finite stocks of resources
   - Carrying capacity of ecosystems
   - Population
   - Élites

2. **Assumptions about Natural Relationships**

   - Hierarchy and control

3. **Agents and their Motives**

   - Élites; motivation is up for grabs

4. **Key Metaphors and other Rhetorical Devices**

   - Overshoot and collapse
   - Commons
   - Spaceship Earth
   - Lily pond
   - Cancer
   - Computers
   - Images of doom and redemption

Survivalism in Practice

What difference has this discourse of survivalism made in environmental affairs? And has any such influence been for the better or for the worse? As I have already noted, survivalism provides the apocalyptic horizon of environmental concern, raising the stakes in environmental affairs. In these terms, its effects may be profound, while hard to trace directly into any particular politics, policies, or environmental outcomes. Certainly the bleak authoritarian prescriptions proposed by the survivalist vanguard (especially in the 1970s) find little reflection in political practice or institutional design, and show few signs of being adopted anywhere, let alone at the global level. The draconian population control attempted briefly and disastrously in India in the mid-1970s, and in China with much greater effect since then, may constitute exceptions. The more pervasive political practice associated with survivalism turns out to take a form somewhat different from the authoritarian political theory I described earlier.

This form does, though, remain an élitist affair, certainly not that of a social movement, or even interest groups involving large numbers of people. As I have noted, survivalism treats most people as "population," effectively denying them agency, the capacity to act. The politics of limits is exclusive. Now, pressure groups devoted to furthering the survivalist agenda have existed and do exist, in the form of organizations such as Negative Population Growth (NPG), the Club of Rome, and the Worldwatch

Institute. Such groups have generally relied upon the largesse of founda-tions and a few wealthy benefactors, rather than on any mass member-ship. It is symbolic of this élitism that the Club of Rome limited its membership to 100 individuals. More broadly based was the Global Tomorrow Coalition of environmental and future-oriented interest groups in the United States, formed to follow up the concerns highlighted in the *Global 2000 Report to the President* after 1980. Some of these affiliated groups had a large membership. But the Coalition itself never played an especially visible role in mobilizing public opinion on particular issues; groups could quite easily declare an affiliation to it without really integrating its efforts with their own activities.

Survivalist pressure groups have for the most part sought the ear of the powerful rather than the mobilization of any broader public (though Worldwatch publications are in fact widely distributed). Sometimes this was successful—as for example, when President Jimmy Carter directed the Council on Environmental Quality and the Department of State to produce what eventually became *Global 2000.*

But in looking for the impact of a discourse we should not necessarily expect to find it only in the instrumental actions of its adherents as they are felt by other political actors. The impact of discourses cannot be reduced to just the impact of interests and organizations that subscribe to them; indeed, it is quite conceivable that impact may be felt in the absence of any such iden-tifiable organization(s). Discourses take effect in largely impersonal fashion, if they can indeed manage to change the language that significant numbers of people use in talking about the environment. So can we trace any initia-tives, policies, agreements, social changes, or other phenomena pertaining to environmental affairs to the limits discourse? Obviously coordinated population control efforts—especially in China—fall into this category. At the all-important global level, perhaps the best example may be found in coordinated international action to halt and reverse ozone depletion in the stratosphere. Certainly this is the success to which survivalists themselves point. Meadows, Meadows, and Randers (1992: 141–60) believe that the ozone issue shows that we can indeed move at the global level "back from beyond the limits." Peter Haas (1992) argues that it was a like-minded "epis-temic community" of atmospheric scientists which was the driving force behind global action, just as it should be in the survivalist discourse.

Ozone depletion was first recognized as an issue in the 1970s; the culprit was identified as chlorofluorocarbons (CFCs), chemicals found in aerosol sprays and refrigerators. Stratospheric ozone is vital in shielding life on earth from solar ultra-violet radiation, which can cause skin cancer in humans and other animals, damage photosynthesis in green plants (so threatening agriculture and forestry), and kill aquatic plankton. The issue was dramatized in the form of an "ozone hole" appearing over Antarctica in the Austral winter, identified and named in 1985. The ozone problem did, then, constitute a classic limit, and one which by the mid-1980s appeared to have been overshot. While studies and global negotiations relating to this issue had been going on for some time, in 1987 there was a dramatic acceleration in the pace of global action. The 1987 Montreal Protocol was signed by 24 nations, covering the main CFC producers and consumers, under the auspices of the United Nations Environment Program. The Protocol committed developed nations to freeze consumption of CFCs almost immediately and impose a series of percentage cuts subsequently. Later revisions strengthened the Protocol, eventually specifying that CFCs be eliminated entirely at the end of 1995, at least for the developed countries. The rest of the world was given longer, and promised aid from developed countries to introduce substitutes and compensate for economic losses caused by lack of access to CFCs.

Meadows, Meadows, and Randers (1992: 159) conclude that the ozone issue shows that "a world government is not necessary to deal with global problems, but it is necessary to have global scientific cooperation, a global information system, and an international forum within which specific agreements can be worked out." Litfin (1994) explains the Montreal Protocol in terms of a global discursive shift on this issue, toward a discourse of limits, or, as she refers to it, precaution. The key event to Litfin was the rhetorical force of the "ozone hole" idea. The hole referred to seasonal and variable (though substantial) reductions in ozone concentrations over Antarctica. A "hole" could capture the imagination in the way reams of data from monitoring stations could not. It should be stressed that by 1987 there was no empirical evidence that CFCs actually damaged the ozone layer, though the chemical reactions required for this to happen had been demonstrated in laboratory settings.

There is no denying that the ozone issue does represent an environmental success. However, some caution is in order before making too much of it, or seeing it as a prototype for global action on other issues, for three reasons. First, the stakes were comparatively small: CFCs are useful chemicals, but substitutes for them can be developed, and have been developed. The stakes are much larger when it comes to dealing with issues such as greenhouse gases, notably carbon dioxide, where the whole basis of the industrial economy in fossil fuels is at issue.

Second, it is possible to reconstruct the history of negotiations on the ozone issue in terms not of rational solving of a collective problem (Meadows), nor of science-driven policy making (Haas), nor a discourse shift (Litfin), but rather in terms of the material interests of key actors, as Berejikian (1995) shows. The negotiations were dominated by two key actors: the United States and the European Community (EC). The United States already had legislation restricting CFCs at the national level. Corporations such as Du Pont feared that the lack of any global controls on CFCs would put them at a competitive disadvantage, as they were devoting resources to the development of substitutes for CFCs. (Meadows, Meadows, and Randers, 1992: 159 praise the role played by "flexible and responsible corporations" such as Du Pont.) So clearly an international agreement was desirable from the point of view of Du Pont, and by extension the United States. The EC, for its part, initially dragged its feet on the issue. However, once it became clear that the United States might ban the import from the EC of products containing CFCs, the EC was much more willing to negotiate. On the ozone issue, it was fortuitous that the material interests of key players could be eventually brought into line with global environmental concerns. This coincidence should not be expected to prevail as anything like a general rule.

Third, there is no guarantee of universal compliance with the Montreal Protocol and its subsequent strengthening. There was little problem in the developed countries delivering on their promises. However, come the end of 1995, five countries of the former Soviet bloc were seeking exemption from a ban on CFC production and use. Less developed countries, notably China, dragged their feet on their proposed gradual phase-out of CFCs; and they found allies in the United States Congress, where an anti-environmental but, more significantly, penny-pinching Republican majority saw the finance of this phase-out by developed countries such as the United States as an undesirable monetary burden, to be avoided if possible. By 1995 India was going full steam ahead on CFC production, and there was an emerging international black market in CFCs.

Survivalism: An Assessment

This problem of limited compliance on the part of some nation states on the ozone issue illustrates what is perhaps the biggest challenge confronting the limits discourse. In this discourse, agency is for elites, and most importantly for elites operating on a coordinated global basis. The survivalist discourse deals in global aggregates (such as resources and population), which can only be addressed at the global level. The slogan "Think globally, act locally" is a frequent exhortation in environmental circles; but for the discourse of limits and survival, the appropriate slogan is "think globally, act globally." Though the ozone issue illustrates some potential for coordinated global action (for discussion of other, less dramatic, cases, see Haas, Keohane, and Levy, 1993), as things stand the requisite global authority is missing. One survivalist—Garrett Hardin—believes it implausible, such that survivalism should be pursued within "lifeboats" in the developed world only. Other survivalists advocate stronger global authority, but give few ideas as to how it might actually be brought into being. As the twentieth century draws to a close, all kinds of political and economic currents point in exactly the opposite direction. The global economy is increasingly governed by principles and regimes of free trade, especially following the culmination of the Uruguay Round of the General Agreement on Tariffs and Trade (GATT) in 1994 and the establishment of the World Trade Organization (WTO). The WTO is perhaps the strongest body for global governance yet established (certainly stronger than the United Nations), but it has no environmental mandate. Within free-trade regimes, nation states are compelled to pursue policies to encourage footloose investors to locate capital in their countries rather than their rivals, and so must toe the line of economic imperatives more strongly than ever. Politically, liberal democracy seems the universal model of choice for the first time in human history. This model is a far cry indeed from the centralized authoritarian forms favored by the more austere survivalists, though real-world liberal democracies are not necessarily so far from the more pervasive elitism of the survivalist discourse.

Survivalism does not, then, sit easily in the real world. It also has to struggle with some powerful competing discourses. Rome is home to a Church as well as a Club. The Roman Catholic Church has consistently opposed any efforts to control human population, inasmuch as such efforts inevitably countenance contraception and abortion as part of population control strategy. The Church played a very visible obstructive role at the 1994 United Nations International Conference on Population and Development in Cairo, in unholy alliance with Islamic Fundamentalists and mostly Protestant fundamentalists from the Christian Right in the United States.

From the left, Marxists who remember Marx's own opposition to Malthus ridicule a discourse of limits, especially when it is propounded by powerful industrialists, and financed by corporate foundations. No less than in Marx's own day, a recognition of limits gets in the way of dreams of a future of communist abundance. Only recently has this scornful tendency among Marxists been questioned by the rise of eco-Marxism, which sees in ecological crisis the possibility of an ally that would hasten the global crisis of capitalism.

From the left more generally, opposition to survivalism comes from those who see talk of population as inherently racist (for the United States, see Chock, 1995; for Australia, see White, 1994). An ontology that stresses "population" and the denial of agency to members of that population looks, from this left/multicultural direction, as if it were designed to control and discriminate against those ethnic groups whose numbers are increasing most rapidly. In the United States, these are generally nonwhites, whose numbers are bolstered by immigration both legal and illegal. On this account, raising the specter of overpopulation of the United States and the need to control immigration is a racist denial of the rights of—especially—Hispanics, who constitute the bulk of low-income and illegal immigrants.

Perhaps most surprisingly, an assault on the discourse of limits now comes from ecofeminism. Ecofeminists affirming pre-patriarchal symbols of fertility contend that population control in practice means control of women by a male power structure (see, for example, Diamond, 1994). For women to regain their places in harmony with a living, fertile earth means breaking free from all patriarchal shackles—including the patriarchy of population control experts and their political masters. The survivalists do give them plenty of ammunition here, as for example when Garrett Hardin (1993: 258) states that "we need to devise acceptable ways of influencing the desires of women in the light of community needs."

The religious, Marxist, left multiculturalist, and ecofeminist arguments against the discourse of limits turn out on closer inspection to miss their target. Religious arguments reduce to dogma concerning fundamental tenets of faith for individual (micro) behavior combined with insensitivity to how these tenets play out at the macro level. Orthodox Marxists, now thin on the ground, disapprove of the limits discourse because of its inconvenient implications, not because they can fault its logic. Left multiculturalists in exposing racist aspects of limits discourse do not thereby solve the problem of population pressure; they sweep it under the carpet, or implicitly assume that the interests of particular ethnic groups must always trump any global interest. In other words, they advocate maintenance and expansion of a commons in the interests of social justice. They actually have nothing at all to say about the reality or otherwise of limits. (A better deployment of social justice concerns here would begin by noting that it is the prosperous peoples of the world who impose the greatest burden on the ecosphere.) The same can be said of those ecofeminists who are against population control; they have nothing to say about the macro-level consequences of their position.

The arguments of these competing discourses cannot easily stand scrutiny—indeed, they are generally not made as arguments, in the sense that they do not take on the limits discourse in any terms that could engage this discourse and the problems it has identified. But these counterclaims are still important, and help explain the real-world fate of survivalism and limits.

There does exist a discourse which has engaged survivalism more directly, and on ground where arguments can be made, as opposed to dogma asserted. This opponent is Promethean, and its defining feature is the denial of limits. Given that it is rooted in industrialism, but only makes sense as a reaction against the limits discourse, it is appropriate to discuss this Promethean discourse and the challenge it presents to survivalism at length in the next chapter. Suffice it to say for the moment that the Promethean viewpoint came to dominate the policy positions of the Reagan administration in the United States in the 1980s, also helping to explain why the United States was so obstructive in so many international negotiations on environmental and population issues (the ozone issue was an exception).

The limits discourse has, then, had limited impact in its own terms. Recall that survivalism seeks coordinated, central action, with foresight built in. Very little such action is apparent, and, as seen in the context of the ozone issue, the action that does occur is more limited than it might at first seem. The time horizons of governments and corporations remain short. The emerging global political economy is thoroughly inhospitable to survivalist concerns. The limits discourse is in evidence at the periodic United Nations conferences on population and the environment (notably the Conference on the Human Environment in Stockholm in 1972, the Conference on Environment and Development in Rio in 1992, and the International Conference on Population and Development in Cairo in 1994), though increasingly these gatherings are dominated by the competing discourse of sustainable development. Today, we find survivalists lamenting time wasted as a result of prior warnings unheeded—which is why Meadows, Meadows, and Randers (1992) believe the world has now gone "beyond the limits." Garrett Hardin (1993) laments the continued dominance of population taboos. He bemoans the fact that the population issue was not on anyone's agenda for Earth Day in 1990, mostly, he believes, as a result of the fear of the corporate sponsors of Earth Day of offending the anti-limits groups I have mentioned (1993: 3).

One other factor which can restrict the impact of survivalism is a silence about environmental problems as they arise at local, regional, and national levels. Survivalism is about both thinking and acting globally. Some of the other discourses have more to say about environmental issues at these other levels. However, it is conceivable that one could be a survivalist for global issues, while subscribing to some other discourse when it comes to local issues.

Nothing in this patchy record means that the survivalist discourse was or is erroneous in its stress on limits, and it may yet find vindication if, for example, the global greenhouse effect comes to the worst. Politically, there has never been enough imagination as to how the agenda might be pursued, and the discourse never really got past the simplistic draconian authoritarianism of the 1970s survivalists. Survivalists do not quite know what to say or do about global capitalism, especially given that some of their financial sponsors are global capitalists. These problems notwithstanding, the impact of the discourse of limits and survival should not be dismissed. If nothing else, it raised the stakes in the establishment of the environment as a key issue, perhaps the key issue, of the late twentieth century and beyond.

3

Growth Forever: The Promethean Response

The Promethean Background

Discourses do not need conscious adherence or articulation. Indeed, some discourse analysts would argue that their hallmark is that nobody articulates their principles, the latter being so ingrained and taken-for-granted that it would never occur to anyone to question them, and so even raise them. (Analogously, most speakers of the English language could not articulate the basic principles of grammar and syntax which they use every day.) Such was the case for a long time with the environmental discourse which can, now that it has been articulated, be styled Promethean. In Greek mythology Prometheus stole fire from Zeus, and so vastly increased the human capacity to manipulate the world for human ends. Protheans have unlimited confidence in the ability of humans and their technologies to overcome any problems presented to them—including what can now be styled environmental problems.

The term "cornucopian" is sometimes associated with this kind of discourse that denies the existence of environmental limits. Cornucopia means abundant natural supply: unlimited natural resources, unlimited ability of natural systems to absorb pollutants, and unlimited corrective capacity in natural systems. However, Julian Simon, one of its leading proponents, protests that this is a misnomer: "The school of thought that I represent here is not cornucopian. I do not believe that *nature* is limitlessly bountiful. . . . our cornucopia is the human mind and heart not a Santa Claus natural environment" (J. Simon, 1981: 41). Simon's protests notwithstanding, I will show that members of this school of thought, including Simon himself, do portray a Santa Claus natural environment at key junctures. So strictly speaking this discourse should be styled Promethean/cornucopian. But that is too much of a mouthful, so let me just call it

Promethean, which really does capture the essence of the discourse better than "cornucopian."[1]

For several centuries, at least in the industrializing and industrialized West, the dominant Promethean order has been taken for granted. The Industrial Revolution produced technological changes that made materials close to home (such as coal and later oil) into useful resources. At the same time, European colonial expansion opened up whole new continents and oceans for exploitation. Against this background, capitalist economic growth became taken as the normal condition of a healthy society. Even those who looked forward to a future beyond capitalism, notably Karl Marx, applauded technological progress, economic growth, and the conquest of nature.

The power of unarticulated Promethean discourse is still felt today, as just about every government, everywhere sees its first task as achieving a "healthy" level of economic growth. The entire way in which economic news is reported assumes that growth is good. This refers to growth in wealth, growth in income, growth in profits, growth in employment, growth in housing starts, growth in passenger miles travelled. That economic growth usually means increased stress on environmental systems—more pollution, more congestion, faster depletion of resources—is never reported along with these economic aggregates (though this stress is increasingly being reported elsewhere). Thus there is a sense in which the political-economic discourse of liberal capitalist systems still generally floats free from any sense of environmental constraints. "Economy" and "environment" are implicitly put into quite different boxes.

Promethean Argument to the Foreground

The rise of survivalism described in the previous chapter meant that Promethean discourse had to be articulated and defended, rather than just taken for granted. Economists were, and still are, in the forefront of the Promethean counterattack. The economists' basic argument was established as early as 1963 with the publication of *Scarcity and Growth* by Harold Barnett and Chandler Morse, produced under the sponsorship of the Washington think-tank Resources for the Future. Economists have always averred that price is a measure of scarcity: if the real price of a good goes up,

---

[1] To complicate matters still further here, there are also cornucopian or Santa Claus environmentalists among the green romantics, and at least one self-styled Promethean environmentalist in the form of Martin Lewis (1992).

that means demand in relation to supply is increasing. Conversely, if the price of a good falls, then demand relative to supply is falling. This logic can be applied to the goods we call natural resources. Thus Barnett and Morse (1963) gathered long-term trend data for the prices of a number of "extractive goods": agricultural products, minerals, fisheries products, and timber. In every case except forest products the story was the same. Barnett and Morse showed that since at least the beginning of the twentieth century, the real price (i.e. after adjusting for inflation) of natural resources had been falling. And if price measures scarcity, this means that natural resources are becoming more abundant with time. Updates of the Barnett and Morse analysis continue to tell a similar story (Smith, 1979; Taylor, 1993).

When the limits to growth argument and its associated survivalist discourse arrived with such a bang in the early 1970s, Promethean economists did, then, have a ready-made argument and plenty of data to throw back at the survivalists. The Oxford economist Wilfred Beckerman (1974) deployed long-run evidence from price trends against the *Limits to Growth* global modellers to argue that there was nothing wrong with projecting economic growth into an indefinite future. It became the standard criticism of the *Limits* modellers that their computer models did not include any role for either prices or technology. Twenty years later, Beckerman saw no difficulty in deploying the same kind of evidence against another generation of survivalists to argue that *Small is Stupid* (Beckerman, 1995; the title's allusion is to E. F. Schumacher's *Small is Beautiful*). Julian Simon put his money where his mouth was in a famous bet with survivalist Paul Ehrlich in 1980. Simon bet that the real price of any set of natural resources that Ehrlich cared to name would be lower at any time in the future than in 1980. Ehrlich specified copper, chrome, nickel, tin, and tungsten, with 1990 as the date. Come 1990, the price of copper was 24 per cent lower than in 1980, chrome 40 per cent lower, nickel 8 per cent lower, tin 68 per cent lower, and tungsten 78 per cent lower. Ehrlich sent Simon a check for $1000 (see Michaels, 1993: 368–9). Later, Simon would renew his challenge in the context of a debate with survivalist Norman Myers; by now, he was so confident that he increased the offer to a month's pay, and extended it to any measure of human welfare in any country or region of the world (Myers and Simon, 1994: 20–1, 115). This time, Simon found no takers.

Why do the prices of natural resources keep falling, so seemingly becoming more abundant? The answer is to be found in the price system itself. If a shortage threatens, there is money to be made in either finding new sources of the resource in question, or in developing substitutes for it. In this light, there is nothing new about resource scarcity, or about the response to it. In sixteenth- and seventeenth-century Europe, wood was the key energy resource, and so when wood supplies seemed to be running out an energy crisis seemed imminent. The response was the development of coal as a fuel, which in turn made the technologies of the Industrial Revolution possible— and coal itself came to be mined more cheaply using these industrial technologies (Nef, 1977). Come the mid-nineteenth century, the economist William Jevons predicted that coal would soon run out, and that the wheels of British industry would stop turning (Jevons, 1865). He need not have worried; not only were more and more deposits of coal continually discovered, but oil was soon developed as an energy resource.

Economists such as Barnett, Morse, Beckerman, and Simon see no problem in projecting such happy trends in resource and energy availability and price into the future. Just how far into the future? "We expect this benign trend to continue at least until our sun ceases to shine in perhaps 7 billion years, and until exhaustion of the elemental inputs for fission (and perhaps for fusion)" (Simon and Kahn, 1984: 25). No modesty here! Though perhaps those not convinced that economists can forecast inflation and unemployment over the next year or so might be a bit hesitant about accepting the 7 billion year forecast.

In the 1980s Julian Simon established himself as the leading American Promethean, and broadened the argument beyond resource prices to encompass trends over time of indicators of human wellbeing such as life expectancy, food supply per capita, amount of arable land, air and water quality, amount of parkland, forest cover, and fish catch. The indicators he sought were mostly global, though national and regional data were adduced too. Life expectancy plays a key role to Simon as a surrogate for pollution. He allows that with time some forms of pollution increase as others decrease; so the introduction of the internal combustion engine saw an increase in pollutants such as carbon monoxide and ozone, but a massive decrease in the horse droppings in which city streets were often quite literally awash. What matters, Simon avers, is the net overall effect of offsetting pollution increases and decreases on human health—and the best summary measure of that is life expectancy (J. Simon, 1981: 130–1). The long-term trend evidence is that in all parts of the world people are living longer; therefore in all parts of the world pollution is falling. In 1995 Beckerman observed that in the previous 15 years life expectancy had fallen only in Sierra Leone and Uganda, and that over the previous 30 years life expectancy globally had risen from 53 to 66 years (Beckerman, 1995: 111).

Simon is not always as scrupulous as he might be in the kinds of evidence he adduces. For example, in 1984 he tried to show that the United States was becoming less crowded through reference to a graph showing a massive increase in the amount of land in national parks over the 1950–80 period

(Simon and Kahn, 1984: 8). In fact, almost the entire increase occurs in 1979. What happens in 1979, which Simon fails to mention, is passage of the Alaska National Interest Lands Conservation Act, which for the first time classified federal government lands in Alaska. Some of these lands were classified as national parks. Many are accessible only by bush plane. One can imagine the sighs of relief in 1979 echoing around the Bronx, South Central Los Angeles, and Chicago, as suddenly their residents all felt less crowded.

While a critic might be able to dispute some of the trend evidence beloved of Prometheans, most of it is actually beyond dispute. The question is what to make of it. And here we may pitch straight into a discourse analysis of the Promethean position.

Analysis of Promethean Discourse

1. BASIC ENTITIES WHOSE EXISTENCE IS RECOGNIZED OR CONSTRUCTED

What such an analysis reveals, strikingly and immediately at the "ontological" level, is that for Prometheans, natural resources, ecosystems, and indeed nature itself, do not exist. This denial can explain just about everything there is worth knowing about the content of the Promethean discourse. This claim about nature's non-existence, at least as anything more than a store of matter and energy, might seem startling. Consider, though, Simon's basic argument about natural resources. He affirms, time and time again, that the supply of natural resources is infinite. Why is this? Because there is no fixed supply of resources: "Resources are only sought and found as they are needed" (1981: 40). Thus there is no point in measuring the quantity of reserves remaining: if more is needed, more will be sought and found. But just what are these things we call natural resources anyway, if, as one Promethean argues, "Not a single natural resource has ever been created by 'nature' " (Taylor, 1993: 378)? The answer is that "natural" resources are in fact created by humans transforming matter. Nature is, indeed, just brute matter; and in their wilder moments (as in the Simon and Kahn 7 billion year projection mentioned earlier) Prometheans believe matter is infinitely transformable, given enough energy. The medieval alchemists believed base metals could be turned into gold. Prometheans believe that with enough energy iron can be turned into copper (Myers and Simon, 1992: 100 n.)— which indeed it can be, though the amount of energy required is massive. Similarly, deserts can be turned into cropland, outer space can be colonized.

With enough energy, more specifically with the fruits of economic growth, we can also take care of any pollution that threatens human health (see Lewis, 1992: 184). As Beckerman (1995: 25–6) puts it, "if you want a better environment in general and, in particular, reasonable access to clean drinking water, adequate sanitation and an acceptable urban air quality, you have to become rich." Pollution is, in the Promethean light, just matter in the wrong place in the wrong form, and with enough skilled application of energy, that can be corrected quite easily.

Nature does not, then, exist as anything more than brute matter. Though Prometheans might occasionally use the word ecosystem, the concept of ecosystem plays no part in their discourse, in which ecosystems do not constrain human activity. Accordingly, for Prometheans "the term 'carrying capacity' has by now no useful meaning" (Simon and Kahn, 1984: 45). That concept does, of course, figure centrally in the survivalist discourse.

Having dealt with absences from the Promethean ontology, what basic entities does it recognize or construct? In short: people, markets, prices, energy, technology. Prometheans talk a lot about population—Julian Simon, for example, became famous mostly as a result of his intervention in debates over global population, in which he celebrated and applauded population growth. But population is not constructed in the way it is for survivalists, as an aggregate entity to be controlled, something more than just "people." I will return to the implications of this difference shortly.

2. Assumptions about Natural Relationships

I have already noted that the Promethean discourse comes close to denying the very existence of nature, which is at most seen in inert, passive terms. The most important natural relationship taken for granted by Promethean discourse is therefore a hierarchy in which humans (and in particular human minds) dominate everything else. This domination does not need to be organized, or consciously maintained; it just exists. In their more extreme moments, Prometheans believe that a total control of nature is within our grasp, once nature is fully understood (for an early explicit statement, see Murphy, 1967).

Beyond human domination, the other relationship seen as natural is competition between humans, for it is through competition that innovative means for overcoming emerging scarcities can best be generated. So when the Organization for Petroleum Exporting Countries organized oil embargoes in the 1970s it was competition which spurred the search for non-OPEC sources of oil, and for cars that would use less gasolene. This emphasis on competition reveals an affinity between the Promethean discourse and proponents of the market as the best means for organizing economy and society. Prometheans see little need for government to do anything much in the way of environmental and natural resources policy: if long-term trends are improving, the best thing government can do is leave well alone. Inasmuch as they attend to government, Prometheans see in it mostly sources only of ill. As the Promethean physicist Bernard Cohen (1984: 566) puts it in reference to the United States, "Given a rational and supportive public policy, science and technology can provide not only for the twenty-first century but for ever." But, he avers, the necessary support for nuclear energy and other constructive endeavors is missing. For:

our government's science and technology policy is now guided by uninformed and emotion-driven public opinion rather than by sound scientific advice. Unfortunately, this public opinion is controlled by the media, a group of scientific illiterates drunk with power, heavily influenced by irrelevant political ideologies, and so misguided as to believe that they are more capable than the scientific community of making scientific decisions (p. 566).

3. AGENTS AND THEIR MOTIVES

In the Promethean discourse, agency—the capacity to act—is for everyone: not as political actors (as the preceding quote from Cohen emphasizes) but as economic actors. People going about their ordinary business, pursuing their selfish interests, will together ensure a bright environmental future. Of course, this is little more than an application to resource and environmental issues of the "invisible hand" working in the market system, first celebrated by Adam Smith in the late eighteenth century.

As seen in the discussion of the survivalist discourse in the preceding chapter, survivalism denies agency to populations, which are treated as problems to be controlled. The Promethean discourse, in contrast, celebrates the people who compose populations. If individuals are problem-solvers, all potentially contributing to the betterment of humanity's lot, then the more people the better. In denying the existence of limits, Prometheans generally also deny the need to worry at all about rising populations, be it on a national, regional, or global scale. Population explosion is simply not a problem. Julian Simon, in particular, has pointed out that rising populations have been accompanied by rising, not falling, life expectancy, and increased, not reduced, income per head. Certainly this is true at the global level: the same decades which have seen population explosion have also seen life expectancy rising to historically unprecedented levels on a global scale, and the prices of natural resources continuing to fall. Why, then, worry about exploding populations? Individuals, Simon believes, make good decisions about the number of children they will have, such that "population size adjusts to productive conditions rather than being an uncontrolled monster" (J. Simon, 1981: 162–3). For Simon, "the ultimate resource is people—skilled, spirited, and hopeful people who will exert their wills and imagination for their own benefit, and so, inevitably, for the benefit of all" (1981: 348). If people are good, then more people will always be better. However, not all Prometheans share Simon's cavalier position on population. Beckerman (1995: 63, 173–4) allows that developing countries do have a population problem. He believes that the world's real environmental problems are associated with the poor in these countries lacking access to clean water and good sanitation. The obvious solution is for them to become rich, and that may be easier the fewer of them there are.

4. KEY METAPHORS AND OTHER RHETORICAL DEVICES

The key Promethean metaphor is mechanistic. Machines are constructed from simple components—ultimately, simple resources—through the application of human skill and energy. Thereafter they do useful things for humans. A solution to any kind of problem can be pieced together in like manner for Prometheans, be it the restoration of malfunctions in the human environment (such as pollution or wilderness destruction), or the creation of natural resources for human use.

The main weapon in the Promethean rhetorical arsenal is the trend. Prometheans are at their happiest when presenting graphs depicted declining resource prices, increasing parklands, croplands, and forests, increasing life expectancy, increasing crop yields and fisheries catches, and so forth. The explicit accompanying message is: the trend can be extrapolated indefinitely into the future. (Over 7 billion years into the future, as we have seen in one case.) Note how different this is from the survivalist modelling of the interaction of different variables (such as population growth, resource use, and environmental damage). The trends presented in graphs or figures by Prometheans are single-variable, and no attempt is made to model interactions. This is not to say that one or the other rhetorical device is better, simply that they are different. Prometheans would say that the interactive models of survivalists are hopelessly inaccurate, simplified, and speculative. The difference underscores the Promethean neglect of the existence of eco*systems*, in which by definition many factors interact.

Box 3.1. **PROMETHEAN DISCOURSE ANALYSIS**

---

1. **Basic Entities Recognized or Constructed**
   - Nature as only brute matter
   - Markets
   - Prices
   - Energy
   - Technology
   - People

2. **Assumptions about Natural Relationships**
   - Hierarchy of humans over everything else
   - Competition

3. **Agents and their Motives**
   - Everyone; motivated by material self-interest

4. **Key Metaphors and other Rhetorical Devices**
   - Mechanistic
   - Trends

The Impact of Promethean Discourse

Promethean discourse flourished alongside capitalism and the Industrial Revolution, with an unbounded faith in the ability of humans to manipulate the world in human interests in ever more effective fashion. Such was human progress. Thus the first place to look for the impact of the discourse would be in our dominant institutions: a capitalist economy geared to perpetual economic growth, and a political system whose main task is to facilitate the conditions for that growth. Of course, these institutions were not put into place under the direction of the discourse. Rather, discourse and institutions co-evolved. When it comes to political institutions, the Promethean discourse may be said to constitute much of their software, if the hardware is composed of formal laws and constitutions. That is, institutions of government such as parliaments, executives, and bureaucracies require sets of understandings shared by the people who work within them in order to coordinate their operations. The main shared understanding in the capitalist democracies has long been that growth is good. As I noted earlier, in the absence of an environmentalist challenge, there was for a long time no need even to articulate the basic tenets of this Promethean discourse; they were just taken for granted.

Once the environmental challenge did arrive in the late 1960s, and especially with the terms of debate set by survivalism in the early 1970s, the Promethean discourse was very much on the defensive, and so pressured to articulate its key tenets for the first time. These newly articulated tenets eventually found a ready and sympathetic ear in the form of President Reagan and his associates. The Reagan presidency does indeed constitute the high point of influence of Promethean discourse on the development of policies and institutions. The early years of the Reagan administration in particular were quite spectacular in this regard.

The anti-government, market-oriented movement with which Ronald Reagan was happy to associate his candidacy in 1980 and his presidency thereafter was quite clear in its enthusiasm for economic growth, and quite clear that the main impediment to growth was excessive governmental regulation. Environmental regulation was a particular target. Candidate Reagan in his acceptance speech to the 1980 Republican Party convention declared that "the economic prosperity of our people is a fundamental part of our environment." A moment's thought will reveal that this is a meaningless sentence; but its rhetorical importance is clearly to declare that environmental goals should be subordinated to economic ones. Just how this would happen became evident as soon as Reagan entered the White House in 1981 (for details, see Vig and Kraft, 1984).

Two key appointments symbolized the Reaganite Promethean approach to the environment. James Watt was appointed Secretary of the Interior, responsible for overseeing the vast bulk of federal lands. Anne Gorsuch (later Burford) was appointed Administrator of the Environmental Protection Agency (EPA), the agency charged with administering the nation's anti-pollution policy. Both Watt and Gorsuch Burford were essentially hostile to most of the legislation they were supposed to be administering. Watt was by background a "Sagebrush Rebel," identified with a movement based in the rural West of the United States keen to transfer ownership of federal lands (including national parks and wilderness areas) to the states, with the idea that the states would then open these areas to loggers, miners, and ranchers. It should be stressed that though their rhetoric was anti-government, Sagebrush Rebels were not especially interested in the free market; they did not want to pay market prices for access to land, timber, or minerals, but rather sought a continuation of heavy government subsidy of these activities, with privilege accorded to established users (such as holders of grazing leases on public land) rather than open to the highest bidder. In this, the Sagebrush Rebels differed from those Prometheans who stress markets and private property. Still, Watt's view was clearly Promethean: resources were there to be used for human benefit, not locked away. He characterized environmentalists as Nazis or Bolsheviks, and anyone who did not share his views as un-American. In 1990 he suggested that "if the troubles with environmentalists can't be solved in the jury box or the ballot box, perhaps the cartridge box should be used" (quoted in Dowie, 1995: 97). Watt's three years as Secretary of the Interior (he was forced to resign over a racist and offensive joke about the composition of a review committee) were turbulent, as he was in constant battle with a Congressional majority that did not share his views. In addition, he proved the best recruiting agent that the environmental movement ever had. Thus the massive policy changes he sought never materialized: nobody could galvanize the environmental opposition into action quite like James Watt.

Except perhaps for Anne Gorsuch Burford. Burford attempted to purge the ranks of the EPA of individuals who actually believed in the mission of the agency, and turned policy making over to the polluters the EPA was supposed to regulate. The involvement of the chemical industry in running EPA's hazardous waste program was eventually shown to have crossed the bounds of legality. Burford, too, clashed repeatedly with Congress, and was forced to resign under fire in early 1983. She left behind an agency with its budget and personnel slashed, its morale shattered, and its mission severely compromised. Her assistant administrator for hazardous waste, Rita Lavelle, received a six-month prison sentence.

Of these two environmental nemeses, Gorsuch Burford had the greater impact. James Watt had minimal effect, mainly because the checks and balances built into the United States system of government stymied his attempts at radical reform. He simply could not manage the federal lands the way he wanted to. Burford, in contrast, was able to paralyze some essential EPA regulatory functions, and severely damage its enforcement capabilities. However, the damage proved not to be lasting: Burford was replaced as Administrator by William Ruckelshaus, who had been the first Administrator of the EPA under President Nixon. Ruckelshaus began the process of restoring the EPA to its traditional mission. However, the Reagan administration continued to operate under an Executive Order (Number 11291) issued in February 1981 which specified that economic criteria should take priority in the formulation of rules and regulations by government agencies.

The later Reagan years did see a retreat from some of the excesses (and flamboyance) of the Watt–Burford era. No longer was the Promethean agenda in the hands of clowns and criminals at the highest level of government (the criminality in question being evident at the EPA). Yet this was mostly a matter of expedience and compromise; clearly the Promethean discourse set the tone for the rest of the 1980s in United States policy making. Nowhere was this more evident than in US actions in the international arena, where wholesale reversal of US commitment to international environmental governance took place (see Caldwell, 1984). Thus the United States withdrew support and finance for international treaties or programs concerning the Law of the Sea, transboundary air pollution (especially acid rain), trade of nuclear materials, and the United Nations Environment Program. Given the weight of the United States in international affairs, such a stance effectively blocked progress toward coordinated international environmental policy. Of course, Protheans would argue that no such policy is necessary. Consistent with a Promethean view, the United States also ended support for international population control programs. Influential here was not just the Promethean argument that there can be nothing wrong with population growth, but also the objections of the Christian Right and the Catholic Church to the use of such funds in programs that involved abortion as an option. In the 1980s, the only real exception to US foot-dragging on international environmental affairs came with the issue of ozone layer depletion, which I discussed in the previous chapter.

The influence of the Promethean discourse in United States policy in the 1980s can be discerned quite clearly in the person of Julian Simon. Simon himself rejected the "spaceship earth" metaphor that appears in survivalist discourse; otherwise, one could describe him as spaceship earth's first science officer in the 1980s.[2] Simon and the like-minded futurist Herman Kahn were originally scheduled to conduct the federal government's interagency review of the survivalist *Global 2000* report produced in the waning months of the Carter presidency. That proposal was blocked by Alan Hill, Chair of the President's Council on Environmental Quality, and Simon and Kahn instead produced their response with financial support from the right-wing Heritage Foundation. This response was published in 1984 as *The Resourceful Earth* (Simon and Kahn, 1984), one of the most visible and influential Promethean documents. The Heritage Foundation played a key role in formulating all kinds of policy initiatives for the Reagan administration, giving policy substance to Reaganism, from the very first days of his presidency.

Come the late 1980s, the power of the Promethean discourse in US environmental affairs receded. George Bush was keen to distance himself somewhat from his predecessor on environmental policy, declaring in 1988 that he wanted to be "the environmental president." Only on the population issue did extreme Protheanism hold its power—and this largely because of the common cause Promethean could make with the Christian Right and the Catholic Church. With the resurgence of the Christian Right in the mid-1990s, and the Republican gains in Congress in 1994 led by House Speaker Newt Gingrich, this natalist alliance gained new ground; and proposals dormant since the Watt–Burford years of Promethean excess were once again heard in Washington. In the early 1980s it had been Congress which had

---

[2] I owe this characterization to Gerald Mackie.

blocked these excesses; come 1995, it was Congress, or at least the Republican majority, which was pushing for weaker anti-pollution laws, the end of the Endangered Species Act, and the opening up of federal lands to loggers, miners, and ranchers. At the same time, the US West saw an echo of the Sagebrush Rebellion in the form of the Wise Use Movement, whose goal again was to remove control of federal lands to the state and local level. The Wise Use Movement combines populist rhetoric with funding from resource industry corporations.

It is in the United States alone that explicit Promethean discourse on environmental affairs has gained significant influence (though there are Promethean publicists in other countries, such as Wilfred Beckerman in the UK). This American exceptionalism was highlighted in the 1980s, when in international gatherings the US sometimes found itself casting the sole vote in the United Nations General Assembly against particular environmental measures—such as the World Charter for Nature in 1982, and a motion against trade in hazardous substances in 1983. (Of course, not all of the countries voting for these measures could be said to be paragons of environmental virtue.) In the United States, Promethean discourse resonates with the interests of both capitalist market zealots and Christian conservatives, not to mention miners, loggers, and ranchers accustomed to subsidized access to resources. Such constituencies are smaller or absent in other countries. But even in the United States, it is noteworthy that large corporations that might be expected to benefit from broad dissemination of a Promethean view tend to prefer discourses with at least a veneer of environmental concern.

Promethean Discourse: An Assessment

An assessment of the Promethean discourse may begin by noting that without a cornucopian adjunct, the discourse is radically incomplete, the protestations of its adherents such as Julian Simon notwithstanding. Why is this?

Private believe that human beings left to their own devices will automatically generate solutions to problems—and that the operation of an invisible hand will guarantee good collective consequences at the macro-level of individual-level decisions. To substantiate this claim, they return time and again to examples such as the introduction of motor vehicles leading to cleaner and healthier city streets with the removal of horses and their droppings. But there is no guarantee that such benign side-effects of individual actions will always occur. It is not only survivalists who stress the centrality in environmental affairs of the tragedy of the commons, the essence of which is that materially rational individual decisions can produce disastrous macro-level consequences. What can Prometheans say about, for example, global warming, where millions of rational individuals contribute to the build-up of carbon dioxide in the atmosphere by burning fossil fuels? Most such individuals are probably unaware that global warming might be a problem. The Promethean answer is simply to deny that global warming is a problem (see, for example, Beckerman, 1995: 79–87; Michaels, 1993; Ridley, 1995: 21–4). Given the uncertainties and ambiguities in the evidence produced by scientists so far, it is not hard to tell such a story, laced with appropriate (though selective) evidence. The Promethean Aaron Wildavsky goes through a whole series of environmental risks to show that really the scientific evidence shows there is no cause for alarm—and has no problem in generalizing this conclusion to all risks, including the ones he has not studied (Wildavsky, 1995: 447). Similarly, Simon suggests that we extend his conclusions from cases where good evidence is available to cases where it is unavailable, such as "the ozone layer, the greenhouse effect, acid rain, and their kin" (Myers and Simon, 1994: xvi). When it comes to loss of biodiversity through species extinction, Prometheans again take great pains to deny that this is a problem, arguing that there are no reliable statistics to show that we are witnessing wholesale extinctions caused by human activities such as deforestation (see Simon's contribution in Myers and Simon, 1994: 40).

What is coming to the rescue of the Prometheans here? Julian Simon claims that the difference between himself and the survivalists is that he bases his arguments on evidence, whereas survivalists rely on theory (Myers and Simon, 1994: 148). But in fact the Promethean argument can only stand with not just a theory of human ingenuity, but also a theory of nature's abundance. The implicit theory is that nature is replete with negative feedback devices that correct for human abuses. (Negative feedback is by definition automatic corrective action in a system which restores it to equilibrium when it is disturbed; in this sense, negative feedback is usually a good thing.) So when Simon discusses biodiversity he refers to the fact that nature is always creating species, as well as extinguishing them (Simon and Kahn, 1984: 23). Never mind the issue of time scale here. Survivalists argue that the rate of contemporary species extinctions caused by environmental destruction far exceeds the speed with which nature can create species; it is the difference between decades and millennia. Wildavsky (1995) in his discussion of global warming alludes to such feedback devices in ecosystems, but this is a rare admission in the Promethean literature. In fact, if the Promethean position is to stand, such devices must have an unbounded capacity to correct for human abuses. In short, what is needed here is an infinitely forgiving nature. Earlier I noted that Simon referred disparagingly to Santa Claus cornucopians. Promethean discourse in fact requires nature to be more generous still than Santa Claus, who brings only coal and no presents to children who misbehave. For the Prometheans—more properly styled Promethean–Cornucopians—nature will bring good things to us even, and especially, when we misbehave.

At the end of the day, who is right, the survivalists or the Prometheans? Are there limits, or are there not? Resolution of this issue is not easy, given the different worlds which survivalists and Prometheans seem to inhabit. The survivalist world consists of finite ecosystems with fixed stocks of resources, where human population explosion and economic growth threaten to overshoot the limits of these systems. In the Promethean world, nature does not exist, save as a source of matter to be rearranged in the human interest through the application of energy and technology (though, as we have seen, an infinitely forgiving nature eventually comes to rescue the otherwise incomplete Promethean world view). Where Prometheans see benign trends heading off into a happy future, survivalists see looming boundaries into which these trends will eventually crash.

On the trend evidence itself, the Prometheans are clear winners. Now, as we have seen, Prometheans are not always overly scrupulous about a little sleight of hand when it comes to presenting statistics. Moreover, the statistics they do present are not always global ones. And given complexity and interdependence in environmental affairs, improvement on one indicator in one place may mask deterioration in another. This is the phenomenon of displacement (see Dryzek, 1987: 16–20). Displacement occurs when, for example, a country exports its toxic wastes, or its polluting industry. In this context, it should be noted that a cleaner environment in developed countries, for which we have more and better figures to compose trends, has been purchased in part by transferring manufacturing to developing countries with comparatively lax environmental standards. Displacement across space can also occur when tall smokestacks are constructed on coal-burning power stations to reduce local pollution—only to cause acid rain elsewhere, as a result of sulfur dioxide spending longer in the atmosphere than it otherwise would have done. Displacement can take place across the media, as when a water pollution problem is solved by capturing effluent, drying, and burning it; or disposing of it as toxic sludge. In short, Promethean statistics should be believed only when they refer to global trends. Caution may be warranted there too—if, for example, growing global agricultural production has been purchased at the expense of the long-term productivity of land (for example, through excessive use of fertilizers and pesticides, or farming techniques that hasten soil erosion). This example shows that displacement can occur across time too. Prometheans ignore such issues. Their confidence in the veracity and power of statistical indicators of environmental trends represents a refusal to recognize complexity and uncertainty in ecological affairs.

These issues notwithstanding, when it comes to long-term global trends in natural resource prices, agricultural production, and life expectancy, the lines on the graphs have indeed been pointing in benign directions. Thus survivalists are tactically mistaken in taking on Prometheans in arguing about which direction the global trends are pointing—though many survivalists have made the mistake of so doing, and ending up with egg on their faces (or, in the case of Paul Ehrlich, a wallet $1000 lighter). Survivalists in their more astute moments will simply argue that the fact that a trend has persisted for long in the past is no guarantee that it will persist indefinitely into the future. The driver of an accelerating car about to hit a brick wall might well say "so far, so good"—but that does not mean the wall is not there. Survivalists have given us all kinds of good arguments for the existence of walls—even though they cannot prove that such walls exist, let alone specify precisely how far in front of the car they are located. However, survivalists have done themselves no favors in producing wild scare stories which Prometheans have had fun debunking. False alarms along these lines include predictions of global *cooling* in the 1970s, and claims about imminent exhaustion of oil or particular minerals.

One way to resolve this issue might be to compare the answers to two questions. First, if we believe the Prometheans and they are wrong, what are the consequences? Second, if we believe the survivalists and they are wrong, what are the consequences?

As a footnote to this analysis of Promethean discourse, it should be observed that on dimensions unrelated to limits and survival, prominent Prometheans can be found on the environmentalist side. So Julian Simon takes pains to stress that he enjoys being in the outdoors, and especially likes birdwatching (Myers and Simon, 1994: 204). And Aaron Wildavsky concludes his Promethean exposé of environmental risks with the question, "What, in my vision, is left of environmentalism? There is respect for nature, for all life. There are moral questions of human relationships to all creation" (1995: 447). Given that there is little in Promethean discourse about aesthetics, there is nothing to stop Prometheans being aesthetic environmentalists. Aesthetics aside, if the Prometheans are right then all other discourses of environmental concern are rendered irrelevant and unnecessary.

PART III

SOLVING ENVIRONMENTAL PROBLEMS

The clash of survivalists and Prometheans detailed in Part II is full of drama, and the stakes involved appear to be massive—nothing less than the fate of the Earth. Yet if we look for specific changes in institutions, policies, and practices directly traceable to these discourses, we are likely to be disappointed. Prometheans would say that the whole point is that nothing much needs changing, though there are in fact a large number of public policy practices they would like to see eliminated, involving some fairly radical changes. In practice, we find more limited policy responses in an environmental context. Governments have not engaged in draconian population control or sought an end to economic growth. Instead, they have opened their doors to environmental lobbyists, passed laws to conserve resources or ameliorate pollution, and created bureaucracies to implement these laws.

I turn then to a less apocalyptic discourse that has had obvious consequences in terms of the way societies, and especially governments, have gone about characterizing and attacking environmental problems. The discourses of environmental problem solving recognize the existence of ecological problems, but treat them as tractable within the basic framework of the political economy of industrial society, as belonging in a well-defined box of their own. The basic story line is that of problem solving rather than heroic struggle. Human interactions with the environment generate a range of problems (rather than one big problem like overshoot of limits threatening social collapse), to which human problem-solving devices need to be turned. Now, different varieties of this discourse reveal different conceptions about how best to organize human problem solving, especially when social problem solving is at issue, which requires the coordination of large numbers of individuals. The three main ways human beings have found to coordinate such efforts are by bureaucracy, democracy, and markets. Corresponding to these three coordination mechanisms are the three discourses which I will address in Chapters 4, 5, and 6: administrative rationalism, democratic pragmatism, and economic rationalism. However much partisans of these three variations may disagree with each other, they share the basic story line of problem solving as I have just defined it; and their differences with survivalists, Prometheans, sustainable developers, and green radicals are striking. Of the three, I will deal with administrative rationalism first because it captures the dominant governmental response to the initial onset of environmental crisis. Democratic pragmatism soon emerges as a corrective to administration. And economic rationalism builds on its advances in all areas of political life to generate alternatives to and remedies for the pathologies it identifies in both administration and liberal democratic governance.

4 Leave it to the Experts: Administrative Rationalism

Environmental issues are typically complex. They also involve systems that have long been the objects of study of natural scientists (and public health engineers). Thus when these issues came to new prominence in the 1960s they could be readily associated with a public policy tradition which accorded substantial status to scientific expertise as harnessed by the administrative state. This sort of nexus of science, professional administration, and bureaucratic structure has been used in many policy settings: defense and national security planning, public health engineering and health-care delivery more generally, agriculture, and natural resources management. Administrative rationalism may be defined as the problem-solving discourse which emphasizes the role of the expert rather than the citizen or producer/consumer in social problem solving, and which stresses social relationships of hierarchy rather than equality or competition. As an institutional style, administrative rationalism figures more strongly in some political systems than in others. So it is very strong in France and Germany, slightly less strong in Britain (where it has been leavened by a culture of generalism among high-ranking civil servants), and it has had a somewhat patchy but none the less significant presence in the United States.

When environmental issues did rise to sudden prominence—and occasional pre-eminence—on the political agenda, their assimilation to this tradition was not planned or debated against the alternatives (such as those that might be generated by the alternative discourses that appear in other chapters). It was simply taken for granted that this was how any such issues should be handled. Thus the onset of environmental problems was met by institutional and policy responses that were remarkably similar in both content and timing across the nations of the developed world.[1] If one seeks the

[1] For the United States, Hays (1987: 393–4) argues that the high-visibility conflictual environmental politics of the late 1960s and early 1970s yielded to environmental administration and

essence of most other environmental discourses, it is to be found in the writings and speeches of theorists and activists. But for administrative rationalism, that essence can be captured by looking at actual practice in the development of policies, institutions, and methodologies. Administrative rationalism does have its theorists, but they tended to come later, as they contemplated ways of building upon or strengthening existing environmental accomplishments. Later on in this chapter we will encounter some of these theorists, but it is more appropriate to begin with a survey of practices, policies, and institutions inspired by administrative rationalism.

The Repertoire of Administrative Rationalism

Administrative rationalism manifests itself in the following institutions and practices.

1. PROFESSIONAL RESOURCE-MANAGEMENT BUREAUCRACIES

"Natural resource management" has been a concern of governments for much longer than has "environmental policy." This is especially true for governments with resource-rich territory, and a significant proportion of economic activity accounted for by the resource sector, notably the United States, Canada, and Australia. The oldest professional resource management bureaucracies are to be found in the United States, the legacy of the American Conservation Movement at the beginning of the twentieth century (see Hays, 1959). This Movement was infused with some German ideas about conservation ecology via its key figure, Gifford Pinchot, who studied in Germany. The Movement's main argument was that the American endowment of natural resources was in danger of being squandered in a free-for-all, such that more rational scientific management coupled with government ownership was required to better put those resources to efficient human extractive use. The movement had no interest in wilderness preservation, environmental aesthetics, or pollution reduction, and in practice sought only to achieve maximum sustainable yield from renewable resources such as forests and watersheds. The Conservation Movement soon

management in the late 1970s, a development he describes as the rise of the environmental professional. In contrast, I would argue that the administration was there all the time in this era, but that in the late 1970s the politics became relatively subdued, leaving the field relatively free for the professionals. Political conflict certainly made a comeback in the 1980s.

achieved ascendancy in Washington DC, and Gifford Pinchot lent his guidance to the administration of President Theodore Roosevelt, a keen supporter of the Movement. The main organizational legacy of the Conservation Movement was the US Forest Service, located within the Department of Agriculture, which was reorganized by Pinchot. However, the Forest Service's ethos of professional resource management based on scientific principles rather than political expediency could not be maintained in the face of sustained political pressure from the timber industry. Today, the US Forest Service functions mainly to service the timber industry—for example, by constructing logging roads into national forests at public cost, so providing an enormous public subsidy to the industry. Welfare logging of this sort presumably has Gifford Pinchot turning in his grave.

Later, President Franklin Roosevelt's New Deal in the 1930s saw the establishment of several more federal resource management agencies, notably the Civilian Conservation Corps, the Tennessee Valley Authority, and the Soil Conservation Service. Creations of a confident presidency, these agencies were deliberately insulated from Congressional influence, thus giving professional resource managers space to move without having to worry about political oversight. Ackerman and Hassler (1981: 4–6) define a New Deal agency in terms of the "affirmation of expertise," which in turn implies insulation of the agency from both political control and judicial oversight. Today, the US federal government is home to a range of resource management bureaucracies such as the Bureau of Land Management, the Fish and Wildlife Service, the National Park Service, the National Oceanographic and Atmospheric Administration, and the US Geological Survey. None of these cases are paragons of scientific management to the exclusion of political influence—especially the influence of extractive industry, be it miners, loggers, oil companies, ranchers, or fishers. But all operate according to at least a public justification of administrative rationalism, however much that may be violated in practice. Certainly, all of them still employ individuals with the relevant scientific and professional expertise, and certainly many of these employees think that rational resource management is what they are doing.

2. POLLUTION CONTROL AGENCIES

Not every country has a vast national estate of natural resources. But every country suffers from pollution; and so every country that can afford it has a pollution control agency of some sort. Many subnational governmental units such as states, provinces, *Länder*, and cities also possess such agencies; they are even emerging at the international level (for example, the United

Nations Environment Program, which has managed to broker pollution control agreements for regional seas).

The oldest such agency is Britain's Alkali Inspectorate, created in 1864. As its name implies, its concern was originally with a limited range of pollutants, though that range expanded with time. The old Alkali Inspectorate is one of the ancestors of the unified Inspectorate of Pollution established in Britain in 1987 as part of the Department of the Environment. The Inspectorate was itself later merged into a still more inclusive Environment Agency. This unification was a bit belated; most developed countries gained such an agency in the early 1970s. So the Netherlands gained a Department for Public Health and Environmental Hygiene in 1971, the US Environmental Protection Agency was established in 1970, and in Germany anti-pollution policy was centralized in the Interior Ministry in 1969, later passing to a free-standing agency. Such agencies are typically charged with implementing laws passed by parliament. Landmark pieces of legislation here include the 1956 Clean Air Act in the United Kingdom (passed in response to London's "killer fog" in December 1952).

The US Environmental Protection Agency (EPA) is sometimes regarded as the paradigmatic anti-pollution agency, but in fact it is a bit of an anomaly, inasmuch as the professional discretion embedded in it is highly constrained. The members of Congress who set up the EPA in 1970 had in mind the experience of regulatory agencies which had been captured by the very industries they were supposed to be regulating (so the trucking industry controlled the Interstate Commerce Commission, the food industry controlled the Food and Drug Administration). To prevent such capture, Congress specified in a number of statutes (such as the Clean Air Act, Water Pollution Control Act, Toxic Substances Control Act, and their various sets of amendments) in great detail exactly what the EPA must do in a variety of areas, setting precise targets and dates for pollution reduction and the means for achieving them. This micromanagement on the part of Congress intensified in the 1980s when Congressional leaders rightly perceived that the Reagan administration wished to dismantle the EPA and its mission (Rosenbaum, 1995: 208–9). The EPA's counterparts in other countries typically have much more discretion in setting standards and deadlines, and in formulating measures to apply in particular cases.

3. Regulatory Policy Instruments

Whether as a matter of legislation (as in the case of the US EPA) or of choice on the part of the agency itself, the most popular policy instrument for pollution control has in all developed countries been regulation (see Opschoor and Vos, 1988 for a survey of countries). Regulation involves the staff of the agency formulating knife-edge standards for particular polluters, who are punished (usually by fines) if and when these standards are exceeded. In addition, regulators can specify the kinds of pollution-control equipment that must be installed to clean emissions (for example, catalytic converters on car exhausts, or scrubbers to clean the emissions of coal-burning power plants), the kinds of materials that can be used (for example, unleaded gasoline, or low-sulfur coal), and the kinds of practices that must be followed (such as inspections and safety checks). Normally regulation has been "end of pipe" in character—that is, regulators have not intervened to specify changes in production processes to make them produce less noxious waste to begin with. Instead, the focus is on reducing discharge of that waste into the environment once the waste has been produced.

Regulation of this sort entails substantial discretion on the part of the regulators, even in the United States. That said, national approaches to regulation differ substantially. In the United States, regulation proceeds in adversarial fashion, and both sides rely a great deal on lawyers to advance their cases for more or less stringent pollution standards. Many decisions end up in the courts: polluters sue the EPA for excessive stringency in enforcing the relevant law and for arbitrary action violating the principles of the US constitution; environmentalists sue the EPA for not enforcing laws with enough vigor, the EPA sues polluters for not complying, corporations sue individuals for defamatory objections to their actions (so-called SLAPP suits—strategic lawsuits against public participation). Thus in the United States it is the courts' interpretation of the legislation in question which is ultimately decisive, and administrative rationalism in practice is highly constrained by this legalistic, adversarial context.

Matters are very different in other countries, where administrative rationalism is allowed a freer hand. In Britain, regulations are developed through consultation between government and officials and polluters. Such a cosy relationship tends to startle US observers; yet the results in terms of pollution abatement and environmental quality appear to be no worse in Britain than in the United States (see Vogel, 1986). This does not mean that regulation in Britain is simply a matter of political negotiation, for both sides at least in principle accept the authority of scientific expertise in adjudicating disputes. In some cases, a scientific body is called on quite formally to render a verdict—for example, the Royal Society played this role on acid rain policy in Britain in the 1980s, effectively arbitrating disputes on this issue (Hajer, 1995: 144–5). Pollution-control discourse in Britain specifies that no regulatory action be taken until conclusive scientific research can demonstrate the harm being caused by the pollutant. As William Waldegrave, Minister of State in the Department of the Environment, put it in 1987, "It is necessary in an area which should be science-based to put up pretty formidable hurdles and tests of a scientific nature if we are to make rational priorities" (quoted in Weale, 1992: 80). This is the exact opposite of the "precautionary principle" applied in countries such as Germany and the Netherlands, which specifies that scientific uncertainty is not a good reason for delaying action against pollution (I will discuss this principle in greater depth in the chapter on ecological modernization).

4. ENVIRONMENTAL IMPACT ASSESSMENT

Environmental impact assessment specifies that government departments (and, in some cases, private developers) must prepare a systematic assessment of the environmental damage likely to be caused by any project, be it an airport, a mine, a shopping mall, a sale of oil or mining or timber leases, a freeway, or a pipeline. Typically only projects with anticipated "major" environmental impacts are included. The target is, then, the decision-making processes of government agencies, with the intent of forcing environmental values and scientific means for the calculation of the project's effect on them into the decision calculus. The US National Environmental Policy Act of 1970 (NEPA) is a landmark in establishing this kind of process, but again the US turns out to be slightly anomalous. Large numbers of impact statements have been prepared in the US, perhaps the most famous being the two prepared for the Trans-Alaska Pipeline immediately following the passage of NEPA. The first was a few pages long; after being ruled inadequate by the courts, a second was prepared in multiple volumes which would occupy many feet of shelf space (ironically, the pressure of the energy crisis in the wake of the 1973 Organization of Petroleum Exporting Countries oil embargo eventually led Congress to exempt the pipeline from NEPA requirements). Again, the courts have played a large role in determining what US legislation actually means. In the case of NEPA, the courts' interpretation has been that an impact statement must be prepared, not that it must actually be used in decision making. Thus US environmental impact statements became long and unreadable documents, designed to defend agencies against accusations that environmental concerns were not being taken seriously. Environmentalist and community objectors to proposals could file suit only on the basis of the adequacy of the impact statement, not on the basis of the substantive merits of the agency's decision. Observers of the environmental impact process in the US are divided on whether it has indeed improved policy making by bringing environmental values and scientific expertise to bear. Even Lynton Caldwell, largely responsible for crafting the NEPA legislation, cannot make up his mind on whether the Act had the desired impact (for a pessimistic assessment, see Caldwell, 1978; for a more positive verdict, see Caldwell, 1982).

The US pioneered environmental impact assessment, but it was soon followed (without some of the quirks imposed by the political and legal environment of policy making in the United States) by Canada, Australia, Germany, and France, among others. Again, Britain dragged its feet, and only accepted the idea of environmental impact assessment at the behest of the European Community in 1985. In these other countries the path of administrative rationalism in environmental impact assessment has been less strewn with legal and political obstacles than in the United States. Not that matters are always smooth. For example, in my own city of Melbourne the state government (Victoria) now routinely exempts the biggest and most controversial projects from assessment. In the mid-1990s these included, most notably, the construction of a grand prix motor-racing circuit in an inner-city park, a freeway network around the city center, and the world's biggest casino.

Environmental impact assessment, even when it can escape legal shackles, is not unalloyed administrative rationalism. That is only part of the story. For typically the process also mandates opportunities for public comment on impact statements and so public participation in the policy process. This latter aspect of impact assessment is more easily joined to democratic pragmatism, and will be discussed in the next chapter.

5. EXPERT ADVISORY COMMISSIONS

Aside from environmental impact assessment, the United States also pioneered the idea of an expert commission to offer advice on environmental affairs. The President's Council on Environmental Quality (CEQ) was set up in 1970 in a section of the National Environmental Policy Act. Quite what the commission would do (aside from offer comment on the environmental impact processes established under NEPA) was never entirely clear, and the role of the CEQ has varied substantially across the different presidencies since 1970. It fell into virtual disuse in the 1980s. At one level, the CEQ might act as a counterweight to the longer-established and more influential Council of Economic Advisors. Both report directly to the President. But the CEQ has never attained the standing of the CEA. In 1993 President Clinton replaced the CEQ with an Office of Environmental Policy in the White

House, a development which had the appearance, though not necessarily the substance, of an upgrading. So it remains ironic that bodies such as Germany's Council of Environmental Experts, established in 1972 and explicitly modeled on the US CEQ, have been able to achieve greater centrality in environmental policy making.

In Britain, as I have already noted, there is a long tradition of deference to scientific expertise, and so to expert advisory bodies. Notable among such bodies is the Royal Commission on Environmental Pollution, established in 1971. As the name implies, its mandate is narrower than that of the US CEQ; but its policy role is greater. In addition, as I have already noted, the Royal Society is occasionally called upon to play a key role in policy determination. None of this means that environmental policy in Britain is made by administrative rationalism untarnished by politics, for science is expected to fall into line with the policy priorities of the government of the day. Given that one of those priorities is normally that more scientific research is needed before any substantial action is taken to protect the environment, it is not hard to find scientists who can tailor their recommendations to government desires.

6. RATIONALISTIC POLICY ANALYSIS TECHNIQUES

The expertise which legitimates administrative rationalism comes largely in the form of access to the methods and findings of environmental science and engineering. The relevant disciplines include forestry, oceanography, meteorology, ecology, hydrology, geology, fisheries biology, biochemistry, and toxicology. But administrative rationalism also involves the application of general-purpose policy analysis techniques, most of them geared to identification of the optimal policy in a given situation. As it turns out, many of these techniques were developed in an environmental context, or at least what we would now recognize as an environmental context.[2] The most widely used such techniques are cost–benefit analysis and risk analysis. Computer modelling of the sort discussed in the chapter on survivalism is also congenial to administrative rationalism, but is less widely used in policy advice and policy legitimation. Other available techniques include technology assessment, decision analysis, and a range of forecasting methods.

Cost–benefit analysis can be either forward-looking, in informing the choice of policy or project, or backward-looking, to evaluate policies already in place. Forward-looking cost–benefit analysis involves the following steps:

[2] Cost–benefit analysis was pioneered in water resources management in the 1950s, before "the environment" was conceptualized.

1. Identify policy options. (The procedure still works if there is only one option to compare with "do nothing.")
2. For each option, list both desirable effects (benefits) and undesirable effects (costs).
3. Attach monetary values to all costs and benefits, using "shadow pricing" when the item in question has no market price.
4. Convert all costs and benefits occurring in future time periods to the present time period using a discount rate.[3]
5. Add up the monetary costs and benefits associated with each alternative to give the net benefit associated with each alternative.
6. Choose the option with the greatest net benefit (provided that this net benefit is positive).

The real substance of a piece of cost–benefit analysis is in shadow pricing, and this is where the analyst's expertise comes into play. Obviously some items can easily have a monetary cost pinned onto them. For example, if the analysis is of a proposal to build a dam, construction costs can easily be expressed in terms of dollars. So can the benefits of the electricity generated by the dam. Other items are more difficult. How does one value in monetary terms the loss of a free-flowing river? Or the benefits to recreational users yielded by the artificial lake that will be constructed? In fact there are a large number of shadow-pricing techniques that can be brought to bear. A lost environment (such as a drowned river valley) can be valued by simply conducting a survey and asking individuals how much compensation they would require as individuals to consider themselves no worse off than before. Alternatively, they can be asked how much they would be willing to pay to prevent the drowning. Alternatively, the amount of time and money individuals expend to reach the valley in question for recreational activities can be observed and summed and, after making a few assumptions concerning the conversion of time to money, used to calculate how much individuals do actually pay to get to the valley.

Among the earliest significant applications of cost–benefit analysis was in the siting and construction of dams in the United States, starting in the 1950s. The main sponsors of the analysis were the US Army Corps of Engineers and the Bureau of Reclamation. One of the more famous pieces of cost–benefit analysis in an environmental context was conducted in the late

---

[3] A discount rate is like an interest rate, except that it works back from the future to the present. So at a discount rate of 5%, $100 expected one year in the future has a present value of $95. The choice of a discount rate can be quite controversial, and different discount rates can impart different conclusions to the analysis.

1960s in Britain by the Roskill Commission, set up to recommend a site for a third major airport for London. Roskill's recommendation in favor of a site at Wing in Buckinghamshire was reached via a cost–benefit analysis of the alternative sites. In its efforts to monetize all costs and benefits associated with each site, the Commission provided plenty of ammunition for its opponents. For example, the price put on a centuries-old church which would have to be demolished to make way for the airport was determined by the increased travel time churchgoers would have to expend to go to more distant churches. (The recommendation in favor of Wing was not accepted by the government of the day.)

Cost–benefit analysis received a major boost with the promulgation in 1981 of Executive Order 12291 by President Reagan. This order specified that henceforth all significant federal regulations, including environmental ones, had to pass a cost–benefit test administered by the Office of Management and Budget. This order owed more to right-wing ideology than to administrative rationalism. The idea was to use cost–benefit analysis as a tool in the Reagan administration's attack on positive government, to free corporations from regulations that harmed profitability.

Cost–benefit analysis is by now the subject of a huge literature, both technical in terms of how to do it (see, for example, Sugden and Williams, 1978), and critical in terms of why it should never be done (for example, Bobrow and Dryzek, 1987: 27–43; Sagoff, 1988). This is not the place to enter the debate on the pros and cons of cost–benefit analysis. From the discourse analyst's perspective, the main cumulative impact of cost–benefit analysis may be in legitimating the idea that public policy formation is a matter for technical, expert choice and not a question on which non-specialists such as elected officials, still less any broader public, have any rightful say. And this is why cost–benefit analysis rests more easily in a discourse of administrative rationalism than it does in economic rationalism. For this technique uses markets only to provide prices for the balance sheet of costs and benefits. Once such prices have been input, it is expert-guided governmental actions which are at issue. Thus cost–benefit analysis has an implicit faith in the welfare-maximizing virtues of government officials, which true economic rationalism lacks, preferring instead that market mechanisms be utilized wherever possible, rather than government control.

Risk analysis covers a family of procedures and techniques, many of them used to quantify the potential harm to humans from environmental hazards, such as ingesting particular pollutants, living downwind of a nuclear power plant, or being exposed to additional ultra-violet radiation as a result of ozone depletion in the stratosphere. In many cases it is possible to compute a dose–response curve, which shows how the risk to health and life varies with the amount of exposure to a hazard. The main sources of information in risk assessment are animal studies and epidemiology. Animal studies are based on the assumption that exposing animals to high doses of a pollutant can yield useful information about what happens when human beings are exposed to much lower doses (in terms of cancer rates, etc.). Epidemiological studies are statistical analysis of human populations that relate degree of exposure to a risk (for example, quantity of suspended particulates in the air) to the incidence of particular kinds of death and disease (for example, lung cancer). Both instruments can be a bit blunt. As Wildavsky (1995: 254, quoting David Ozonoff) puts it, "a good working definition of a catastrophe is an effect so large that even an epidemiological study can detect it."

Risk analysis also involves study of risk perceptions by ordinary people. Almost invariably, the scientific evidence shows that people wildly overestimate the potential damage to them from environmental risks such as having a toxic waste dump in the vicinity (Wildavsky, 1995), and behave quite inconsistently in relation to risks. Given that both animal studies and epidemiology are extremely blunt instruments, public skepticism and alarmism become a bit more understandable. Also, risk assessment is not very good at dealing with the interaction effects of multiple environmental hazards. Still, thinking of the place of risk analysis in environmental discourse, its function is quite clear: the assessment of true risks is a matter for the experts, and the ordinary public usually gets it wrong. However, it should be noted that many of the psychologists who study risk give greater credence to public skepticism (for example, Fischoff, Slovic, and Lichtenstein, 1982). Public skepticism can be explained by, for example, distinguishing between risks that are borne voluntarily, like driving a car, and those that are incurred involuntarily, like being exposed to fumes from a nearby factory. People have a much higher tolerance for risks they bear voluntarily. They also tend to have a low tolerance for low-probability catastrophic events (such as the meltdown of a nuclear reactor), and so overestimate the risks from them.

Discourse Analysis of Administrative Rationalism

Administrative rationalism seeks to organize scientific and technical expertise into bureaucratic hierarchy in the service of the state. As such, it rests on the following components.

1. Basic Entities whose Existence is Recognized or Constructed

Administrative rationalism is a problem-solving discourse, and so takes the structural status quo of liberal capitalism as given. Within this *status quo*, the discourse has a strong conception of the nature of government. Government is the administrative state, treated in monolithic terms. Governing is therefore not about democracy, but about rational management in the service of a clearly-defined public interest, informed by the best available expertise. Managers and experts have well-defined roles within the administrative monolith.

Administrative rationalism is quite agnostic about many of the entities that so energize survivalism and its Promethean critics—entities such as ecosystems, finite stocks of resources, population, energy (at least in the key role Center stage, nor do they condition the very nature of the quest as they do for survivalists and Private). There is nothing to stop administrative rationalism coming across such concepts in the problem-solving quest; but they are not at center stage, nor do they condition the very nature of the quest as they do for survivalists and Prometheans.

2. Assumptions about Natural Relationships

While not explicitly concerned with the fundamental character of relationships between human and nonhuman worlds, administrative rationalism does assume that nature is rightfully subordinated to human problem-solving, though not in the forthright and confident celebration of human domination of nature found among Prometheans. (Green radicals would still detect a latent human arrogance.)

Within human society, administrative rationalism assumes two complementary kinds of hierarchy. The first subordinates the people to the state. The second puts experts and managers in their properly dominant places in the state's own hierarchy, which is justified on the basis of expertise. The discourse pretty much denies the existence of politics of any sort.

3. Agents and their Motives

Agency is granted to both collective and individual actors. The state as a collective actor is the primary agent, but this does not imply that all individuals working for the state have an equal capacity to act. Technical experts and managers have a greater capacity than anyone else. Motivations are treated as entirely public-spirited, and the public interest is conceptualized in unitary terms. Thus discovery and application of the public interest is itself a technical procedure (see Williams and Matheny, 1995: 11–17), which is why (for example) cost–benefit analysts or risk assessors know better than the public itself what is in the public interest.

4. Key Metaphors and other Rhetorical Devices

Administrative rationalism is much poorer and less vivid in its metaphors than survivalist and Promethean discourses. Doom and redemption are not at issue, which makes for muted rhetoric. At one level, environmental problems are serious enough to warrant attention; at another level, they are not serious enough to demand fundamental changes in the way society is organized. Thus the rhetoric combines a mixture of concern and reassurance, both of which can be drawn upon at particular stages in problem-solving efforts. So government officials can reassure people that there is no cause for alarm when a particular environmental risk surfaces (be it alar on apples, asbestos in schools, or radon in basements). The same actors may also point out that policy measures need to be taken in response to the risk, though normally in ways that treat the risk in piecemeal fashion, rather than as a manifestation of anything more deeply wrong with industrial society.

If there is a metaphor that characterizes the discourse, it is that of a unitary and omniscient administrative mind. This is like the human mind, only collective and embodied in the administrative state. Just as the human mind controls the body, so the administrative mind controls the state. As Torgerson (1990: 120–1) puts it, "The image of the administrative mind is one of an impartial reason exercising unquestionable authority for universal well being; it is an image which projects an aura of certain knowledge and benign power."

The Justification of Administrative Rationalism

I argued earlier that the search for administrative rationalism in environmental affairs should begin not with the writings of theorists and the proclamations of activists, but with an examination of actual policy practice. I have defined that practice in terms of the sixfold repertoire of administrative rationalism discussed earlier in this chapter. These items are for the most part institutional and policy hardware, with very tangible existence. As bits of hardware, some of them can be appropriated by competing discourses, or

---

BOX 4.1. DISCOURSE ANALYSIS OF ADMINISTRATIVE RATIONALISM

1. Basic Entities Recognized or Constructed
  - Liberal capitalism
  - Administrative State
  - Experts
  - Managers

2. Assumptions about Natural Relationships
  - Nature subordinate to human problem solving
  - People subordinate to state
  - Experts and managers control state

3. Agents and their Motives
  - Experts and managers
  - Motivated by public interest, defined in unitary terms

4. Key Metaphors and other Rhetorical Devices
  - Mixture of concern and reassurance
  - The administrative mind

---

at least by the other problem-solving discourses set out in the next two chapters. The essence of administrative rationalism is to be found in the discursive "software" that unites these six items around a common purpose. As a problem-solving discourse, administrative rationalism takes the political-economic status quo of liberal capitalism as given. It then puts scientific and technical expertise, organized into bureaucratic hierarchy, motivated by the public interest, to use in solving environmental problems without changing the structural status quo. With this characterization in hand, it is possible to identify more clearly the justification on which administrative rationalism rests.

The twentieth century was greeted by the German sociologist Max Weber with an announcement that bureaucracy was the supremely rational form of social organization (see Gerth and Mills, 1948). Weber was not happy about this, but saw increasing rationalization of society through bureaucratic organization as inevitable. Why? Because increasing complexity in social and economic problems could not be confronted by individuals acting in isolation, but only by the coordinated problem-solving efforts of large numbers of individuals. The best way to cope with a large, complex problem is to break it down into smaller sets and then into still smaller subsets. Each subset should then be assigned to an individual or small group to craft a solution. These partial solutions are then aggregated into a solution for the complex problem as a whole (see H. Simon, 1981). Clearly somebody needs to formulate the initial breakdown into sets and subsets; somebody needs to keep an eye on the people dealing with each subset; and somebody needs to piece together the elements in the aggregation process. That "somebody" is the apex of organizational hierarchy. Hierarchy is justified on the basis of access to both principles of administrative management and substantive expertise in the issue area in question. And the structure of problem disaggregation and solution aggregation describes too the standard organization chart of a bureaucracy.

When Weber was writing, environmental problems were not conceptualized as such. But when these problems did reach the agenda, it is unsurprising that Weberian bureaucracies were constructed to deal with them. How is an anti-pollution agency organized? It is normally divided into offices dealing with air pollution, water pollution, hazardous wastes, and solid wastes. Each of these offices is then disaggregated further, perhaps on a regional basis, perhaps to deal with different kinds of pollutants, perhaps to deal with different industries. For example, the air pollution office could be divided into "stationary sources" (smokestacks) and "mobile sources" (vehicles). The stationary source unit could then be divided further into units dealing with power generation and manufacturing. Power generation could be divided into suspended particulates (smoke), greenhouse emissions (carbon dioxide), and sulphur dioxide (acid rain). Particular kinds of scientific and engineering expertise can then be assigned to the appropriate unit or sub-unit.

This kind of Weberian bureaucratic ideal is rarely realized in practice, where political factors intervene to confuse the organizational chart. These factors include interventions by elected officials, political parties, lobbyists for interest groups, and occasionally even the public. When this happens, policy making can become decidedly more complicated and messy. The response on the part of a number of structural reformers is to try to depoliticize and centralize decision making. For that especially politicized agency, the US EPA, Walter Rosenbaum (1985:299–300) recommends four measures along these lines: a fixed five- or seven-year term for the Administrator (head of the EPA) so that he or she cannot be dismissed at will by the President; the replacement of political appointees by professional civil servants; the establishment of an inspector-general to oversee the professional conduct of the EPA and its employees; and external scientific review of the EPA's use of technical information in decision making.

This sort of insulation is also recommended by Bruce Ackerman and William Hassler (1981) at the end of their analysis of the disastrous consequences of subjecting the US EPA to political micro-management by Congress. The consequence of that micromanagement is that battles are fought in the congressional arena over the means of policy—and questions of means, they argue, are surely a matter for the experts, not politicians and lobbyists. The particular case they analyze in depth is the Clean Air Act

Amendments of 1977, which mandated the installation of expensive scrubbers to clean the emissions of all new coal-burning power stations. This proposal was supported by both high-sulfur coal producers from the Eastern States and Western-based environmentalists concerned only with pristine air and minimal intrusion into wilderness in the West. The proposal was both hugely expensive and likely to lead to an increase in the quantity of acid rain produced rather than a decrease, the latter because it discriminated against low-sulfur coal mined in the West. Surely no expert agency would ever have produced such a perverse policy. The solution to the EPA's woes, they argue, is to have Congress force very precise ends on the agency—expressed, for example, in person-years of life expectancy added to the US population by a particular date (p. 124). This precise specification will protect the agency against industry capture, the fear of which was the reason for Congressional micromanagement of the agency to begin with. Once these ends have been imposed, EPA professionals should be left alone to craft appropriate solutions; no means should be forced upon them by Congress.

If politics and political conflict cannot be banished from environmental administration, the next best thing for the administrative rationalist may be to channel them more productively. Along these lines, Kai Lee (1993) argues that the proper function of political conflict is to raise issues which mangers might otherwise miss. Lee's ideal is "ecosystem management," in which professional resource managers trained in ecology take charge of whole ecosystems. He regards the Northwest Power Planning Council, which attempts to manage the Columbia River Basin (and on which he has served) as an exemplary effort in this direction, though it was not in fact governed by ecologists. For Lee, ecosystem management cannot be entrusted to politicians, who do not have the patience to learn, the willingness to tolerate failure for the sake of learning, the ability to operate on a biological rather than an electoral timescale, or to look beyond the short-term interests of their particular human constituencies. But recognizing that political conflict cannot be eliminated, he suggests taming it by establishing forums in which political actors can express their concerns to ecosystem managers, and the establishment of alternative dispute-resolution mechanisms in which people can reason through their differences in a productive manner, rather than waste energy in adversarial processes which produce only stalemate or uncreative either/or decisions.

Administrative Rationalism in Crisis

Among those who have recently reflected upon administrative rationalism in an environmental context, increasingly few have done so in order to defend or advance it. Part of this is due to the association with bureaucracy: it is hard to find anyone who actually likes bureaucracy (recall that even Max Weber did not welcome the bureaucratic world whose arrival he announced; indeed, he described it as an "iron cage," a "polar night of icy darkness and hardness"). It is more common to find bureaucracy defended as necessary rather than attractive. Still, a discourse can soldier on without reflective defenders—indeed, particular discourses may persist precisely because nobody at all is reflecting on them, whether in attack or defense. Unfortunately for administrative rationalism, it is meeting with reflection, much of which turns out to be very critical.

Prosaic and uninspirational though it might be, administrative rationalism could always sustain itself so long as it delivered the goods. In an environmental context, that would mean cleaner air and waters, fewer toxins circulating in the human environment, an environmentally secure future, improving aesthetic standards in city, suburb, countryside, and wilderness, more securely protected ecosystems and species. But the administrative state's performance on these standards has been called into question. This questioning can often be put under the heading of "implementation deficit"—a substantial gap between what legislation and high-level executive decisions declare will be achieved and what is actually achieved at street level in terms of attainment of environmental standards (Weale, 1992: 17–18; implementation deficit is originally a German expression, but the phenomenon is universal).

More generally, the administrative state may be running out of steam in the environmental arena, or experiencing diminishing returns to effort. This would accord with experience in other policy areas such as crime, public health, industrial development, and education. It is relatively easy to achieve substantial initial gains, because the relatively easy and most visible problems will be attacked first. It is very hard to show sustained improvement on any dimension once these initial gains have been made (though occasionally a technological breakthrough may allow more substantial change). For example, in air pollution control it tends to be suspended particulates in cities which get attacked first: these are (literally) visible and easily remedied by technical fixes (such as mandating smokeless fuels). More insidious pollutants such as lead from car exhausts take longer to come to attention and receive their fix—but eventually they get it in the form of unleaded gasoline. More complex, invisible, and contentious issues like acid rain eventually come to the fore, but prove much harder to conceptualize, to even define the problem at hand, and to craft solutions. As Lindblom (1977) puts it, centrally administered systems have "strong thumbs, no fingers."

What lies at the root of these apparent problems in administrative rationalism as an orientation to environmental affairs? To begin with, administrative rationalism implies hierarchy based on expertise, with both power and knowledge centralized at the apex of the administrative hierarchy. Those at the apex are assumed to know better than those at subordinate levels, so as to be able to assign tasks and coordinate operations. But problems of any degree of complexity defy such centralization: nobody can possibly know enough about the various dimensions of an issue such as acid rain, global climate change, ozone depletion, or the interacting cocktail of urban air pollutants, not to mention the social and economic aspects of these issues, to sit with any confidence at any such apex. As the philosophers Karl Popper (1966) and F. A. von Hayek (1979) have argued at length (though never in the context of environmental problems), the relevant human knowledge is dispersed and fragmentary. The closed, hierarchical style of administrative rationalism simply has no way to aggregate these pieces of information in intelligent fashion. Popper's solution is the give and take of liberal democracy; Hayek's is the market. Popper's critique is especially devastating because it is rooted in a model of science, which is for Popper the exemplary human problem-solving activity. To Popper, the hallmark of the scientific community is not authority based on expertise, but free, open, and equal criticism and test of the conjectures of scientists by other scientists. Just as hierarchy and deference to expertise can only obstruct scientific problem solving, so it can only obstruct problem solving in policy and politics.

The Weberian approach to problem disaggregation and assignment of chunks of the problem to different units within the organization requires that such aggregation be done in intelligent fashion. The main principles of disaggregation here are that interactions within problem subsets as defined should be rich, and interactions across different subsets should be weak (Alexander, 1964). But for truly complex problems, those with a large number and variety of elements and interactions facing a decision system, no intelligent disaggregation may be possible. For a defensible disaggregation requires minimization of interactions across the problem chunks with which each organizational unit is dealing. High orders of complexity mean that such interactions will always occur, no matter how intelligently the disaggregation is done. When that happens, there is little in the way of problem solving that occurs, but a great deal in the way of problem displacement (see

Dryzek, 1987: 16–20, 99–100). Such displacement occurs when an air pollution problem is solved by creating a water pollution problem—for example, prohibition of the burning of waste may lead a company to discharge the waste in watercourses instead. It occurs when tall smokestacks are built to alleviate air pollution in the vicinity of a factory, thus leading emissions to fall somewhere else and, in the case of coal-burning power plants, for sulfur dioxide to stay in the atmosphere long enough to constitute acid rain. It is noteworthy that most anti-pollution agencies operate under single-medium statutes such as various clean air acts and clean water acts. Such statutes increase the likelihood of problem displacement across the media.

This question of displacement has been recognized by administrative rationalists, but rarely answered effectively by them. The US EPA has experimented with a "cluster" approach to pollutants, to coordinate rules coming from different pieces of legislation for (say) an industry (Fiorino, 1995: 210). The EPA has also tried "integrated environmental management" of particular geographical pollution hot spots (see Mosher, 1983). But these efforts have to date been unable to transcend the divisions across the single-medium statutes under which the EPA continues to operate.

In Britain, the unified Inspectorate of Pollution was created in part to integrate anti-pollution efforts, and so help identify courses of action that would best reduce environmental damage for any given cost level (the costs in question being to both industry and government). But this new Inspectorate was still composed of single-medium units, dealing with industrial air pollution, "wastes," radioactivity, and water quality. For a number of years its water operations still faced competition from the single-medium National Rivers Authority, though eventually the competitors were merged into the Environment Agency. Legal changes which would have allowed the Inspectorate and its successor to try to operate in holistic fashion were very slow in coming. Thus the integration that has been achieved in the UK remains limited (Weale, 1992: 104–7).

To date, the most effective integration has been achieved in Sweden, though even that is confined to the plant level, such that there is little integration above this level, still less across national boundaries (Weale, 1992: 98–9). So problem displacement across space and time remains likely even in Sweden. The real problem with all these attempts is that the very idea of holistic pollution control flies in the face of Weberian administrative logic. While organization theorists have talked a great deal about how this logic can be changed to make bureaucracies more flexible and effective, little action along these lines is observable, in environmental policy or elsewhere. The usual reaction of administrative rationalists to the failure of rigid rules is to specify still more rules (Levine, 1972).

A more straightforward reason that helps to explain implementation deficit under administrative rationalism is the problem of compliance with policy decisions. Compliance is required in two stages: first, "street level" agency officials must comply with legislative direction and the desires of their superiors, and second, polluters, developers, and resource users must comply with directives emanating from the administrative structure. Both kinds of compliance are problematical. As Weale (1992: 18–19) notes, the latter kind of compliance is rarely a matter of actors being told what to do by public officials and then doing it; more often, compliance is negotiated. So, for example, the degree of pollution reduction, the timetable at which it is achieved, and the kinds of equipment to be installed can all be a matter for negotiation, no matter what legislation and regulation say. Negotiated compliance makes sense for street-level bureaucrats because they need to cultivate working understandings with polluters, and there is every reason for them to make their own discretionary judgments about who is to blame and what negotiation strategy is likely to pay off in the long run. Policies made centrally are rarely sensitive to the local circumstances in which street level bureaucrats must operate.

These local circumstances put such officials in a position where they can learn about what works and what does not. Unfortunately the structure of administration is normally such as to prevent that learning being communicated up the administrative hierarchy, such that learning for the organization as a whole is far more problematical. As one ascends the administrative hierarchy, the limited time and information-processing resources of individual administrators means that much information is inevitably lost. So administrative rationalism is faced with a conundrum here: the more an organization is disciplined, the less it can be expected to learn (see Torgerson and Paehlke, 1990: 9–10). The more it learns (by developing an open and decentralized structure), the less easy will it be to maintain discipline by administrative means, and so the more likely becomes implementation deficit.

Given the locally variable and negotiated ways in which administrators secure compliance, it is ironic that opponents of administrative rationalism have been able to stigmatize it by attaching the term "command and control" to regulatory policy. This is a rhetorical accomplishment which has no real basis, as very little commanding and controlling actually goes on in the implementation of environmental regulations. But since the late 1980s economic rationalists have managed to gain broad acceptance for their re-designation of what used to be called quite accurately "regulation" as, quite inaccurately, "command and control." Command and control sounds ugly, as something that belongs in the military, or discredited Soviet-style economic systems.

As if all these difficulties confronting administrative rationalists were not enough, the liberal capitalist context in which administration must operate—and which, as a problem-solving discourse, administrative rationalism cannot call into question—can be quite debilitating. The first concern of all states operating in a market context must be to secure the confidence of actual and potential investors. If they make such investors unhappy, for example by putting costly anti-pollution laws and regulations into place, then the likely result is disinvestment and capital flight to locales more hospitable to business interests (see Lindblom, 1982). Disinvestment means economic recession and unpopularity of the government in the eyes of the voters; it also means falling tax revenues to finance whatever it is that governments want to do. These constraints are exacerbated in the emerging era of free trade and capital mobility across national boundaries. If I am correct in postulating diminishing returns to effort in environmental administration, then in the early days this was not a problem, because demonstrable improvements in environmental quality could be achieved at little cost to business. But as diminishing returns set in, each increment of environmental improvement becomes more costly to achieve.

This issue of the constraints imposed by the capitalist market context applies to all problem-solving discourses, not just economic rationalism. Other discourses contain solutions to the problem. Survivalists and green radicals would eliminate it by eliminating liberal capitalism. Prometheans would deny that it is a problem, on the grounds that capitalist growth automatically brings environmental benefits. And ecological modernizers would dissolve the problem by pointing to the potential of designing a capitalist system that is compatible with ecological values.

For better or for worse, administrative rationalism has clearly had substantial impact in the environmental arena. Today it may be running out of steam and facing crisis, but its past achievements should not be forgotten. The countries of the developed world have an environment which is cleaner, safer, and more aesthetically pleasing than it would have been without the last thirty years of administrative rationalism. This evaluation does not mean that administrative rationalism was the most effective conceivable response to environmental crisis, or even an adequate one. Nor are past achievements any guarantee of future success. So let me turn to the two other problem-solving discourses, which are presented by their adherents as containing effective remedies for the contemporary ills of administrative rationalism.

5 Leave it to the People: Democratic Pragmatism

Ours is a democratic age; it is decidedly unfashionable for anyone, anywhere in the world to proclaim themselves to be anything but a democrat. Francis Fukuyama (1989, 1992) recently declared that we have arrived at the "end of history," where there are no plausible global competitors to the basic ideology of liberal democracy in a capitalist economic context. Even military dictators take pains to argue that they are just stabilizing the situation so that democracy can be restored or attained in the fulness of time (of course, they also find ways of making that time a very long one). Thus it is increasingly easy to proclaim one's faith in democracy, just as it is increasingly hard to proclaim one's faith in bureaucracy and administrative rationalism. As I noted in the previous chapter, administration is not necessarily very popular as an ideal; rather, it is just what a lot of people, and a lot of institutions, actually end up doing. Even the people doing it rarely admit to liking it. Democracy is different; everyone wants to be a democrat. Whether they truly are democrats is a different question, made harder to answer by the sheer variety of meanings and models of democracy.

In this chapter I will treat democracy not as a set of institutions (elections, parliaments, parties, etc.), but rather as a way of apprehending problems. I will be concerned with democracy as a problem-solving discourse, which means it is reconciled to the basic status quo of liberal capitalism. Other discourses of democracy do exist, some of which challenge this status quo, advocating for example radical participatory alternatives to established institutions (see Dryzek, 1996a), and I shall return to some of these alternatives in later chapters. But for the moment it is appropriate to focus on what I call democratic pragmatism, which involves more or less democratic problem solving constrained by the structural status quo. For this is indeed the version of democracy which dominates today's world, especially after the revolutions of 1989 destroyed the credibility of some Marxist alternatives.

Democratic pragmatism may be characterized in terms of interactive problem solving within the basic institutional structure of liberal capitalist democracy. The word "pragmatism" can have two connotations here, both of which I intend. The first is the way the word is used in everyday language, as signifying a practical, realistic orientation to the world, the opposite of starry-eyed idealism.[1] The second refers to a school of thought in philosophy, associated with names such as William James, Charles Peirce, and John Dewey. To these pragmatist philosophers, life is mostly about solving problems in a world full of uncertainty. The most rational approach to problem solving, in life as in science, involves learning through experimentation. For problems of any degree of complexity, the relevant knowledge cannot be centralized in the hands of any individual or any administrative state structure. Thus problem solving should be a flexible process involving many voices, and cooperation across a plurality of perspectives. As long as this plurality is achieved, there is no need for more widespread public participation in problem solving. So the degree of democratic participation with which pragmatists are happy corresponds roughly to the limited amount found in existing liberal democracies, and this is why there is an essential congruence between the demands of rationality in social problem solving and democratic values, a happy coincidence indeed![2]

Pragmatist philosophy has recently received an explicit environmental twist with the arrival of "environmental pragmatism," which takes its bearings from philosophical debates in the field of environmental ethics. Environmental pragmatism does battle with all attempts to propose moral absolutes to guide environmental affairs, which are treated instead as ripe for tentative problem-solving efforts in which a plurality of moral perspectives is always relevant (see Light and Katz, 1996). In this chapter I will be concerned less with the finer points of environmental pragmatist philosophy, more with the way democratic and pragmatic discourse plays out in the real world of environmental affairs.

It should be emphasized that democratic pragmatism does not have to proceed within the formal institutional structure of liberal democracy; that is, it does not have to involve debate in legislatures. This style of problem solving can also be found within administrative structures, in negotiations between parties to a legal dispute, in international negotiations, in informal networks, and elsewhere.

---

[1] One connotation I do not intend is that pragmatism is anti-theoretical. Pragmatists still have to think!

[2] For a recent refinement of pragmatism as public philosophy, see Anderson (1990).

Democratic Pragmatism in Action

Democratic pragmatism is often proposed in order to deal with manifestations of the crisis of administrative rationalism detailed at the end of the last chapter. If environmental administration involves adjustment within the basic structure of capitalist democracy in order to ameliorate ecological problems, then democratic pragmatism can involve readjustment of administration. On this account, there is nothing wrong with administration that a healthy dose of democracy cannot fix. This dose comes not in the form of taking problem solving away from administration and putting it in the hands of representative institutions such as legislatures; rather, it is a matter of making administration itself more democratic. This task can be accomplished in a variety of ways, many of which have in fact been pioneered in environmental policy (and are slowly diffusing to other policy areas).

In the previous chapter I noted that environmental administration is in crisis indicated by diminishing returns to administrative effort. Administration turns out not to be an effective problem-solving orientation in the context of complex problems: the relevant knowledge cannot be centralized in administrative hierarchy, and Weberian compartmentalization of bureaucratic structure tends to produce problem displacement rather than problem solution. Moreover, compliance with high-level administrative decisions proves problematical, leading to implementation deficit. Democratic pragmatism can speak directly to these aspects of administrative crisis, and later I will assess its performance in these terms. But in practice, the main reason for the democratization of environmental administration has been a felt need to secure legitimacy for decisions by involving a broader public. A number of devices are available for this task.

1. Public Consultation

In the previous chapter I noted that an important item in the repertoire of administrative rationalism is environmental impact assessment, under which a statement is prepared detailing the anticipated impact of a project proposal (be it for a freeway, a pipeline, or a land-use plan) on the environment. At one level, impact assessment is simply designed to force administrators to consider environmental values and scientific evidence that they might otherwise have excluded or overlooked. But impact assessment is invariably accompanied by opportunities for public comment on the document produced. Sometimes this is mere symbolism, if there is nothing to force the department in question actually to take into account the substance of public comment in its subsequent decision on the proposal. Still, policy makers must both anticipate and respond to comment that is made. In the process set up in the United States, which pioneered environmental impact assessment with the passage of the National Environmental Policy Act in 1970, the responsible federal agency must produce a draft statement, release that document for comment, compile responses (from other government agencies, other levels of government, environmental and community groups, interested corporations, resource users, and ordinary citizens), and respond to these comments in the final version of the statement. Thus information from a variety of perspectives that might otherwise have been excluded from administrative decision making is systematically sought out. This information will rarely have direct, traceable impacts on agency decisions; but more subtly it may alter the context in which administrative decisions are made and implemented, by changing the discourse surrounding policy determination in a way that makes both environmental and democratic values more legitimate and more visible than before. The way Bartlett (1990) puts it, environmental impact assessment can constitute a "worm in the brain" of the administrative state, one that moves it in simultaneously more democratic and more environmentally sensitive directions.

Public consultation can also proceed without being tied to particular documents such as impact statements. For example, several European countries (Sweden, the Netherlands, and Austria) initiated extensive consultative efforts in the late 1970s concerning the future of nuclear power (see Nelkin and Pollack, 1981). These exercises did not involve anything much in the way of transfer of power from the state to the citizenry. But they did have real consequences: for example, in 1979 the Swedish government decided not to construct any more reactors, and to begin phasing out nuclear energy.

2. ALTERNATIVE DISPUTE RESOLUTION

Opportunities for public comment do not formalize any particular role for nongovernmental participants. One way of recognizing and involving particular interested parties is through the practice of alternative dispute resolution (ADR). ADR has arisen in legalistic systems—notably the United States—as an alternative to the expensive stalemate that prolonged legal actions entail. The idea is to bring the parties to a dispute together under the auspices of a neutral third party (often a professional mediator) such that they might reason through their differences and achieve a consensus sensitive to all their interests. Thus ADR is appropriate in any realm of life where conflict exists. It began to appear in the environmental realm in particular in the 1970s under the heading of environmental mediation, and since then disputes have been mediated on a wide variety of issues. These issues include construction of dams, irrigation schemes, mines, shopping malls, and roads; watershed management; siting of hazardous waste disposal operations; and anti-pollution measures. Mediation functions not just as an alternative to the courts. Government agencies can also use and sponsor it when encountering resistance to their proposals. The relevant participants might include community representatives, environmental groups, corporate developers, government departments, and local governments. Thus mediation can play a role in policy making rather than dispute resolution narrowly defined. Kai Lee (1993), in the context of a discussion of the Columbia River Basin in the United States, believes that this is a productive way of channelling political conflict into administrative decisions. In particular, he believes ADR has an essential role to play in effective ecosystem management, providing creative ways for conflicts to end in learning rather than in victory for one side and defeat of the other, as happens under the basically adversarial processes of environmental impact assessment. Other observers are more skeptical, seeing ADR mainly in terms of the co-option and neutralization of troublemakers by the administrative state (for example, Amy, 1987). It is perhaps best to note that ADR has an ambivalent potential. At a minimum, it demonstrates that administrative rationalists must legitimate their decisions through participatory procedures. These procedures can involve neutralization and co-option; but they can also involve democratic principles eating away at the administrative state, forcing it to open its ways. So it is up to democratic pragmatists and perhaps even proponents of more radical democracy to make the most of these cracks in the citadel of the administrative state (Torgerson, 1990: 141–5).

3. POLICY DIALOGUE

Environmental mediation and other forms of ADR often tend to be case-specific or site-specific. However, the same principles of reasoned discussion oriented to consensus can also be applied to more strategic policy issues, though the success rate (in terms of reaching an agreement and having it put into policy practice) is lower than for more circumscribed cases. An early example came with the National Coal Policy Project in the United States, which operated in the late 1970s to bring several national environmental groups and coal producers together to jointly devise a strategy for coal mining and coal burning (McFarland, 1984). The two sides achieved agreement on a number of issues: so, for example, the environmentalists agreed to a simplified one-stop permitting process for new coal-burning power plants, and in return the coal producers agreed to public funding of environmental objectors to such plants. However, the recommendations of the project were never put into policy practice, in part because public officials from government agencies with interests of their own were not included in the negotiations (nor were coal workers or their unions).

A clearer example of policy dialogue more explicitly connected to—indeed, sponsored and funded by—government may be found in Australia, with the Ecologically Sustainable Development (ESD) process initiated under Prime Minister Bob Hawke in 1990. ESD began with an invitation to the main national environmental groups and the relevant industry representatives to participate in a series of discussions oriented to the generation of strategic policy recommendations in a number of areas: agriculture, energy, fisheries, forests, manufacturing, mining, and tourism. In each area a working group was set up, and a report eventually produced. The four invited environmental groups were the Australian Conservation Foundation, World Wildlife Fund, Greenpeace, and the Wilderness Society. The Wilderness Society withdrew immediately due to its unhappiness with other government policies contrary to sustainability; later, Greenpeace withdrew. However, both groups remained in contact with the two groups that continued to participate. When it came time for the ESD groups to report, Hawke had been replaced by a Prime Minister committed to confrontation rather than consensus who placed a much lower priority on environmental issues, which had also faded from public prominence with the arrival of economic recession. Thus few of the recommendations found their way into public policy.

A more successful translation of policy dialogue into policy practice may be found in the Canadian province of Alberta, the only place in North America where a solution has been found to the NIMBY (Not In My Back Yard) problem for hazardous wastes. Nobody wants a hazardous waste treatment facility in their backyard. Given that everywhere is someone's backyard, and given the relative ease of access to veto power in the Canadian and US political systems (reinforced in the United States by the prominent role of the courts), the normal condition of policy on this issue is impasse. Recognizing this problem, the government of Alberta in the late 1980s initiated a process of dialogue with local community groups and industry, which eventually produced consensus on a site and principles for its development and operation. The process involved a referendum on the basic idea of siting, funding to communities to employ experts, regular seminars and public meetings. Once the site was selected and the treatment plant built, communities in the vicinity received further funding and access to monitoring reports and expert advice, so public participation did not end with site selection (for details on this case, see Fischer, 1993: 176–7; Rabe, 1991).

4. PUBLIC INQUIRIES

Public inquiries resemble impact assessment in that they are oriented by a specific project proposal. But rather than just producing a document and allowing public inspection and comment, a public inquiry involves a specific and visible forum in which proponents and objectors alike can make depositions and arguments. Obviously a great deal depends upon the terms of reference with which the inquiry begins, and the way these terms are interpreted by the individual presiding over the inquiry. The terms and their interpretation can be narrow and biased toward the project proponent. This is how inquiries into proposed nuclear installations in Britain typically proceed. So Kemp (1985) chronicles the case of a 1977 inquiry into a Thermal Oxide Reprocessing Plant (THORP) proposed for Windscale in Northwest England (then, as now, a notorious site of radioactive pollution). The project proponent, British Nuclear Fuels Ltd., was allowed to introduce evidence on the economic benefits of THORP, but objectors were not allowed to bring to bear economic evidence against it. The legalistic rules of the inquiry were congenial to the well-funded proponents, not to the resource-poor objectors; and the proponents could deploy the Official Secrets Act at key points. Not surprisingly, Mr Justice Parker presiding over the inquiry came down in favor of THORP. Contrast this with the contemporaneous inquiry into proposed oil and gas pipeline construction from the Arctic to Southern markets conducted in Canada by Mr Justice Thomas Berger. Berger took pains to make sure that resource-poor interests, especially indigenous peoples, were provided with funds, access to expertise, and an ability to testify in a forum under conditions with which they were familiar (the inquiry travelled to remote villages). He interpreted the terms of reference broadly, to encompass development strategies for the Canadian North, not just whether or not pipeline should be built. In this sense, the inquiry became more like a policy dialogue. Berger's report (Berger, 1977) proposes a reinvigorated renewable-resource based economy for the Canadian North, in which oil and gas development have little place. Berger pushed democratic pragmatism to its limits—and perhaps beyond, to the kind of participatory process favored by green radicalism.

5. Right-to-Know Legislation

Obviously if individuals from outside government are to be effective participants in more or less democratic processes they need access to the relevant information. Sometimes this access will be facilitated by general freedom of information laws under which governments must operate. These apply to some governments more than others. For example, the British counterpart to freedom of information is the Official Secrets Act, which essentially presumes that everything is secret if it has the remotest connection to national security (this comes into play, for example, on anything relating to nuclear power). More specific to environmental politics is right-to-know legislation which specifies that corporations must disclose information relating to (say) the risks to workers of particular chemicals, the routes and timetables of shipments of noxious substances, and the toxicity of wastes being stored, transported, and dumped. Such laws exist in a number of Canadian provinces and US states.

These five developments all involve injections of democratic pragmatism into the administrative state, with a concomitant displacement of administrative rationalism. In every case experience has been mixed, and a lot of skepticism remains, especially from those committed to more radical expression of both environmental and democratic values. But in some cases, notably that of the Berger inquiry, we can glimpse the possibility of a more radically participatory and discursive democracy that transcends the limits imposed by the basic structure of capitalist democracy. If so, then political change beyond problem solving is at issue. At any rate, taken together these five developments indicate the degree to which the development of environmental policy has over the past thirty years been accompanied by greater openness and participation in decision making. Indeed, the environmental area has typically led all other policy areas in this respect. As Paehlke (1988) notes, all this is a far cry from the gloomy prognostications of survivalists who argued that environmental limits could only be confronted by centralized and authoritarian government. Of course, survivalists might still say that all the policy effort of the last three decades has not really confronted the issue of environmental limits head-on, and that we are still on course for overshoot and collapse. Paehlke says nothing about the reality or otherwise of limits.

Democratic Pragmatism as a Way of Governing

Democratic pragmatism describes an orientation to governing in its entirety, not just the inspiration for a variety of specific reforms and exercises of the kind described in the preceding section. This orientation stresses interactive problem solving involving participants from both within government and outside it. Such interaction can occur in the context of committee meetings, legislative debate, hearings, public addresses, legal disputes, rule-making, project development, media investigations, and policy implementation and enforcement; it can involve lobbying, arguing, advising, strategizing, bargaining, informing, publishing, exposing, deceiving, image-building, insulting, and questioning. In this light, the real stuff of liberal democratic government is not to be found in constitutions and formal divisions of responsibility. Rather, it is to be found in interactions that are only loosely constrained by formal rules. Quiet conversations in the bar may matter as much as speeches to parliament.

These interactions occur whether or not constitutions, laws, rules, and organization charts say they should. If we observe political interaction in liberal democracies, we find all kinds of complex paths of communication. To the administrative rationalist, this might sound like chaos and subversion. But arguably, this apparent chaos has its own rationality, what Charles Lindblom (1959) has called "the science of muddling through," or, later, "the intelligence of democracy" (Lindblom, 1965). This "science" is the exact opposite of administrative science, for it revels in unclear divisions of responsibility, political conflict, bending the formal rules so as to make things work, and substituting ordinary knowledge for analysis. Problems are solved piecemeal, usually through series of rough compromises among the different actors concerned with an issue. Interaction substitutes for analysis; different actors bring different perspectives and concerns, which are somehow agglomerated into policy decisions.[3]

I have already noted that pragmatists believe such processes are the best means for attacking public problems. A justification for the essential rationality of liberal democracy has also been advanced (quite famously) by Sir Karl Popper (1966).[4] Popper's model problem-solving community is found in successful sciences, where the rational attitude is to advance theories capable

[3] There are numerous case studies of this kind of process in the political science literature. Among the best may be found in the work of Aaron Wildavsky (Wildavsky, 1988; Pressman and Wildavsky, 1973).

[4] Popper differs somewhat from the pragmatists in believing that there can be general laws of nature and of society which natural scientists and social scientists alike can discover. Pragmatists believe only that there are particular problems to be solved, not laws to be discovered.

of being put to the test, then seek criticism of them through as many tests as possible, especially experimental tests. Popper believes that this attitude should apply in politics and policy making too. Public policies are like experiments. Nobody knows in advance if a particular policy (for example, a regulatory regime for pollution control) will succeed or fail. So it should be tried first on a limited scale, and reactions sought from as many different directions as possible about its positive and negative effects. Popper calls this kind of policy making "piecemeal social engineering." The only way to ensure feedback from as many different directions as possible is to have policy proceed in a liberal democratic setting, where different interests and actors (such as environmental and community groups, professional associations, different kinds of scientists, elected representatives, corporations and their officials, labor unions, and journalists) are all able to give their opinions without fear, and in the knowledge that will find an audience among policy makers. Real-world liberal democracies are only imperfect approximations to Popper's "open society" ideal, but no closer style of politics has yet been found.

Is this sort of policy making by interaction appropriate to an ecological context? To begin, the apparent chaos of piecemeal, interactive politics might belie a deeper organization, even if nobody in the system perceives it or really understands why and how this organization happens. Liberal democracies in one sense resemble ecosystems, for both are self-organizing systems (diZerega, 1993). That is, complex structures of order evolve without anyone designing them, as a result of the relatively simple and short-sighted choices and actions of the individual organisms within the system. In this light, the real order of liberal democracy is not to be found in constitutions, but in the informal, interactive processes at the heart of democratic pragmatism. Of course, the precise structure of order in any self-organizing system matters a great deal. By definition, an environmentalist can have little quarrel with the kind of order that ecosystems have produced by evolution (though he or she might wish for fewer deadly viruses and other living things that hurt human beings). That liberal democracy is a self-organizing system (as is the capitalist market) does not mean that it is at all defensible or adequate in the light of ecological criteria.

Ecosystems are self-organizing systems full of negative feedback devices that correct for disturbances to them. For example, a forest fire is normally followed by pioneer species of plants springing up in the burnt area, which in turn provide the growing conditions for more mature forest species to return. The idea of negative feedback also defines the metaphor of the thermostat. So what kind of "thermostat" does democratic pragmatism possess? The answer lies in the variety of individuals, organizations, parties, and movements which can bring pressure to bear in and on political interaction in response to environmental disturbances. For example, one would expect wilderness advocates to keep their eyes on old growth forests, so that if clearcutting threatens to get out of hand they can protest, lobby, hold press conferences, issue legal challenges, and so forth. Or if a proposal for a toxic waste incinerator in an urban neighborhood threatens life and health, the local community can organize against it. Survivalists would argue that these kinds of actions are all reactive and so incapable of anticipating limits before we hit them, though it should be noted that survivalist groups such as Zero Population Growth also participate in liberal democratic politics.

Whether or not these negative feedback devices are ecologically adequate depends crucially on the values of the people through whom the devices act. If people value tangible material goods above all else, then feedback will be impaired (though even these individuals might protest against any immediate environmental threat to their life and health). So is there anything in liberal democracy that is intrinsically conducive to ecological values? Let me take a look at two arguments which claim that there is.

Democratic pragmatism involves talk and written communication, not just strategizing and power-plays, and such communication works best when it is couched in the language of the public interest, rather than private interests. Steven Kelman (1987) believes that such talk is not cheap, and that people actually internalize public interest motivations. Adolf Gundersen (1995) applies this sort of analysis to public deliberation about environmental affairs. Deliberation is necessary for democratic pragmatism to work. Problem solving in democratic pragmatism, recall, is never a matter of individuals acting in isolation or under command from anyone else. Instead, problems always get discussed. Gundersen believes that the very act of discussion or deliberation about issues activates a commitment to environmental values, or, more precisely, "collective, holistic, and long term thinking." Long-term thinking might even extend to the wellbeing of future generations, who cannot of course participate directly in current debates. Gundersen's evidence is a series of 46 "deliberative interviews" which he conducts with a variety of people who did not in the beginning identify themselves as environmentalists. By the end of these discussions, all espoused environmental values more strongly. On this account, everyone has latent positive dispositions which only need to be activated into specific policy commitments. Discussion in liberal democratic settings forces people to scrutinize their own volitions and dispositions in a way that promotes such activation.

The idea that participation in democratic settings activates environmental values is shared by the environmental philosopher Mark Sagoff (1988). Sagoff believes that every individual has two kinds of preferences: as a consumer and as a citizen. These preferences may point in quite different directions for the same individual. His running example concerns the Mineral King Valley in California's Sierra Nevadas, where the Walt Disney Corporation wanted to build a ski resort. Confronting his students with this possibility, it turns out that many of them would enjoy visiting such a resort to ski and enjoy the après-ski nightlife. Few had any interest in backpacking into the existing Mineral King wilderness. But when asked whether they would favor construction of the resort, none did. The answer is that while as consumers they would love to ski there, as citizens they object to wilderness destruction. The implication is that citizen preferences are more concerned with collective, community-oriented values, as opposed to the selfish materialism of consumer values. While one might dispute the degree to which such public-spirited motivation pervades real-world liberal democratic politics, Sagoff's critique of economic reasoning and market rationality as applied to environmental policy is devastating. He also deploys his argument to excuse some of his more disgusting personal habits, notably driving a car that leaks oil everywhere which sports an "ecology now" bumper sticker (Sagoff, 1988: 53). The sticker proclaims his citizen preferences, the oil slick under his car his consumer preferences. The citizen in him would like the government to crack down on the consumer in him.

Discourse Analysis of Democratic Pragmatism

1. Basic Entities whose Existence is Recognized or Constructed

Like administrative rationalism, democratic pragmatism takes the structural status quo of liberal capitalism as given. However, the treatment of government is very different. Government is treated not as a unitary state, but rather as a multiplicity of decision processes populated by citizens. *Homo civicus* figures large, *homo bureaucratis* hardly at all. In short, government is carried out by liberal democracy, not the administrative state. Democratic pragmatism has little or nothing to say about ecosystems and the natural world; very different conceptions on this score are welcome in liberal democratic debate.

2. Assumptions about Natural Relationships

Both administrative rationalism and democratic pragmatism place nature as subordinate to human problem-solving efforts. Whether nature contains self-regulating ecosystems or is just a storehouse of brute matter and energy makes little difference here. The natural relationships within human society postulated by the two discourses are in contrast quite different. Democratic pragmatism celebrates equality among citizens (of course, the reality of liberal democracy may be very different). Everyone has the right to exert political pressure, be they scientists, elected officials, pressure group leaders, ordinary voters, or ordinary non-voters. Beyond this basic equality, political relationships are seen as interactive and far more complex than those in a bureaucratic hierarchy. Interactions feature a mix of competition and cooperation. Certainly cooperative problem solving can occur; but so can political conflict between partisans of competing interests (such as environmentalists and developers).

3. Agents and their Motives

Agency in democratic pragmatism is for everyone, be they individual citizens and political activists or collective actors such as corporations, labor unions, environmentalist groups, community organizations, and government agencies. Motives are mixed. Many of these actors much of the time pursue selfish material interests, such as profit, increased property values, higher wages, more secure employment, or subsidized access to a favorite natural area. But the discourse also allows, indeed requires, that at key junctures agents can be motivated by the public interest. In the first instance, this public interest will have to be defined in plural terms. So what the Wilderness Society takes as being in the public interest will not necessarily be the same as for the Chamber of Commerce. Some democratic pragmatists would leave it at that, arguing that plurality here is irreducible, and that we can expect only piecemeal compromises across partisans of different views. But others I have discussed, such as Kelman, Gundersen, and Sagoff, hope for something more: reasoned public dialogue that will produce convergence on a common conception of the public interest (see also Williams and Matheny, 1995). If a single public interest does emerge through dialogue it is a very different matter from the unitary public interest that exists for administrative rationalists, for whom the public interest is something for analysts to discover, rather than the public to debate.

4. Key Metaphors and other Rhetorical Devices

No vivid metaphors pervade democratic pragmatism in action. But two scientific metaphors are advanced by reflective defenders of this discourse. The first treats public policy as the resultant of forces acting upon it from different directions. These forces differ in the direction in which they want to pull public policy, and in their relative power, exercised by all the individuals and groups with the capacity to act. Such a metaphor is likely to be employed by those who think there can be no unitary conception of the public interest. Indeed, this metaphor was long a staple of pluralist accounts of the US political system developed by American political scientists.

A second metaphor is that of science in its entirety. As we have seen, Popperians believe that public policies are like scientific experiments, and that the proper attitude for scientists and policy makers alike is an open, critical, and democratic one.

Another metaphor I mentioned earlier is that of the thermostat, designed to trigger interventions (heating and cooling) as soon as temperature departs from a desirable range. Democratic pragmatism allows attention to a wide range of target variables analogous to temperature (economic and political as well as environmental ones), and many ways in which negative feedback can be brought to bear. Foremost among these is the possibility for aggrieved citizens and groups to mobilize when they perceive an environmental abuse.

Box 5.1. **DISCOURSE ANALYSIS OF DEMOCRATIC PRAGMATISM**

1. **Basic Entities Recognized or Constructed**
   - Liberal capitalism
   - Liberal democracy
   - Citizens

2. **Assumptions about Natural Relationships**
   - Equality among citizens
   - Interactive political relationships, mixing competition and cooperation

3. **Agents and their Motives**
   - Many different agents
   - Motivation a mix of material self-interest and multiple conceptions of public interest

4. **Key Metaphors and other Rhetorical Devices**
   - Public policy as a resultant of forces
   - Policy like scientific experimentation
   - Thermostat

The Limits of Democratic Pragmatism

Democratic pragmatism has much to be said on its behalf. As an orientation to solving problems within the liberal capitalist political economy, it accepts many problems that baffle administrative rationalism. This transfer is often made for reasons relating to the need to legitimate policy decisions in the eyes of a broader public but, as we have seen, it can be justified in terms of more effectively resolving (or at least attacking) the problems too. If we look around today's world, we see that the countries that have progressed most in terms of environmental conservation and pollution control are the capitalist democracies (though it should be stressed that the most capitalist are not the best performers). The latter piece of evidence does not provide quite the comfort to democratic pragmatism than it might. For the acknowledged leaders in the environmental stakes include countries such as Germany and Japan (see Jänicke, 1996), whose policy-making structures impose substantial restraints on democratic pragmatism, especially on who can have access to policy making and under what terms. So in Japan policy making is monopolized by business and government elites; in Germany, labor union leaders also have a say. In each of these cases, usually described as corporatism, participation is through highly formalized channels, allowing little of the self-organizing give and take celebrated by democratic pragmatists. Moreover, some of the best-performing countries are adopting a discourse quite different from democratic pragmatism, as we will see in Chapter 8.

Skeptics might also argue that it is the prosperity of the capitalist democracies that allows them to cope better with their environmental problems than anyone else, as opposed to the intrinsic problem-solving qualities of democratic pragmatism. And there is always the possibility that they have succeeded in offloading many of their environmental problems onto poorer countries. So a clean and pleasant environment in Japan is purchased in part by the dirtier elements of manufacturing industry being transferred to other East Asian countries, not to mention deforestation of South East Asia to meet Japanese timber needs.

The main limit to democratic pragmatism is the simple existence of political power (which goes unrecognized by enthusiasts such as Gundersen and Sagoff). Politics in capitalist democratic settings is rarely about disinterested and public-spirited problem solving in which a variety of perspectives are brought to bear with equal weight. Often there are powerful interests with large financial resources at their disposal which will try to skew the outcomes of policy debates and decision-making processes in their direction. Now, sometimes that direction will coincide with ecological values. More often it will not, as the interests with by far the greatest amount of resources and the strongest incentives to deploy them in political interaction are business interests.

Business can influence the terms of debate by producing glossy advertising material to tout the environmental friendliness of its products. It can (and does) sponsor Earth Day festivities. It can produce television advertising to promote the corporate environmental image: so in the United States Weyerhauser promotes itself as "the tree growing company" with film of a bald eagle flying over a forest. The clearcutting of old growth forests which is also one of Weyerhauser's activities is unmentioned. Corporate actors also have greater access to expert counsel in public inquiries. Alternative dispute resolution can be manipulated by these actors and their sympathizers in government in order to co-opt and neutralize troublemakers from community and environmental groups. ADR can be oriented toward a "responsible development" gloss on projects which will generally go ahead, and toward treatment of environmental values as on a par with business's material interests (Amy, 1987). Participation by environmentalists in impact assessment might dissipate energies that would be better spent on other activities, if the impact assessment process merely legitimates decisions already made elsewhere on the basis of economic values or corporate profit (Amy, 1990: 60–4). Corporations can even offer employment to environmental activists. For example, leading British Green Jonathan Porritt signed on as an advisor to Sainsbury's, the food retailing giant, though this does not mean that the British Green Party has become the political wing of Sainsbury's.[5]

Such pressures do not go all one way; public opinion does exist as something more than the creation of business public relations departments, and public interest groups can mobilize expertise and support, even money. Still, so long as the structural status quo of the capitalist market economy is taken as given, business has a "privileged" position in policy making, for government relies greatly upon business to carry out basic functions such as employing people and organizing the economy (Lindblom, 1977: 171–5). Yet more fundamentally, the same state imperatives that constrain administrative rationalism, and which I discussed at the end of the previous chapter, also constrain democratic pragmatism, for as long as the latter remains a problem-solving discourse. These imperatives involve, first and foremost, maintaining the confidence of actual and potential investors. Any measures for environmental protection, conservation, or pollution control which threaten to undermine this confidence will be automatically punished by disinvestment. This possibility casts a long shadow over policy deliberations, however democratic they may be (see Press, 1994). And once business publicists realise this, they can make good strategic use of the disinvestment threat, even when there is no real intention to disinvest.

Democratic pragmatism as a discourse recognizes citizens as a basic

---

[5] This title was once held by the rump Social Democratic Party, when its main funding came from the Sainsbury family.

entity, and a natural relationship of equality across citizens. But this imagery of reasoned debate among equals is in practice highly distorted by the exercise of power and strategy, and by state imperatives lurking in the background. Matters appear still more doubtful in an ecological light when one further considers the character of actors and their interests. One advantage of democratic pragmatism stressed by its adherents is that it enables views on policy proposals to come from a variety of directions. Some directions represent conceptions of what is in the public interest. These conceptions may vary: to some, the public interest may involve mostly economic efficiency, to others distributional equity in society, to others still ecological integrity, to others social harmony. When liberal democratic enthusiasts such as Gundersen and Sagoff in an ecological context, and Dewey and Popper more generally, think of democratic debate, this is presumably what they have in mind.[6] But other interests involved are motivated mostly by their own material interests: corporations and industry associations concerned with maximizing profit and avoiding environmental controls on their operations, or labor unions concerned with the income and employment of their members, even if that means employment in unsustainable practices such as clearcutting of ancient forests. The pluralist aspect of democratic pragmatism treats all such interests and concerns as equally legitimate (see Williams and Matheny, 1995: 19–24). The mere fact of participation in liberal democratic settings does not lead actors to discard their motivations as consumers and producers in favor of more public-spirited citizen preferences, or to conclude that pursuit of their economic interests should be confined to the market place rather than allowed to enter politics.

More insidious still are special interests which masquerade as general principles. So, for example, the "Wise Use" movement in the American West in the 1990s has a name that connotes commitment to sensible use of resources, but in practice it seeks a regime of subsidized access for local communities and corporations to minerals, grazing rights, and timber located on public lands in the region.

Political rationality in democratic pragmatism means that all actors have to be mollified, pretty much in proportion to their ability to create difficulties for government officials, irrespective of whether they are motivated by conceptions of the public interest or more selfish material interests. This does not necessarily coincide with ecological rationality, which is concerned

---

[6] For a more explicit statement about the degree to which "public spirit" actually pervades even US politics, see Kelman (1987). According to Kelman, presidents, congresspersons, and bureaucrats alike are all motivated mainly by the desire to make an honest effort to achieve good public policy. But even Kelman recognizes that special interests will sometimes upset this happy situation.

with the integrity of natural life-support systems (see Dryzek, 1987: 118–20). So in 1993 the Clinton administration took a small step toward ecological rationality when Secretary of the Interior Bruce Babbit proposed reforming grazing law to end subsidized access for cattle ranchers to public land. It soon became evident that the politically rational thing to do was back off on these reforms for fear of the electoral weight of the Western states where these reforms would take effect, and where welfare ranchers and their sympathizers could tip the balance come election day.

Democratic pragmatism in some respects merits a similar summary judgement to administrative rationalism: plenty of achievements to look back upon, but limits to effectiveness increasingly apparent. This similarity applies mostly at the level of specific policies and institutions inspired or justified by the two discourses. But as a discourse, democratic pragmatism has one striking advantage: it is more conducive to an awareness of the limitations of its own institutional manifestations, and so to efforts to overcome these limits.

Democratic pragmatism as a political style developed mostly in the context of distributive issues, where the main task is to allocate the gains and losses of government activity. Thus when environmental issues reach the agenda, they too are treated in distributive terms, with the main question being how to strike a balance between winners and losers, such as economic and environmental interests. General interests in (say) the integrity of ecosystems or the quality of commons resources are less easily represented. As we shall see in Part IV, sustainability discourses dissolve such problems by dissolving the conflict between economic and environmental values. This raises the prospect of environmental values being assimilated in to, rather than overridden by, the economic imperatives of states in capitalist societies. But first, another problem-solving discourse merits examination.

6 Leave it to the Market: Economic Rationalism

When it comes to theories to guide public policies and other social practices, democratic pragmatists are quite agnostic. The only test they are inclined to apply is the pragmatic one of whether the policy or practice inspired by the theory works out in reality. Liberal democratic politics of the sort these pragmatists favor is usually home to believers in many different theories and perspectives. In the last two decades, the most prominent such perspective on policy in general has been an economic one. This perspective goes by different names in different places: market liberalism, classical liberalism, neoliberalism, and free-market conservatism. Sometimes it is even personalized, and becomes Thatcherism in the UK, Salinastroika in Mexico (after President Salinas de Gotari) or Rogernomics in New Zealand (for finance minister Roger Douglas). Now, many of those who sail under these banners are Prometheans, who believe that the only task for government in environmental affairs as in all affairs is to leave markets well alone, such that human ingenuity can be given full rein. Yet there are others just as committed to market principles, who recognize that, whatever the case in other areas, markets in environmental goods do not always exist, and so often need to be created and managed. Thus their discourse is rationalistic, entailing substantial cogitation, calculation, and design on the part of policy makers.

Economic rationalism may be defined by its commitment to the intelligent deployment of market mechanisms to achieve public ends. It differs from administrative rationalism in its unremitting hostility to environmental management on the part of government administrators—except, of course, in establishing the basic parameters of designed markets. In this one key aspect economic rationalism turns out to depend on the administrative rationalism it otherwise so despises. The commitment to markets might imply that economic rationalism's natural political home is on the political right. Yet some people with left and/or green credentials are also attracted by the use of markets in an environmental context (for example, Daly, 1992; Roodman, 1996), and countries with governments organized along more social democratic lines (for example, Germany, the Netherlands, and France) have pioneered economic rationalist environmental policy instruments. But the rise of economic rationalism in environmental affairs has much to do with the broader ascendancy of market-oriented thinking, within a shared context of economic slowdown and budget deficits.

Economic rationalism has become increasingly popular in the environmental arena in recent years. William Reilly, Administrator of the Environmental Protection Agency under President George Bush and before that head of the Conservation Foundation, declared that "The forces of the marketplace are powerful tools for changing individual and institutional behavior. If set up correctly, they can achieve or surpass environmental objectives at less costs and with less opposition than traditional regulatory approaches" (quoted in Yandle, 1993: 188). A change of president did not dampen this enthusiasm: in 1992 president-elect Bill Clinton spoke of "harnessing market forces" to induce companies to incorporate "environmental incentives into daily production decisions" (quoted in Nelson, 1993: 1).

As we shall see, economic rationalism plays out in different ways in different societies, though nowhere with quite the enthusiasm it generates in the United States. At the international level, in recent years market-type policy instruments have been promoted by the Organization for Economic Cooperation and Development, the rich man's club of the world's developed countries (see OECD, 1989), and the European Community. These instruments were even endorsed by the 1987 Brundtland Report, *Our Common Future*, which launched the era of sustainable development on the international stage.

My discussion of economic rationalism begins with its purest strain, emphasizing the conversion of environmental resources to private property. I then move to less radical strands which stress market incentives but not necessarily private property.

Privatizing Everything

Markets are systems based on commodity exchange, in which goods, services, and financial instruments are exchanged for each other. Markets work smoothly to the extent that participants in transactions can be confident that they do in fact have a right to sell or buy the goods in question—in other words, they have property rights, be it to a car, a can of beans, a company, a bond, or a piece of land. If we are to have markets in environmental goods, then we need private property rights in these goods too. According to economic rationalism, specification and enforcement of these rights is the main task of government when it comes to environmental matters.

Why are private property rights and markets so desirable? The answer is straightforward: people tend to care more for what they hold privately than for what they hold in common with others. This is why (for example) there is more litter in public parks than in private gardens, or why public grazing land in the American West is more degraded than private land. The metaphor of the commons plays a much smaller role than it does in survivalism, but economic rationalism has a clear solution to the tragedy of the commons: divide it into chunks of private property. Once the commons is so divided, these chunks can be bought and sold according to who is prepared to pay the most for them. Economic rationalists tell us that, given a few assumptions, markets maximize social welfare; and markets in environmental goods should be no exception. The private property right to the good in question will be bought by the individual or firm or other entity that values it most, and can make the most profitable use of it.

It is easy to see how this logic of property and markets works for ordinary material goods, services, education, even human labor power, much less easy to see how it applies to the environment. But economic rationalists see no real difficulties in applying the same logic here. Meiners and Yandle (1993: viii) believe that "environmental controversies seem to boil down to arguments about property rights." Of itself, this recognition does not imply that it is going to be easy to specify, enforce, and adjudicate an appropriate set of rights. Yet economic rationalists are adamant that the failure to do so lies at the heart of environmental problems: as Mitchell and Simmons (1994: 148) put it, "environmental problems must be understood more as failures by government to specify property rights than as offshoots of private profit-seeking."

What, then does an appropriate set of property rights look like? When it comes to land, the answer is easy, as systems of private property are well established. All that needs doing is extend private property rights to all land. This is really only a political issue in countries with large amounts of land in public ownership, such as the United States. American free-market environmentalists are obsessed with the public lands issue. Much of this land is in the Western states, and most of it is controlled by agencies of the federal government, especially the National Park Service, the Defense Department, the Forest Service, and the Bureau of Land Management. With the exception of the Pentagon, these are notionally professional land management agencies. In practice, as economic rationalists argue, these agencies often act as conduits for the abuse of land at the hands of special interests (see Anderson and Leal, 1991: 51–9 for a catalogue). Thus ranchers are able to graze their cattle on public land at below-market prices, and have little incentive to care for the land in question, because they do not own it. Logging companies gain heavily subsidized access to national forests, as the Forest Service constructs roads into the forests at public expense. Often, the Forest Service receives less money for a timber lease than it pays to construct these roads into the lease area. This amounts to publicly subsidized wilderness destruction. Wilderness lovers for their part get free and often subsidized access to the back country, leading to its overuse and degradation. Tourists get heavily subsidized roads and facilities in the more accessible parts of National Parks, which again become overused and abused. Mining companies can make use of antiquated nineteenth-century laws which allow them to stake claims to minerals on public lands while paying virtually nothing.

According to economic rationalists, none of these abuses would occur if the land in question were privately owned. Ranchers would have every incentive not to overgraze land, and to invest in soil and vegetation conservation. Owners of forests that could not be logged economically would keep them as wilderness areas, or invest in wildlife conservation in order to attract hunters or photographers, who would be charged admission to provide income for these conservation investments. If parks were privatized, tourists and backpackers alike would have to pay the market price for access to them, and the private owners would again have every incentive to use the income to enhance the recreational value of the park. If anyone wanted to preserve wilderness for its own sake or for the sake of the species that inhabit it rather than for recreational opportunities, then they could buy it and do so. This is exactly what the Nature Conservancy, a private organization, currently does, to the applause of free-market environmentalists. If mineral rights were privatized there would be a more orderly and efficient market in mining, rather than an inefficient scramble to make (subsidized) claims.

Privatization of land is only a major issue in North America, because in most other developed countries most land is already private. Not so air and water, and here a little more ingenuity in the specification of private property rights is called for. The argument becomes applicable to more countries, because all of them have air and water in problematical condition.

Air as such is hard to privatize because, of course, it moves around in the way land does not (barring the occasional earthquake, landslide, or soil erosion). But the useful properties of air can indeed have private property rights attached to them, normally in tandem with a parcel of land. So a right to breathe clean air can be attached to ownership or occupation of a piece of residential or commercial land. Anyone violating that right by emitting pollutants into the atmosphere can then be notified of that fact and pursued for compensation sought for taking away the property right in question. If necessary, action could be taken through the courts to either secure compensation or prevent violation of the property right to clean air. The legal system would come to play an expanded role in any such regime.

The immediate problem here is one of identifying polluters and tracing the effects of pollution on human health. This can be extraordinarily difficult, especially when there are multiple polluters, as in many urban areas. The air in my garden may not be clean, but am I coughing because of the methane given off by the nearby landfill, the heavy metals emitted from a local toxic waste incinerator, smog coming from car exhausts, or sulfur dioxide from the city's coal-burning power station? Or is it because my neighbor is burning her garbage? Clearly what is needed here are vast improvements in monitoring technology, and until that technology arrives, it is not surprising that property rights in air have made little headway anywhere. Market zealots such as Anderson and Leal (1991: 165–6) recognize this problem, which is why they fantasize about adding tracers to all pollution sources, and about advances in lasimetrics, satellite tracking of atmospheric chemicals.

Some of the same problems apply when it comes to water, though private property rights to clean water have in fact been established in some cases. Most notably, in Britain the private recreational fishing rights attached to a stretch of river or lakeside come with a right to water clean enough for fish to flourish. So any polluter, upstream or elsewhere in the lake, can be sued by the individual or fishing club holding the fishing rights. The Anglers Cooperative Association has been zealous in bringing cases against polluters, and often very successful. The result is that British waterways, while rarely pristine, are much cleaner than they would be otherwise. Those benefiting include not just the fish and the anglers, but also the (very few, given the climate) people who swim in rivers and lakes, the (more numerous) people who rely on rivers as sources of drinking water, and the plants and animals of aquatic communities.

In arid regions, the main water issue concerns not water pollution, but water supply. Again the US West offers the most contentious and troubled cases. Water rights to portions of stream flows have generally gone to the first person who could claim them; thereafter, the "use it or lose it" doctrine applies, which means that users must waste water when they do not need it, for fear of losing their right to it once they do need it. It does not require an economic genius to realize that it would be more efficient to allow individuals and corporations to buy and sell rights to particular portions of the flow of a river or creek. Water policy in the US is also blasted by free marketeers for its enormous degree of public subsidy for questionable schemes that build dams and canals to supply agribusiness corporations and a few other wealthy interests. The main villain here is the Bureau of Reclamation, long regarded as one of the more powerful empires in the US government (see Reisner, 1993). Essentially, the Bureau's aim is to create agriculture in the desert. The massive ecological costs of its efforts include elimination of stream flows, siltation behind dams, and soil salination. None of these public subsidies and ecological costs would apply, economic rationalists aver, if Western agribusiness, cities, and industries had to pay market prices for the water they consumed. Welfare irrigation in this light is no more defensible than welfare logging, welfare ranching, welfare backpacking, welfare tourism, and welfare mining. All are both costly and environmentally devastating.

Land, air, and water together cover a lot of what we normally mean by "environment," so if all can be privatized then we would, according to the marketeers, be well on the way to solving all environmental problems. We could go still further by privatizing species, wildlife, and fish. Species might be privatized through property rights to their genes. For example, many rare plants in endangered tropical forest ecosystems could be claimed by pharmaceutical companies for the sake of their actual or potential role in producing new drugs. Wildlife might be privatized in conjunction with land, or, when animals wander across property boundaries, tracked by means of radio collars. Anderson and Leal (1991: 34) suggest that whales could be treated as private property: "Whales also can be 'branded' by genetic prints and tracked by satellite." Conservationists wanting to save the whales could therefore buy them, as could whalers wanting to hunt them. The market would determine the most appropriate use for whales. But note that whalers would not hunt to extinction, for once they had private property rights to them, they would have every incentive to invest in the health of the whale stock, just as farmers invest in the health of their animals.

A free-market zealot would insist that solutions to environmental problems would begin and end with the establishment of private property rights. In fact, as Coase (1960) demonstrated for the case of pollution, it does not even matter who has the right, the polluter or the sufferer from pollution, so long as it is legally clear. For if there is a legally unrestricted right to pollute, then market solutions to pollution can be generated by the sufferers banding together and offering to pay the polluter to cut back on emissions. Depending on what the sufferers are willing to pay, and whether this is larger or smaller than the profit the polluter is making from the activity, cutback will or will not occur in a fashion that is optimal in market efficiency terms. The fact that nowhere in the world can we observe sufferers offering to pay polluters to stop polluting does not stop Coase's article being regarded as a classic by economists.[1] (Scandinavian governments have effectively offered to pay Poland to stop polluting their atmosphere, but this is a matter of governmental action, not citizen-sufferers approaching polluters with an offer.)

Those who believe that if it moves you should privatize it, and if it doesn't move you should privatize it, represent the radical fringe of economic rationalism. This fringe has little representation outside the United States, where its stronghold is in think tanks such as the Foundation for Research on Economics and the Environment (FREE) in Seattle, the Political Economy Research Centre in Bozeman, Montana, the Pacific Research Institute in San Francisco, the Cato Institute in Washington, DC, and to a lesser extent mainstream conservative think tanks such as the American Enterprise Institute. Even in the United States, it must be said, the privatizers have had little impact on the content of public policy. Mostly they just rail from the sidelines.

More influential, and in more countries, have been the economic rationalists who advocate not wholesale privatization and private property rights, but rather the use of market-type mechanisms and economic incentives to induce environmentally appropriate behavior, and to these I now turn.

If You Can't Privatize it, Market it Anyway

When it comes to air and water pollution, the hard-line economic rationalist position would be that private property rights in air and water need to be established and enforced, and that thereafter there is nothing more that needs doing. However, given the substantial difficulties with this hardline position, economic rationalists enamoured of markets have often turned to the next best thing: government-managed markets, and failing that quasi-market incentives. The most popular proposals for managed markets in the environmental realm involve pollution rights. The basic idea here is that government defines an airshed or watershed, determines the maximum level of pollution that should be allowed, divides that level into a number of rights, then auctions off those rights to the highest bidder. After the initial

---

[1] There are good economic reasons why they do not. As Mancur Olson (1965) pointed out in his classic analysis of the logic of collective action, the fact that individuals share an interest does not mean they will act upon it. Each person has an incentive to take a "free ride" on the efforts of others. This logic parallels that of the tragedy of the commons introduced in Chapter 2, in that rational individual decisions lead to collectively bad outcomes.

auction has been held, polluters can buy and sell rights from one another. Polluters for whom it is easy and cheap to reduce emissions will cut back rather than pay for pollution rights, whereas polluters for whom emissions reduction is expensive will purchase rights to pollute. Thus the government-specified level of pollution abatement will be achieved in the most cost-effective manner. Environmentalists who believe abatement should be greater still can always purchase quotas themselves and leave them unused (for arguments in favour of tradeable quotas, see Anderson and Leal, 1991: 145–7; Mitchell and Simmons, 1994: 155–7; Yandle, 1993).

Tradeable quotas have been introduced to a limited extent in the United States, where since 1979 the federal Environmental Protection Agency has sponsored use of the "bubble" concept in a few localities. However, in practice bubbles cover only a particular plant, and so the emissions "trades" occur only within a company (that is, allowing the company in question to decide in which part of the plant it can most cheaply reduce emissions, rather than have government regulators instruct the company in what standards and technologies to use in particular parts of the factory). Bubbles and related emissions trading practices promoted by the EPA have resulted in hardly any trades in emission rights across companies, at least of the kind sought by economic rationalists (see Hahn, 1995: 134–7).

The 1990 US Clean Air Act Amendments allow for emissions trading on a larger scale, at least for sulfur dioxide from coal-burning power plants. Under this Act, pollution credits beginning in 1995 were granted to 110 of the country's dirtiest coal-burning power plants, representing between 30 and 50 per cent of the sulfur dioxide currently emitted by them. The Chicago Board of Trade was then to hold auctions for additional credits. But this is still a highly restricted initiative and a far cry indeed from the purist economic rationalist position on tradeable quotas; the same can be said for all real-world US experiments so far. And the United States is ahead of other countries on such measures. On a still larger scale, the 1987 Montreal Protocol for the protection of the ozone layer provided for trades between countries in quotas for the emission of chlorofluorocarbons (the chemicals that deplete ozone), though no such mechanism has yet been established.

Tradeable quotas can also be established in resources such as fish. The quota would refer to an allowable catch for a particular fishery for a specified time. Obviously some government agency is needed to establish the quotas (and perhaps change them in response to the changing health of the fishery), but once established the quotas can be bought and sold on the market. Australia uses such a system for its southern bluefish tuna fishery. Fisheries throughout the world have been notoriously subject to the tragedy of the commons, resulting in overfishing, depletion, and overcapitalization as fishers rushed to beat their competitors to the catch. So far, tradeable quotas have been far less widely used than other forms of regulation (such as regulation restricting numbers of boats, fishing seasons, kinds of equipment, and total allowable catch for the fishery as a whole).

More widely adopted than tradeable quotas are quasi-market incentives using standards and charges for pollution control, or "green taxes" as they are sometimes known. Government sets an ambient environmental standard (for example, for level of carbon monoxide in urban air), and then impose taxes or charges on the activities which threaten that standard. The taxes in question can be levied on the goods whose production causes pollution, or directly on the pollution itself. Examples of the former are quite rare, though the European Community applies a tax on cadmium batteries, and several years ago the UK government mooted a proposal to impose an environmental tax on walking boots, on the grounds of the damage caused by the boots to footpaths in National Parks and other scenic areas of Britain. Examples of levies on pollution itself might include charges per kilogram of sulfur dioxide emitted by smokestacks, or per kilogram of BOD (biological oxygen demand) for organic pollutants in rivers.

The economic rationalist's argument for a regime of green taxes is essentially that they leave discretion in the hands of the polluter in terms of how much to reduce pollution and what kind of technology to use. If the polluter chooses to pursue abatement, then it has every incentive to find the most cost-effective way to do so. Polluters for whom abatement is expensive will prefer to pay the charge and continue to pollute. All polluters have an incentive to continuously search for less-polluting methods of production, for that will always save them money. Government should set the charge per unit of pollution at a level sufficient to induce the required degree of abatement (for arguments in favour of green taxes, see Anderson *et al.*, 1977; Kneese and Schultze, 1975; Moran, 1995).

The idea of green taxes captured the terms of policy discourse most effectively in Britain in the late 1980s and early 1990s, where an upsurge in environmentalism coincided with a national government committed to market values. The Prime Minister remembered that she had studied chemistry long ago at Oxford University, and so could recognize chemical pollution when she saw it. The key document was produced by the environmental economist David Pearce for the Department of the Environment in 1989, entitled *Blueprint for a Green Economy* (Pearce, Markandya, and Barbier, 1989), which advocated a comprehensive regime of green taxes. This report was followed up by a 1990 government white paper entitled *This Common Inheritance*, which curiously relegated the Pearce recommendations to an appendix. However, by late 1992 green taxes found more official favor, as the government announced that "In future, there will be a general presumption in favour of economic instruments" (quoted in Jacobs, 1995: 114). This presumption has yet to be reflected in the content of policy measures for pollution control. Part of the problem in Britain is that the Treasury sees green taxes in primarily revenue-raising terms, and wants to set levels without reference to environmental departments of government. This worries industry, which foresees charges rising and falling, most likely rising, in response to government's revenue needs. And it worries environmentalists, for it gives government a vested interest in pollution, for the more pollution that occurs, the more revenues does government receive (see Jacobs, 1995: 124).

Other countries have made more progress in actually implementing green taxes, especially on water pollution. Most notably, France, Germany, and the Netherlands make use of per-unit pollution charges in their repertoire of environmental policy instruments (see Andersen, 1994). The experience of these countries is decidedly mixed. In France, charges are used mainly as a revenue-raising device, and are not set high enough to affect dramatically the environmental behavior of polluters. In the Netherlands, charges are successful and widely supported by environmentalists. In Germany, green taxes play only a secondary role within a more traditional regulatory system. German municipalities retain substantial control over policy implementation, and so happily dump pollution downstream. So the German experience is mixed. In all three countries revenue raised by charges is earmarked for projects to improve water quality. As Hahn (1995: 146–7) notes, "charges and marketable permits schemes . . . are rarely, if ever, introduced in their textbook form." The same might be said of all the policies and practices inspired by economic rationalism: the textbook explication and advocacy is crystal clear, the real-world implementation very murky indeed.

One international environmental problem that has received attention from advocates of green taxes is global warming, caused mainly by the build-up of carbon dioxide in the atmosphere resulting from the burning of fossil fuels. This issue was firmly on the agenda at the United Nations Conference on Environment and Development (the "Earth Summit") in Rio de Janeiro in 1992, where developed countries promised to stabilize their carbon dioxide emissions. In response, both the European Union and the OECD have explored a carbon tax, levied per tonne of fossil fuel burned. Denmark, Finland, the Netherlands, Norway, and Sweden already have such a tax.

Before leaving green taxes in order to conduct a more systematic discourse analysis of economic rationalism in general, it should be noted that radical free-market zealots oppose them on the grounds that such taxes require competent and benign action on the part of government administrators in, for example, setting and changing tax rates (see, for example, Mitchell and Simmons, 1994: 148). Such zealots, recall, believe that the real cause of environmental problems is inadequate or inappropriate government specification of private property rights, and until that situation is rectified, any other policy actions are useless or counterproductive, and that includes green taxes.

Analysis of Economic Rationalism Discourse

1. Basic Entities whose Existence is Recognized or Constructed

Economic rationalism's world is populated by economic actors.[2] *Homo economicus* can appear as a consumer or producer; and if producers are organized into firms, the firm still behaves like an individual. Markets, prices, and property have real existence. At some level government exists too as something more than a collection of economic individuals. However, economic rationalist discourse is ambiguous and troubled on this point. Some economic rationalists treat government as staffed entirely by *homo economicus* individuals, all concerned only with their own material interest, and all exploiting the public for personal benefit. This is why these economic rationalists always prefer markets to politics (see for example Mitchell and Simmons, 1994). But even these die-hard economic rationalists require someone, somewhere to be steering the system in the public interest, otherwise who is going to put into practice the appropriate arrangement of private property rights they seek?

Notably missing from economic rationalism are citizens (of the sort populating democratic pragmatism). Also, environments do not exist in any strong sense. At most, "the environment" is only a pathway for some human decisions to have effects on other people—for example, through pollution. The existence of ecosystems, let alone ecosystems that often defy understanding, cut across chunks of private property, and impose constraints on human activity, is not perceived. There is no such thing as wilderness, only wilderness experiences (that is, human perceptions of wilderness amenity). Unlike the Prometheans, economic rationalists recognize the existence of natural resources, which is why it is so crucial to establish the right kinds of property rights to these resources. In further contrast to Prometheans, eco-

---

[2] Many feminists would argue that they really are economic men, just as the old terminology had it.

nomic rationalists would not necessarily dismiss the existence of limits to human activity imposed by finite resources.

2. Assumptions about Natural Relationships

Economic rationalism assumes that the basic relationship across individuals and collective actors (such as firms) is competitive. Thus the sort of cooperative problem solving sought by democratic pragmatists is ruled out. Corresponding to its thoroughly ambiguous attitude toward the existence of government as anything more than an assemblage (or sometimes tool) of rational egoists out to plunder the public purse, economic rationalism is confused about the existence of hierarchy within government. Administrative rationalism, as seen in a previous chapter, happily accepts natural hierarchy based on expertise. When it comes down to it, economic rationalists have to do the same, because some experts must be in a position of authority to implement the establishment of appropriate private property rights, or to design green taxes to produce the desired results. Of course, the experts themselves must be economic rationalists; but they cannot be economic actors, for if they were they would devise schemes in their own personal interest, not in the public interest!

The other kind of hierarchy implicit in economic rationalism is between humans and the natural world. Economic rationalism is thoroughly anthropocentric: nature exists only to provide inputs to the socio-economic machine, to satisfy human wants and needs. The appropriate expertise to use and manipulate these environmental inputs is taken for granted. Once appropriate property rights and incentives are in place, individual actors have no problem in deploying expertise to produce good results for society as a whole.

3. Agents and their Motives

As should be clear by now, the main agents for economic rationalists are *Homo economicus* ones, motivated by material self-interest, and pursuing it rationally. But, as I have just noted, exemption is granted for a few agents in governmental positions, who are allowed to be motivated by concern for the public interest, albeit defined in economic rationalist terms. Of course, the governmental actors who populate horror stories are not allowed any such public interested motivation; they are treated as rational egoists, whose interaction produces all kinds of perverse outcomes. Missing from economic rationalism is any notion of active citizenship; indeed, economic rationalism abolishes citizenship. When I receive a circular from the economic rationalist government of the state of Victoria, where I live, it is addressed "Dear Customer". There are no citizens in Victoria.

4. KEY METAPHORS AND OTHER RHETORICAL DEVICES

Like the Promethean discourse as analyzed in Chapter 3, the basic metaphor of economic rationalism is mechanistic. That is, the social world is treated as a machine whose products meet human needs and wants, which can be understood through reference to its components and their functions. UnlikePrometheans, economic rationalists believe the machine may need to be reassembled, through for example redefinitions of property rights. Once we get the property rights in order, the machine will work smoothly. Environmental resources are treated as inputs to the social machine, be they raw materials for production or amenities such as wilderness and clean air.

Economic rationalists have proven to be skilled rhetoricians. They have scored a notable rhetorical success in recent years in gaining acceptance of the term "command and control" to describe intervention by government administrators in the environmental affairs of industry and commerce. Such intervention used to be known, accurately and simply enough, as "regulation." Economic rationalists oppose regulation, so getting it stigmatized as "command as control" obviously helps them. Of course, as my earlier discussion of administrative rationalism makes clear, precious little command and control actually occurs in environmental administration; there is much more in the way of informal cooperative relationships between government officials and polluters. So as a description of the real world, the term command and control is laughable; but as a rhetorical ploy, it is brilliant. Following the collapse of Soviet-style systems which really did work by command and control, who could possibly favor such a system (except perhaps the military)?

An equally successful rhetorical ploy involves use of the adjective "free," especially to describe markets. A market is a market is a market; so why does it need to be called a free market, especially given that markets can only operate if government supplies a supportive legal context? Relatedly, why are capitalist corporations styled free enterprise? The answer is that the standard set of freedoms existing in liberal democratic societies are very popular. In free markets and free enterprise, coercion is abolished if not in fact, then in rhetoric.

A third pervasive rhetorical strategy in economic rationalism is the horror story, usually involving governmental action that produces perverse, inefficient, and costly results (for good selections, see Nelson, 1993; Stroup and Shaw, 1993). In the United States, one of the most widely circulated environmental horror stories picks up on the analysis of the 1977 Clean Air Act Amendments carried out by Ackerman and Hassler (1981) (who ironically are not themselves economic rationalists). Ackerman and Hassler demonstrate the disastrous results of a particular episode in legislation for environmental regulation. Eastern producers of high-sulfur coal combined with environmentalists to persuade Congress to mandate that all new coal-burning power plants install scrubbers to remove sulfur dioxide from their emissions, irrespective of how low the sulfur content of the coal being burned, and so how much sulfur dioxide was being emitted. This measure effectively discriminated against Western low-sulfur coal producers, and ensured that the ambient air quality targets of the legislation would be met at a cost billions of dollars greater than could have been achieved with a switch to low-sulfur coal. Moreover, the legislation allowed existing coal-burning plants to operate with no additional controls, thus ensuring that such old and dirty plants would gain a competitive edge over new plants, and so stay in use much longer, thus actually encouraging increased pollution.

Other good horror stories include the Superfund, which shuffles toxic waste around at enormous expense; water policy which, bizarrely, promotes water-intensive crops such as rice and cotton in the desert; and timber policy, which heavily subsidizes otherwise uneconomic logging. Most of these horror stories are true. Their rhetorical weight comes with the economic rationalists' generalization from these stories, nearly all of which are about the United States government, to all the environmental activities of all

---

Box 6.1. **DISCOURSE ANALYSIS OF ECONOMIC RATIONALISM**

1. **Basic Entities Recognized or Constructed**
   - Homo economicus
   - Markets
   - Prices
   - Property
   - Governments (not citizens)

2. **Assumptions about Natural Relationships**
   - Competition
   - Hierarchy based on expertise
   - Subordination of nature

3. **Agents and their Motives**
   - Homo economicus: self-interested
   - Some government officials must be motivated by public interest

4. **Key Metaphors and other Rhetorical Devices**
   - Mechanistic
   - Stigmatizing administrative regulation
   - Connection with freedom
   - Horror stories

governments. Perhaps the fault lies with the US federal government in particular, rather than government in general.

An Assessment of Economic Rationalism

Economic rationalism in environmental affairs has been around a long time now. The analysis and advocacy of quasi-market incentive systems has been the staple of environmental economics since the late 1960s, and more radical market-oriented arguments gained ground in the early 1980s. Within the community of environmental policy analysts, there has been little serious opposition to economically rationalist arguments. All these arguments were quite consistent with the dominant political discourse of the 1980s, at least in the Anglo-American world, and with worries about budget deficits and the excessive size and scope of government action that surfaced in developed countries more generally in this period. Not surprisingly, international bodies with an economic mandate such as the OECD have been pushing such policies for a long time. Yet if we look for the diffusion of economic rationalism into environmental policy practice, we find the pace has been glacial. Traditional regulatory policy instruments still dominate anti-pollution policy everywhere, and we have to look very hard to find cases of tradeable quotas in access to resources, still harder for any evidence of privatization of resources and environmental goods. Even when policy instruments are adopted, we find no evidence of the wholesale institutional change that economic rationalists seek. Regulatory agencies are still with us and, far from being replaced by regimes of property rights or by economistic calculators of green taxes, they end up administering such schemes. When it comes to institutions, economic rationalism has had much less impact than administrative rationalism and democratic pragmatism which, as we saw in the two previous chapters, have been major factors in the evolution of environmental institutions in the last 30 years. Economic rationalism's lack of influence at the policy level may in some ways reflect its failure at the institutional level, for the policy prescriptions have not been able to find a hospitable institutional home. Less commodious homes provide only for piecemeal and distorted adoption of economic policy advice. But to explain policy failure in terms of institutional failure merely begs the question of why the discourse has fallen short in influencing practice at any level.

No doubt part of the explanation for the glacial progress of economic rationalism in environmental affairs lies in simple inertia, and the resistance of established routines. Yet if inertia is so powerful, why has economic rationalism made greater inroads more rapidly in areas such as labor-market deregulation, business deregulation, privatization of state-owned industries and utilities, even redesign of the welfare state? A related explanation might note that proposals for economic instruments can never enter in the clean and straightforward fashion of the economics textbooks. Instead, their entry and so their design is heavily dependent on the configuration of political forces and the prevailing political-economic context. We have seen in the case of Britain, for example, how the revenue-raising potential of green taxes has attracted the Treasury, but in doing so has made both industry and environmentalists nervous. The fairyland of neoclassical microeconomics in which economic rationalist argument for market-oriented policy instruments is rooted is very different from the real world. The good fairies are not in charge of policy design and implementation. But still, the environmental area is hardly unique in this respect.

To get at the real reasons for resistance to economic rationalism we need to treat it as a discourse rather than just a set of proposals for policies and institutions. Recall that the basic agents and motives recognized by economic rationalism treat people only as *homo economicus* consumers and producers. There are no citizens in economic rationalism. In the previous chapter I noted that Mark Sagoff (1988) points out that all individuals have both consumer preferences and citizen preferences, and that these may point in different directions. As a consumer I may want to make use of freeways to get to work more quickly, as a citizen I may demonstrate against construction of the freeways because they destroy communities and natural areas. As Sagoff argues, we normally put our citizen preferences first. But economic rationalists count only consumer preferences. So the world as constituted by economic rationalists is one where citizen preferences, and so citizens, count for nothing. This is not a world likely to please environmental citizen activists, which is why environmentalists have often opposed economic rationalist schemes, without always being able to explain exactly why. When we visit a National Park, we do so as citizens. Part of the experience of being there is that it is indeed a *National* Park, emblematic of what it means to be a Canadian, an American, a Costa Rican, or a Japanese; a repository of common trust and community pride. And visiting National Parks in other nations can also involve recognition of and respect for the identity and citizenship of others. These are experiences that Walt Disney could never provide.

Such opposition, again often unarticulated, may also arise as a result of the way economic rationalism treats or, rather, does not treat the environment. Recall that in economic rationalist discourse, the environment exists only as a medium for the effects of some human actions on other humans, and as a source of inputs for the socio-economic machine. Thus it has no intrinsic value, and chunks of it can be bought or sold at will, depending only on the most profitable human use. When it comes to pollution, economic rationalism attaches no stigma: rights to pollute are just like any other commodity, to be bought or sold. As Kelman (1981) notes, this failure to stigmatize pollution in moral terms makes many environmentalists uneasy. Goodin (1994) compares this selling of pieces of the environment by governments to the selling of indulgences by the medieval Catholic Church. In both cases, individuals can have their sins forgiven if they can afford to pay. But just as places in heaven were not the church's to sell (only for God or St Peter to decide), so pieces of the environment are not government's to sell. Martin Luther and opponents of green taxes have more in common than they might think.

In short, no matter how attractive economic prescriptions may be in instrumental terms, even to committed environmentalists, they help constitute a discourse, and a world, which those according higher priority to citizenship, democratic, and ecological values find unattractive (see Dryzek, 1995).

A further limitation of economic rationalism arises from its basically mechanistic metaphorical structure. The idea that the world may be full of complex systems, ecological systems and social systems interacting in variable and uncertain ways, is implicitly denied by economic rationalism. Economic rationalists have no way to deal with such interactions, which may well violate the boundaries of private property rights, no matter how carefully drawn. For example, proposals for tradeable quotas in ocean fisheries inevitably treat species in isolation. But rational management of a single species is impossible. Whether the species survives or flourishes depends not just on how many tons of it are caught per year, but on what is happening to other species that are predators, prey, or competitors for the same ecological niche. Moreover, other factors such as pollution or development may affect the habitat of the species.

Finally, economic rationalism as a discourse gets into all kinds of tangles in its treatment of government. I have already noted that its attitude to government is thoroughly ambiguous: at one level government is populated by rational egoists feeding at the public trough, plundering the public purse, and thoroughly indifferent to environmental values. At another level public-spirited government action is needed in order to put economic rationalist prescriptions into institutional and policy practice, and in this sense economic rationalism depends crucially on administrative rationalism. The "public choice" school of economic rationalists has thrived on horror stories about government in theory and practice; in fact, without quite realizing it, the public choice school has demonstrated that political order is impossible if everyone is a rational egoist (see Dryzek, 1992*b*). When it comes to environmental affairs, if everyone is a rational egoist, then the commons will always be abused, polluters will continue to generate externalities, and government will do absolutely nothing to remedy the situation. The obvious inference is that economic rationalism is inadequate as an orientation to environmental affairs (see Dryzek, 1996*b*, for a more elaborate justification of this point). In this light, economic rationalism's real usefulness may come in detailing very precisely the destructive effects of *homo economicus*, and the need for his proclivities to be controlled by more socially, politically, and ecologically benign human motivations. Economic rationalism, unlike democratic pragmatism and green radicalism, has had nothing to say about these alternative wellsprings of human behavior and action.

This concludes my discussion of the three discourses of environmental problem solving. While all three have their problems, it is fair to say that the real-world achievements of administrative rationalism and democratic pragmatism are more substantial than those of economic rationalism. This conclusion will not necessarily dismay die-hard economic rationalists, who argue that the problem is precisely that their proposals have not been tested fairly. Still, for administrative rationalism and democratic pragmatism, their problems are revealed through examination of several decades of real-world influence. For economic rationalism, in contrast, the problems are revealed by contemplation of the reasons for lack of impact. Partisans of each one of these three discourses often make their case through reference to the deficiencies of the other two, while remaining within the basic parameters of problem solving within the political-economic status quo of liberal capitalism. But the manifest difficulties of all three discourses lead others to be a bit more creative in looking for alternatives. Let me turn now to emerging discourses which remain reformist in their orientation to industrialism, but are more imaginative in seeking ways to dissolve familiar dilemmas and impasses.

Part IV

The Quest for Sustainability

The apocalyptic horizons of environmental concern were set firmly in the early 1970s by survivalists who argued that economic growth and population expansion would have to yield to global environmental limits, sooner rather than later. Prometheans denied the existence of these limits. The problem-solving discourses surveyed in Part III are essentially agnostic about global limits, focusing instead on the work to be done in the here and now, rather than contemplating the fate of the earth. Yet for the most part problem solving is energized by the need to achieve some kind of resolution to conflicts between ecological values and economic values.

Life would certainly be less troublesome if such conflicts did not exist, or, failing that, could be dissolved. The unresolved dispute between survivalists and Prometheans could be put behind us, and environmental problem solving could proceed with renewed vigor in the knowledge that solutions are available which, while not pleasing everyone, can respond effectively to a range of key ecological and economic concerns. Throw in commitments to global justice through the eradication of poverty and to the wellbeing of future generations, and the prospect would surely be irresistible. But what could possibly combine ecological protection, economic growth, social justice, and intergenerational equity, not just locally and immediately, but globally and in perpetuity? The answer is "sustainable development," which specifies that we can have them all.

Since the early 1980s, sustainable development has become hugely popular as an integrating discourse covering the whole range of environmental issues, from the local to the global, as well as a host of economic and development concerns. Just what sustainable development means in practice is a matter of some dispute, as is the question of whether it can actually deliver on some, most, or all of its promises.

The notion of sustainability receives greater precision in the second discourse covered in Part IV: ecological modernization. Ecological modernization concerns itself with the restructuring of the capitalist political economy along more environmentally defensible lines. The key is that there is money to be made in this restructuring. At one level ecological modernization is about the search for green production technology. But this search also opens the door to intriguing possibilities for more thoroughgoing transformation, involving political change as well as technological change. So although at first sight ecological modernization looks like a rescue mission for industrial society, albeit an imaginative one, it also points to political and economic possibilities beyond industrial society.

7

Environmentally Benign Growth: Sustainable Development

What is Sustainable Development?

Sustainable development is nowhere an accomplished fact, save in small-scale hunter-gatherer and agrarian societies that have existed in harmony with their local environment at low levels of economic and technological development. Such societies are becoming increasingly scarce. Sustainable development refers not to any accomplishment, still less a precise set of structures and measures to achieve collectively desirable outcomes. Rather, it is a discourse. And it is not just any discourse. Since the publication of the report of the Brundtland Commission in 1987 (World Commission on Environment and Development, 1987) it is arguably the dominant global discourse of ecological concern. As Torgerson (1995: 10), puts it (perhaps overstating the point), "public discussion concerning the environment has become primarily a discourse of sustainability."

It is at the discursive level that dilemmas are dissolved by sustainable development, not at the level of policies and accomplishments. That is, sustainable development is not proven or demonstrated but, rather, asserted. But just what is sustainable development?

This question is a hard one to answer. The most widely quoted definition is Brundtland's: "Humanity has the ability to make development sustainable—to ensure that it meets the needs of the present without compromising the ability of future generations to meet their own needs" (World Commission on Environment and Development, 1987: 8). Later in the report Brundtland declares that "In essence, sustainable development is a process of change in which the exploitation of resources, the direction of investments, the orientation of technological development, and institutional change are all in harmony and enhance both current and future potential to meet human needs and aspirations" (p. 46).

Now, sustainable development as a concept did not begin with Brundtland. The two words have been joined occasionally since the early 1970s, and the concept has a deeper history in the renewable resource management concept of maximum sustainable yield. The latter is the maximum catch from a fishery, or cut from a forest, or kill of game animals, that can be sustained indefinitely. But the maximum sustainable yield concept says nothing about growth in resource use (indeed, rules out growth), or about how management of different resources might interact, or what to do with non-renewable resources. Sustainable development is a much more ambitious concept in that it refers to the ensemble of life-support systems, and seeks perpetual growth in the sum of human needs that might be satisfied not through simple resource garnering, but rather through intelligent operation of natural systems and human systems acting in combination.

Brundtland's definition did not satisfy everyone, and other definitions of sustainable development have proliferated. By 1992 the count was 40 and rising (Torgerson, 1994: 303). In the early 1990s the Transportation Research Board of the United States National Academy of Sciences spent a million dollars to try to come up with a definition. However, the Board failed to do anything more than simply agglomerate the concerns of its members, rather than converging on a concise definition. By 1996 the United Nations Educational, Scientific, and Cultural Organization (UNESCO) was sponsoring a project to clarify the meaning of the concept in a number of disciplines, with a view to making the concept a scientifically usable one—implying that at the moment it is not a scientific concept.[1] Yet the UNESCO project has a difficult task. For the proliferation of definitions is not just a matter of analysts trying to add conceptual precision to Brundtland's rather vague formulations. It is also an issue of different interests with different substantive concerns trying to stake their claims in the sustainable development territory. For if sustainable development is indeed emerging as a dominant discourse, astute actors recognize that the terms of this discourse should be cast in terms favorable to them. So environmentalists might try to build in a respect for intrinsic values in nature that is conspicuously missing in Brundtland. Third World governments and advocates would stress the need for global redistribution. Local resource managers might note that it is not only global systems that require sustainable management. Business groups equate development with economic growth, such that sustainable development mainly means continued economic growth. Partisans of the limits discourse re-cast their survivalism in the language of

---

[1] This project is under the auspices of UNESCO's Management of Social Transformation Program, and organized through the Institute for Social-Ecological Research in Frankfurt, Germany.

sustainability. After endorsing Brundtland, those arch-survivalists Meadows, Meadows, and Randers (1992: 209) go on to say that "From a systems point of view a sustainable society is one that has in place informational, social, and institutional mechanisms to keep in check the positive feedback loops that cause exponential population and capital growth." For Meadows and colleagues sustainability means an end to economic growth; for the Business Council on Sustainable Development, sustainability means the perpetuation of economic growth. As the Council declares, "Economic growth in all parts of the world is essential to improve the livelihoods of the poor, to sustain growing populations, and eventually to stabilize population levels" (Schmidheiny, 1992: xi).

Does this variety of meanings mean we should dismiss sustainable development as a mere slogan, an empty vessel that can be filled with whatever one likes? Not at all. For it is not unusual for important concepts to be contested politically. Think, for example, of the word "democracy," which has at least as many meanings and definitions as does sustainable development. Part of what makes democracy interesting is this very contestation over its essence. Democracy is doubly interesting because just about everyone who matters in today's political world claims to believe in it. The parallels with sustainable development are quite precise. Just as democracy is the only game in town when it comes to political organization, so sustainable development is emerging as the main game (though not quite the only game) when it comes to environmental affairs, at least global ones. Or, to put the issue in the terms in which we are working, sustainable development, like democracy, is a discourse rather than a concept which can or should be defined with any precision. The discourse itself does, though, have boundaries, and later I will undertake an analysis of sustainable development in these terms to show exactly where the boundaries with other discourses lie. For the moment, though, it should be noted that sustainable development is different from survivalism because it recognizes no fixed limits to growth (the attempts of Meadows, Meadows, and Randers, 1992, to subsume sustainable development under survivalism notwithstanding). It is different from Promethean discourse because it requires coordinated collective efforts to achieve goals, rather than relying on human spontaneity and ingenuity. And it is different from the varieties of environmental problem solving surveyed in the previous three chapters because it is much more imaginative in its reconceptualization of the terms of environmental dispute and in its dissolution of some long-standing conflicts.

The Career of the Concept

The term "sustainable development" has been around for some time. Prior to the 1980s, it was part of the environmentalist lexicon, especially in the context of discussions of developing societies in the Third World. Advocates were interested in the potential of what they called appropriate technologies or intermediate technologies, which were low-cost, low in the environmental stress they imposed, and consistent with local cultural norms (see, for example, Schumacher, 1973). They preferred energy generation from cattle dung over nuclear power stations or large dams, small workshops over large factories. The concept's prominence grew, and its meaning began to change, in 1980 with the publication of the International Union for the Conservation of Nature's (1980) *World Conservation Strategy*. But the real beginning of the contemporary discourse of sustainable development can be dated slightly later, and quite precisely, to December 1983, when Gro Harlem Brundtland, Prime Minister of Norway, was asked by the Secretary-General of the United Nations to chair an inquiry into interrelated global problems of environment and development. Brundtland's World Commission on Environment and Development published its report, *Our Common Future*, in 1987. The report contains many detailed analyses and recommendations pertaining to the international economy, population, food, energy, manufacturing, cities, and institutional change. But its main accomplishment was to combine systematically a number of issues that have often been treated in isolation, or at least as competitors: development (especially of Third World countries), global environmental issues, population, peace and security, and social justice both within and across generations. Brundtland developed a vision of the simultaneous and mutually reinforcing pursuit of economic growth, environmental improvement, population stabilization, peace, and global equity, all of which could be maintained in the long term. Such a vision was seductive, though as I have already noted, Brundtland did not go so far as to demonstrate the feasibility of the vision, or indicate the practical steps that would be required to bring it about.

Since 1987 the discourse of sustainable development has been kept alive and expanding at the international level, especially inasmuch as international society is constituted by international governmental organizations (IGOs) and nongovernmental organizations (NGOs). In 1991 the International Union for the Conservation of Nature, United Nations Environment Program, and World Wildlife Fund (1991) published a joint strategy for sustainable development. The Earth Summit, more formally the

United Nations Conference on Environment and Development, held in Rio de Janeiro in 1992 was a high point, and sustainable development underwrote its proceedings. The 171 national government delegations, many with heads of government present, gave sustainable development their stamps of approval (though the various delegations may have held to different meanings of the term). The Earth Summit endorsed *Agenda 21*, a lengthy and detailed follow-up to Brundtland's efforts, which argued that the global environmental problems had arisen mainly as a result of the profligate consumption and production of the richer countries. After the conference the United Nations established a Commission on Sustainable Development to implement *Agenda 21*, with special reference to how national governments might act, and how conflicts between First World and Third World notions of development and environmental protection might be resolved. Third World governments made it abundantly clear that they were not going to modify their developmental paths for the sake of the global environment without substantial financial compensation.

Even the World Bank, long castigated by environmentalists for its record of complicity in ecologically disastrous development projects (such as large dams and high-technology agriculture), has tried to improve its environmental image by establishing an Environment Department, appointing a Vice-President for Sustainable Development, and sponsoring a series of publications on environmentally sustainable development. The main theme of the Bank's 1992 *World Environment Report* was that environmental management and economic development could proceed together. The Bank has also sponsored research on the development of indicators of sustainable development as alternatives to more established measures of national well-being such as gross national product (see, for example, World Bank, 1995). Whether the development projects sponsored by the Bank will become more environmentally sensitive as a result of these developments remains to be seen.

While the sustainability discourse is most evident at this international level, it has made some inroads within states. In 1990 Japan established a sustainable development program, with an eye to maximizing Japanese opportunities in the emerging sustainable eco-economy (opportunities which are not hurt by the existing energy-efficiency of the Japanese economy). In Brundtland's own Norway, ProSus (Program for Research and Documentation for a Sustainable Society) is a think tank committed to sustainable development for Norway and the world. In Australia, the federal government in 1990 set up an ecologically sustainable development process, with working groups on agriculture, energy, fisheries, forestry, manufacturing, mining, transport, and tourism. Symbolizing sustainable development's positive-sum approach to economy and environment, each working group contained representatives of both industry and environmental groups (along with government and trade-union officials). The working groups reported in 1992, and their efforts were incorporated into a National Ecologically Sustainable Development Strategy, though for a number of domestic political reasons the process and the strategy have subsequently languished (see Christoff, 1995). In the United States federal government the sustainable development torch is carried by the President's Council on Sustainable Development, which could draw support from Vice-President Al Gore's personal views (at least as expressed in Gore, 1992). In Britain, the government endorsed Brundtland's stress on sustainable development but—astonishingly—asserted that existing British economic policy met these principles, giving further proof of just how far the concept can be stretched (Department of the Environment, 1988; see also Jacobs, 1991: 59). Thus the British government saw no need to embark on any particular policy initiatives in this area, confirming its position as a laggard in the sustainability stakes.

International business has also hitched itself to the sustainability bandwagon. The International Chamber of Commerce and the Business Council on Sustainable Development, chaired by Stephan Schmidheiny of the Swiss company UNOTEC, were both active in the process leading up to the 1992 Earth Summit. The Business Council was formed in 1990 to participate in this process at the invitation of Maurice Strong, secretary general of the Summit. Not surprisingly, the Council is committed to economic growth, but with an environmentally sensitive face. Its component corporations such as 3M, Du Pont, Shell, Mitsubishi, and ALCOA can point to success stories in their own operations of environmentally aware practices such as recycling, efficiency benefits achieved by waste reduction, sustainable forestry, and energy-efficient production (see Schmidheiny, 1992 for a compilation). By 1995 the World Business Council on Sustainable Development was composed of 130 of the world's largest corporations, and chaired by Rodney Chase, chief executive of BP. (It should be noted that not all of these 130 companies have exemplary environmental records.)

Where are the environmentalists in these developments? After all, sustainable development began life as one of their concepts. Though not completely displaced by international organizations, states, and business, environmental groups are less visible than they might be. But some environmentalists, such as Friends of the Earth Europe, have indeed tried to keep up with the discourse, to remind everyone that sustainable development requires wholesale reductions in the stress that economic activity imposes on the environment, and respect for intrinsic values in nature.

Discourse Analysis of Sustainable Development

The core story line of sustainable development begins with a recognition that the legitimate developmental aspirations of the world's peoples cannot be met by all countries following the growth path already taken by the industrialized countries, for such action would over-burden the world's ecosystems. Yet economic growth is necessary to satisfy the legitimate needs of the world's poor. The alleviation of poverty will ameliorate what is one of the basic causes of environmental degradation, for poor people are forced to abuse their local environment just to survive. Economic growth should therefore be promoted but guided in ways that are both environmental benign and socially just. Justice here refers not only to distribution within the present generation, but also to distribution across future generations. Sustainable development is not just a strategy for the future of developing societies, but also for industrialized societies, which must reduce the excessive stress their past economic growth has imposed upon the earth.

1. BASIC ENTITIES WHOSE EXISTENCE IS RECOGNIZED OR CONSTRUCTED

Sustainable development's purview is global; its justification rests in present stresses imposed on global ecosystems. But unlike survivalism, it does not rest at that global level. Sustainability is an issue at regional and local levels too, for that is where solutions will have to be found. Thus the basic entities stressed in sustainable development are nested systems, ranging from the global to the local. The systems in question are both social and biological. Natural systems are not something separate from humanity: as the Brundtland report puts it, "The environment does not exist as a sphere separate from humans ambitions, actions, and needs . . . the 'environment' is where we all live" (World Commission on Environment and Development, 1987: xi). Certainly the biological components of systems are treated as much more delicate than the brute matter which is all that Prometheans see in nature. While survivalists see problems in terms of global limits and solutions in terms of global management, sustainable development takes a much more disaggregated approach. Particular resources and systems can be used and developed more or less wisely, imposing more or less environmental stress.

The Brundtland report itself is a bit ambiguous on the existence of limits. A statement that "Growth has no set limits in terms of population or resource use beyond which lies ecological disaster" in part because "accumulation of knowledge and the development of technology can enhance the carrying capacity of the resource base" is followed immediately by a recognition that "But ultimate limits there are" (World Commission on Environment and Development, 1987: 45). In fact, these ultimate limits too prove capable of being stretched by technology. As Brundtland herself later put the point, "The commission found no absolute limits to growth. Limits are indeed imposed by the impact of present technologies and social organization on the biosphere, but we have the ingenuity to change" (quoted in Hardin, 1993: 205).

When it comes to social systems, sustainable development takes the capitalist economy pretty much for granted. However, the structure of political systems is not taken as given, and can be highly problematical. The reorientation in problem solving that sustainable development prescribes may require shifts in power between different levels in order to more effectively meet the challenge of sustainability. The frequent appeals to coordinated international action and grassroots participation suggest that these shifts would be away from the nation-state as presently constituted to both higher (transnational) and lower (local) levels of political organization.

2. Assumptions about Natural Relationships

The most important relationship regarded as if not exactly natural then at least attainable is the positive-sum one: economic growth, environmental protection, distributive justice, and long-term sustainability are mutually reinforcing. In the world of sustainable development there are few hierarchies in human affairs. Instead, there is cooperation. However, there is a hierarchy which puts human beings above the natural world. Though some efforts have been made to introduce respect for nature into its definition, for example in the joint statement of the International Union for the Conservation of Nature, United Nations Environment Program, and World Wildlife Fund (1991), for the most part sustainable development remains anthropocentric. It is sustainability of human populations and their wellbeing which is at issue, rather than that of nature. Relationships of competition are de-emphasized, though as I have noted the existence of the capitalist economy is taken for granted as a background condition. Sustainable development is to be achieved through cooperative rather than competitive effort, thus further distancing the discourse from both economic rationalists and Prometheans.

3. Agents and their Motives

Sustainable development's key agents are not the global managers of the survivalists or the experts with a managerial hierarchy at their disposal of the administrative rationalists. Instead, the relevant actors can exist at many levels, consistent with basic notions about the existence of nested social and biological systems. In practice, sustainable development de-emphasizes national governments and state actors. It was established in the 1980s as a discourse of international society, especially as that society is populated by intergovernmental organizations (such as the United Nations and its branches, and the World Bank) and nongovernmental organizations (such as global environmental groups). There is a role for the grassroots too: the green radical slogan "think globally, act locally" can be adopted here. The Earth Summit's *Agenda 21* called for more citizen participation in environment and development decisions. And, as I have already noted, corporations have clambered on board the bandwagon to show that business too can play a constructive role. In sum, sustainable development is a discourse of and for global civil society (see Conca, 1994; Lafferty, 1996; Wapner, 1996). Civil society is normally defined in terms of political action and interaction not encompassed by the state.

4. Key Metaphors and other Rhetorical Devices

Prometheans and economic rationalists alike rely on mechanistic metaphors, treating the world as a machine whose bits can be arranged to better meet human needs. In contrast, sustainable development's metaphorical structure is organic. Organisms grow and develop; so can societies. Growth here is not just a matter of physical maturation that happens automatically, for sustainable development also stipulates self-conscious improvement. As such, it is consistent with notions of personal human growth that stress education and growing awareness, enabling the individual in question to negotiate his or her social environment in more effective fashion. The image is of an increasingly sensitive, caring, and intelligent human being—only, of course, it is sensitive, caring, and intelligent political-economic systems which become at issue, and the environment to be negotiated is not just a social one, but also a natural one. Just as in fashionable models that portray human development in terms of lifetime learning, the growth in political-economic capacities is seen as open-ended. The only difference is that individual humans eventually die, whereas for sustainable development the growth in political-economic capacities can go on in perpetuity.

Sustainable development in its very name links itself to the idea of progress, and progress is one of the most powerful notions in the modern world. Whatever their other differences, Victorian industrialists, Marxists, social democrats, liberal democrats, and market liberals have all believed in the essential idea of history moving in the direction of social improvement. Sustainable development carries this idea into an environmental era.

Sustainable development also involves a rhetoric of reassurance. We *can* have it all: economic growth, environmental conservation, social justice; and not just for the moment, but in perpetuity. No painful changes are necessary. This rhetoric of reassurance is far from the images of doom and redemption found in survivalism, or the horror stories beloved of economic rationalists. Advocates of sustainable development are far more likely to highlight local success stories of sustainability than they are to dwell on instances of unsustainability (see, for example, Schmidheiny, 1992: 181–333).

Box 7.1. DISCOURSE ANALYSIS OF SUSTAINABLE DEVELOPMENT

1. **Basic Entities Recognized or Constructed**
   - Nested social and ecological systems
   - Capitalist economy
   - (No limits)

2. **Assumptions about Natural Relationships**
   - Subordination of nature
   - Economic growth, environmental protection, distributive justice, and long-term sustainability go together

3. **Agents and their Motives**
   - Many agents at different levels, notably transnational and local rather than the state; motivated by the public good

4. **Key Metaphors and other Rhetorical Devices**
   - Organic growth
   - Connection to progress
   - Reassurance

Whither Sustainable Development?

If we were to look for sustainable development, where would we find it? As discourse, there is a lot of it about. At the institutional level, a number of international initiatives have embodied the ideal—the United Nations Environment Program, the World Bank's environmental facility, the Earth Summit, and so forth. At the national level, some special-purpose institutions with a sustainability mandate have appeared (see my earlier references to Norway, Australia, Japan, and the United States). But can we identify any practices and policies inspired by, committed to, and achieving sustainable development?

This question turns out to be a harder one. Certainly there are success stories to be found in the operations of individual corporations, which can tout (for example) the way mining operations now involve protection for and rehabilitation of ecosystems in the vicinity of the mine. And given the concept's elasticity, any environmentally sensitive economic activity can be recruited as an example. But the question remains: is anyone, anywhere, effectively pursuing and implementing a policy of sustainability? Examples here are harder to find.

Kai Lee believes that "sustainable development has been successfully launched" in the Columbia River Basin in the United States (Lee, 1993: 16), as part of the "World's largest attempt at ecosystem rehabilitation" (p. 49). The Columbia Basin had been developed since the 1930s in decidedly unsustainable fashion, featuring series of large dams, mainly to provide cheap power for industries and cities in the region. The results proved disastrous for the ecosystems of the basin, especially in terms of the near-elimination of salmon from the Columbia and its tributaries. To Lee, sustainable development is mostly a matter of systematic social learning by ecosystem managers; but, consistent with the discourse's stress on cooperative problem solving, the managers do not simply have a free hand in applying their expertise. Instead, they listen to the voices of a variety of political groups in the basin, such as the representatives of commercial and recreational fishers, indigenous peoples, and environmentalists. The adaptive management of the basin is now entrusted to the Northwest Power Planning Council, a basin-wide authority composed of representatives from the various states the basin covers. Adaptive management emulates science in its experimental and open approach to problem solving; unlike many political structures (especially administrative ones), it must be able to tolerate policy failure for the sake of learning, and to operate on an ecological time-scale, not a bureaucratic or electoral one. But however much there is to be said on behalf of the process of adaptive management in the Columbia basin, it should be noted that after ten years of this practice the salmon still have not returned, the large dams are still there, and nobody knows quite how to reconcile the industrial and economic growth values which the dams represent with the ecological values symbolized by the salmon (the salmon have a potentially large economic value too). So sustainable development as a policy outcome has not been achieved, though Lee himself argues that it is wrong to think of it in terms of a goal. Rather, sustainable development represents "a direction in which we strive" (Lee, 1993: 200), and in that sense the management of the Columbia Basin seems to be striving in the right direction, dead salmon notwithstanding.

Lee stresses that one element of social learning must be experimentation with what sustainable development can really mean, both as a concept and in practice. This approach to sustainability is consistent with an emerging strand in the discourse which emphasizes decentralized, exploratory, and variable approaches to the pursuit of sustainability. I have already noted that sustainable development (unlike survivalism) is a multi-layered and multi-faceted enterprise, though still oriented by some common commitments. Rather than try to impose a common definition replete with an associated set of precise goals (which is what survivalists and administrative rational-ists would do), a "de-centered" approach would see local experimentation as the essence of the search for sustainable development (Brooks, 1992; Torgerson, 1994; 1995). This search would be incremental, pluralistic, and piecemeal. In this search, the very fact that agreement on the essence of sus-tainable development has been elusive proves to be a help rather than a hin-drance, for no avenues are ruled out by stipulation, and so all kinds of new possibilities might be unearthed (Torgerson, 1994: 310–13; see also Thompson, 1993).

But if the pursuit of sustainability is to be de-centered and piecemeal, what would actually harness all these disparate and myriad efforts to the common good? The answer lies in the necessity for widespread commitment to the discourse itself, which provides the only conceivable glue to hold these various efforts together. In this light, the sought-after restructuring of power relationships becomes understandable. Sustainable development is, as I observed earlier, primarily a discourse of and for global civil society, not states. Luke (1995: ch. 6) interprets this feature quite cynically as simply serving the interests of managerial "ecocrats" employed in IGOs and NGOs, increasing their power at the expense of nation states. Luke's argument would be plausible if sustainable development did indeed constitute a uni-fied approach. But with the de-centered, piecemeal twist, the role played by global civil society becomes democratic rather than managerial, a welcome antidote to state governments increasingly under the sway of market liberal ideas and committed to reducing environmental controls, expanding trade, and promoting economic growth at all costs (Lafferty, 1996). It is citizens, not ecocrats, who can use the discourse as a resource against ecologically recalcitrant governments.

None of this guarantees that widespread commitment to and pursuit of sustainable development in piecemeal fashion will deliver the goods. Economic rationalists see the whole enterprise as just the latest in a long line of futile attempts to replace markets by political management, trying to impose a discipline on peoples' decisions which is properly exercised by the market's price system (see Anderson and Leal, 1991: 167–71).[2] Radical environmentalists deny that development (interpreted as economic growth) can ever be sustainable, and denounce the anthropocentric arrogance implicit in the discourse (for example, Merchant, 1992; Richardson, 1994). Survivalists attack the denial of limits and carrying capacity explicit in the discourse; so Garrett Hardin (1993: 204–6) takes Brundtland to task for failing even to ask whether the population growth she sees as inevitable and the economic growth she sees as desirable can be accommodated by the earth's resources (see also Milbrath, 1989: 320–3). Similarly, Herman Daly (1993) believes that Brundtland's vision of a world economy five to ten times larger than its present size is impossible given that the present human economy already appropriates 25 per cent of the world's "net primary product of photosynthesis." The more pessimistic among conservation biologists argue that resources are very rarely managed with sustainability in mind until after they have collapsed, for only then does their overuse become apparent (Ludwig, Hilborn, and Walters, 1993; but for a catalogue of local cases where resources have been managed sustainably, see Ostrom, 1990).

There are, then, those who still keep their distance from sustainable development, thus refuting claims that sustainable development is the only discourse of our environmental times. Still, there is no denying its power, which might suggest that those interested in environmental goals of any sort should try to hitch a ride on it, with the intention of moving it in whatever directions they favor. So Lafferty (1996) argues that as of 1996, there is simply no better vehicle for environmentalists to pursue their various goals. The different strategic choices made by some eminent survivalists are noteworthy in this context. Meadows, Meadows, and Randers (1992) disguise their survivalism in the words of sustainable development, and praise Brundtland; Garrett Hardin (1993) rubbishes sustainable development and berates Brundtland.

The success or failure of sustainable development rests on dissemination and acceptance of the discourse at a variety of levels, but especially that of global civil society, followed by action on and experimentation with its

---

[2] Anderson and Leal should be embarrassed by their treatment. On the one hand, they regard sustainable development as sufficiently important for its contrast with their free-market environmentalism to form the conclusion of their book, which is widely regarded as the definitive statement of economic rationalism applied to environmental affairs. On the other hand, they wrongly assert that sustainable development involves a globally administered regime of zero economic growth and zero use of nonrenewable natural resources. In other words, they mistake sustainable development for survivalism—indeed, an extreme form of survivalism.

tenets. Yet the ten years which have seen sustainable development establish itself as the leading transnational discourse of environmental concern have seen very little in the way of the wholesale movements in policies, practices, and institutions at global, regional, national, and local levels which its advocates regard as imperative. Those same ten years have seen a more effective global movement in a very different direction about which sustainable development is strangely silent. That competing direction involves the increasing transnationalization of capitalism, symbolized by the culmination of the Uruguay Round of negotiation of the General Agreement on Tariffs and Trade (GATT) in 1994, which established the World Trade Organization and inaugurated a new era of free trade. The World Trade Organization joins the International Monetary Fund and the World Bank in policing international economic regimes. Free trade, capital mobility, and governments all over the world committed to market liberalization and ordinary (unsustainable) economic growth as their first imperatives run directly counter to sustainable development. It is not so much that global civil society has fought on behalf of sustainable development against transnational capitalism, global economic institutions, and national governments increasingly committed to market liberal principles and lost; it is rather than no real battle has been fought. But even if combat were to be engaged, sustainable development would surely still lose against these massive structural forces and powerful institutions now directing the global economy.

That is, sustainable development would surely lose unless it could be demonstrated that environmental conservation were obviously good for business profitability and economic growth everywhere, not just that these competing values can be reconciled. As we shall see in the next chapter, this is exactly the claim advanced by ecological modernization, which has developed the case with far greater precision than the vague formulations on this score of sustainable development.

8   Industrial Society and Beyond: Ecological Modernization

Cleanest and Greenest

Which countries have turned in the most successful environmental policy performance in the 1980s and 1990s? Among developed nations, my nominations for the top five are (in alphabetical order):

- Germany
- Japan
- The Netherlands
- Norway
- Sweden

Of course, different indicators of environmental policy success produce different rankings, and some dimensions of environmental conservation (such as endangered species protection) are not easily measured. So any such ranking is likely to be controversial (especially from the point of view of those not on my list). However, these five countries are established as the leaders on the basis of indicators such as:

- high energy efficiency of national income (in terms of the amount of energy required to produce a unit of national income).
- low per capita emissions of pollutants such as carbon dioxide and sulfur dioxide.
- low per capita generation of household garbage and other solid wastes.

At issue here is not just the level of these indicators, but also their rate of change with time. These five countries have been particularly successful in increasing the energy efficiency of national income, reducing emissions, and reducing garbage over the last twenty years or so. Moreover, they have committed themselves to support of global initiatives requiring reduction in carbon dioxide emissions for the sake of global climate stabilization, and those requiring elimination of chlorofluorocarbon production for the sake of protection of the ozone layer. These countries come out well in cross-national comparative studies of performance on pollution indicators. The most systematic studies have been carried out by a team based at the Research Unit for Environmental Policy at the Free University of Berlin (see Jänicke, 1992; 1996; for raw data, see Organization for Economic Cooperation and Development, 1991). Support for my ranking of the top five countries can be found in these comparative studies.

Comparative statistics of the sort produced by the Berlin team tell only part of the story. If we dig a little deeper we find that these five states have adopted innovative and advanced procedures, policies, and institutions for dealing with environmental issues. Around 1970, most of the environmental policy innovations were made in the developed English-speaking countries, especially the United States, and then copied elsewhere. But by the 1980s, the English-speaking countries had slipped from leaders to laggards in the environmental stakes. Let us take a look at what the clean and green five have been doing.

In 1989 the Netherlands adopted a National Environmental Policy Plan designed to integrate environmental criteria into the operations of all departments of government. The Plan is oriented by a set of environmental quality targets along with a timetable for achieving them, and grounded in a sophisticated theory of how pollutants are generated in and travel through human social systems. Thus rather than control pollutants at "the end of the pipe," the Dutch Plan seeks to identify and change the activities which cause pollution in the first place. The changes in question are identified in consultation with the relevant industry and with citizen groups and responsible government officials, especially those from the departments responsible for industry, agriculture, and transport. In terms of substantive issues addressed, the Plan encourages more energy-efficient manufacturing and transport, agriculture that can achieve good yields while minimizing use of herbicides and pesticides, and so forth. None of this is done on a piecemeal basis, but rather in the context of the targets of the Plan as a whole. The environment is not treated as a discrete policy area, to be dealt with in isolation from other policy areas. Instead, environmental concerns are woven into all the relevant areas of government.

The National Environmental Policy Plan has had its political ups and downs. Notably, soon after its inception in 1989 one of the parties in the governing coalition withdrew its support for a provision in the Plan which specified the end of a commuting expenses tax break, and so precipitated a general election (see Weale, 1992: 142–5). And there have been inevitable disappointments in the implementation of the Plan. However, the Plan remains alive and functioning in the late 1990s. As a process for forcing environmental concerns into the whole range of government operations, or "turning government green" as Weale (1992: 122–53) puts it, the Plan remains a landmark.

In Germany, concern over the "implementation deficit" associated with earlier environmental policies led in the 1980s to the adoption of the *vorsorgeprinzip* or precautionary principle as the guiding force for policy. This concept has since diffused beyond the borders of Germany. Essentially, the precautionary principle specifies that scientific uncertainty is no excuse for inaction on an environmental problem. Thus if there are good reasons for thinking a problem may be serious, then it will be addressed, even in the absence of scientific proof. As in the Netherlands, the action in question will not take merely remedial form. Instead, it will be incorporated as far as possible in the design of the activities generating the pollution or other kind of problem.

The precautionary principle was strongly resisted—indeed, barely comprehended—by the national governments of Britain and the United States in the 1980s. In the US, the Reagan and Bush administrations used scientific uncertainty as an excuse for taking little or no action on the acid rain issue, especially over claims that sulfur emissions in the United States caused acid rain that damaged lakes and forests in Canada. In Britain, the absence of conclusive science became the standard governmental excuse for inaction on every major regional and global pollution issue: acid rain, carbon dioxide, chlorofluorocarbons, coastal pollution, and sludge dumping in the North Sea, among others.

In Germany, in contrast, the precautionary principle became solidified in law in the 1980s, and so Germany moved ahead in tackling all the pollution problems that Britain denied. Defenders of the principle argued that even in the presence of uncertainty, it was on balance better to nip incipient pollution problems in the bud. Dealing with a problem immediately and cheaply is better than waiting for it to get worse, by which time the amount of money required to fix the problem may have multiplied many times over.

Japan stands out in the environmental stakes in large part due to the energy-efficiency of its economy. This efficiency may be explained to a degree by the extent to which Japan depends on imported oil, and so was shaken by the energy crises of the 1970s. We find in Japan environmental policy made with a minimum of fuss and a maximum of consensus. As in Japanese policy making on all major issues, the key players are government officials and business executives. As I noted in the previous chapter, Japan has adopted a program for sustainable development of its economy, and is maximizing export opportunities for green technologies and pollution-control equipment.

Norway has its environmental blemishes, most notably its continued support for commercial whaling, explained by the historical economic importance of whaling to a few coastal communities. But, as befits the home of Gro Harlem Brundtland (the Sultana of Sustainable Development), Norway has made strenuous efforts to incorporate environmental values into policy making. As in a number of European countries, the policy-making structure of Norway is corporatist. That is, economic and social policies are made behind closed doors by a small number of leaders from government, the labor-union federation, and the business sector. Norway, however, is unique in admitting environmental groups to corporatist policy making. Thus Friends of the Earth Norway is both partially funded by government and its leadership welcomed into the inner sanctums of policy making. This situation is very different from that in the United States and Britain, where Friends of the Earth is a campaigning group that tries to influence government, but has no privileged access to policy making beyond the pressure that any interest group can try to apply.

Sweden, for its part, has pioneered the idea of integrated pollution control (see Weale, 1992: 97–100). In most countries, anti-pollution policy is organized around single-medium and single-substance legislation and regulation. The result is that one pollutant may be reduced, but another pollutant increased as a result. For example, a pollutant discharged into a watercourse may be eliminated by collecting it as a toxic sludge, which might then be dried and burned, leading to air pollution. In Sweden, licenses for new manufacturing plants are issued only after a consideration of the total emissions of the plant, and what might be done to reduce that total to an acceptable level.

What do Germany, Japan, the Netherlands, Norway, and Sweden have in common that might explain their superior environmental performance compared to other developed countries? The first three are densely populated countries that have largely destroyed their native ecosystems (replaced by agro-ecosystems and urban ecosystems), and so have strong incentives to find a way to accommodate a dense population while minimizing further environmental damage. But the same might be said for environmental laggards like Britain, Belgium, and Denmark. And Norway and Sweden have a relatively low population density (at least by European standards). The environmental movements are not any stronger in these countries than comparable others. True, the Green Party has played a key role in German policy development, mostly by forcing other parties to adopt green positions and policies for fear of losing votes to the Greens. But the other four countries lack a green party of comparable force.

More strikingly, what these countries have in common is a political-economic system where consensual relationships among key actors prevail. In discussing Norway, I introduced the idea of corporatism. These five countries are all, to greater or lesser degrees, corporatist systems. Japan can be described as "corporatism without labor," leaving only government officials and business leaders to cooperate in policy formation (Lehmbruch, 1984). Thus the five countries all eschew both adversarial policy making and unbridled capitalist competition. Their polar opposites in these respects are the English-speaking developed countries: Britain, the United States, Canada, Australia, and New Zealand. This consensual and corporatist political-economic structure does not by itself guarantee any concern with environmental values. Until the 1970s, corporatist systems were all organized to emphasize issues of economic growth and income distribution pretty much exclusively. In Germany, environmentalists long battled a seemingly unyielding corporatist state. Yet once environmental values were taken on board, corporatism eventually enabled these values to be addressed in a particular fashion: that of ecological modernization. Here lies the key to explanation of the superior performance of the clean and green five.

The Idea of Ecological Modernization

Ecological modernization was first identified in the early 1980s by the German social scientists Joseph Huber (1982) and Martin Jänicke (1985), who observed and interpreted its development in Germany. The idea was given an international boost in 1984 at the Organization for Economic Cooperation and Development's Conference on Environment and Economics. Ecological modernization refers to a restructuring of the capitalist political economy along more environmentally sound lines. Environmental degradation is seen as a structural problem which can only be dealt with by attending to how the economy is organized, but not in a way that requires an altogether different kind of political-economic system (Hajer, 1995: 25). Environmental criteria must be built into the re-design of the system, along the lines found in the Dutch National Environmental Policy Plan.

Conscious and coordinated intervention is needed to bring the required changes about. It is no good relying on any supposed "invisible hand" operating in market systems to promote good environmental outcomes (of the sort Prometheans stress). Yet this intervention does not take place in adversarial fashion, in terms of government imposing design criteria and other policy measures on industry. Industry itself cooperates enthusiastically in the design and implementation of policy. For the key to ecological modernization is that there is money in it for business. Thus business has every incentive to embrace rather than resist ecological modernization, provided only that business is sufficiently far-sighted, rather than interested only in quick profits. Business is not always so far-sighted, even in Germany, where executives mutter about having done enough already on the environmental front.

What exactly is in it for business? First, "pollution prevention pays," as a popular slogan has it. Pollution is a sign of waste. Less pollution means more efficient production. Second, if a problem is not solved in the present, solving it in the future may be vastly more expensive for both business and government. For example, poorly managed toxic waste dumps become a stew of dangerous chemicals leaking into ground water, soil, and the air. To clean them up is extraordinarily expensive (as the experience of the federally financed Superfund in the United States demonstrates). Far better and far cheaper not to let such problems develop in the first place. Third, an unpolluted and aesthetically pleasing environment means healthier, happier, and more productive workers, who may even happily sacrifice wages and salaries for these environmental rewards. Fourth, there is money to be made in selling green goods and services. Consumers increasingly demand products that are not excessively packaged, that do not contain artificial and toxic ingredients, and that are not produced in environmentally damaging ways. Fifth, there are profits to be had in making and selling pollution prevention and abatement products.

Traditionally, increased national income per head has gone hand-in-hand with increased stress on the environment. As an old Yorkshire saying has it, "where there's muck there's brass." The sign of successful ecological modernization is that muck and brass would be decoupled, such that income per head could go on increasing without any additional strain on the environment. This possibility would, it seems, dispel the darkest fears of the survivalists. A qualitatively different kind of growth would not have to hit ecological limits, even if those limits did have a real existence.[1]

Ecological modernization is sometimes treated as a merely technical concept, referring only to the re-tooling of industry and agriculture along more environmentally sensitive lines. Yet if this is the case, there is nothing

---

[1] Some survivalists would remain unconvinced by even demonstrably successful ecological modernization. For even if the rate of increase of resource depletion slows to zero, the depletion is still occurring, and so eventually the resources will still run out.

truly "ecological" about it, for it would say little about human interactions with ecosystems (see Christoff, 1996). In fact, there really has to be something more to the discourse than narrow engineering and technical concerns. For, as I have already indicated, ecological modernization is not something that can be accomplished by business managers and engineers operating voluntarily and independently on their own products and processes. It requires much in the way of political commitment, to the enlightened long term rather than the narrow-minded short term, and to a holistic analysis of economic and environmental processes rather than piecemeal focus on particular environmental abuses. And it is here that its potential as a discourse rather than a technical concept becomes at issue, for its subject matter encompasses nothing less than how capitalist society shall be guided into an environmentally enlightened era. In this sense, ecological modernization involves commitments on the part of the entire society, not just industry. These commitments include foresight, attacking problems at their origins, holism, greater valuation of scarce nature, and the precautionary principle.[2]

Clearly ecological modernization bears a family resemblance to sustainable development. Hajer in his seminal book on the subject even categorizes the Brundtland report as a key ecological modernization document (Hajer, 1995: 26). But equally clearly, ecological modernization has a much sharper focus than does sustainable development on exactly what needs to be done with the capitalist political economy, especially within the confines of the developed nation state.

Discourse Analysis of Ecological Modernization

The story line of ecological modernization is that the capitalist political economy needs conscious reconfiguring and far-sighted action so that economic development and environmental protection can proceed hand-in-hand and reinforce one another.[3] This story line is constructed from the following discourse elements.

[2] More detailed treatments of the components of ecological modernization as a discourse may be found in Hajer, 1995 and Weale, 1992: 75–9. Weale refers to it as an ideology rather than a discourse.

[3] Hajer (1995: 65) defines the "credible and attractive story-lines" of ecological modernization as "the regulation of the environmental problem appears as a positive-sum game; pollution is a matter of inefficiency; nature has a balance that should be respected; anticipation is better than cure; and sustainable development is the alternative to the previous path of defiling growth."

1. BASIC ENTITIES WHOSE EXISTENCE IS RECOGNIZED OR CONSTRUCTED

Ecological modernization is a systems approach which takes seriously the complex pathways by which consumption, production, resource depletion, and pollution are interrelated. This is most explicit in the Dutch National Environmental Policy Plan, which, as Weale (1992: 128) points out, is rooted in general systems theory. The key to effective action is therefore to anticipate and prevent unwanted environmental ramifications of production and consumption decisions. This orientation is very different from the more atomistic underpinnings of Promethean and economic rationalist discourse, which have little time for system complexity. However, ecological modernization's embrace of the system concept is incomplete, for it can still view natural systems in limited terms, as mere adjuncts to the human economy. Nature is treated as a source of resources and a recycler of pollutants—in a sense, a giant waste treatment plant, whose capacities and "balance" should not be overburdened. Denied are any notion that nature might spring surprises on us, defy human management, have its own intrinsic value, and its own open-ended developmental pathways. This limited view of nature warrants green radical suspicion of ecological modernization.

Like sustainable development, ecological modernization pushes limits to growth into the background. Limits are not so much explicitly denied as ignored. Certainly the idea of limits becomes fuzzier once economic growth is decoupled from growth in environmental stress, which seems to be happening in the five clean and green countries I identified at the beginning of this chapter. More explicitly than for sustainable development, the existence of the capitalist political economy is taken for granted. Unlike sustainable development, economic redirection does not necessarily require a de-emphasis of the state and concomitant promotion of international society and the political grassroots. Germany, Japan, the Netherlands, Norway, and Sweden are strong states which if anything become stronger as a result of their promotion of ecological modernization, which in their hands at least is very much a statist strategy (but see Mol, 1996: 314–15 for an argument that ecological modernization can allow a more participatory and decentralized state).

2. ASSUMPTIONS ABOUT NATURAL RELATIONSHIPS

Ecological modernization implies a partnership in which governments, businesses, moderate environmentalists, and scientists cooperate in the restructuring of the capitalist political economy along more environmentally defensible lines. This partnership is an anthropocentric one, in that the natural world itself is put in a clear position of subordination to human desires and calculations. Whether or not there is much in the way of hierarchy in human affairs is an open question. Certainly there are those who would want to make ecological modernization into a doctrine for managers of the political economy; on the other hand, there is room for more egalitarian political relationships across different actors. There is also a crucial natural relationship between environmental protection and economic prosperity, in that the two are seen as properly proceeding hand-in-hand.

3. AGENTS AND THEIR MOTIVES

The key agents in ecological modernization are the partners I have just identified: governments, businesses, reform-oriented environmentalists, and scientists. Their motivations have to do with the common good or the public interest, defined in broad terms to encompass economic efficiency and environmental conservation. For its achievement, ecological modernization requires widespread commitment to and action upon its principles. If it is resisted by key actors, as in Britain, where the government first flirted with the idea in the 1980s but then explicitly rejected it in favor of more conventional "end of pipe" anti-pollution strategies (see Hajer, 1993), then ecological modernization simply will not happen.

The question of agency under ecological modernization does, on closer inspection, provide a doorway into a potentially more far-reaching change in the way developed societies organize their economic and—especially—political systems. For the partnership is in a major enterprise: the ecological restructuring of capitalism. But the partnership itself might prove to constitute a major restructuring of political life, because its scope will be extended to questions of economic organization that have traditionally been placed off-limits to collective political control. Shortly I will turn to the radical ramifications of this possibility.

4. KEY METAPHORS AND OTHER RHETORICAL DEVICES

The words economics and ecology both derive from the Greek *oikos*, meaning household. In a sense, ecological modernization returns both ecology and economics to their household root, and re-establishes their commonality. For the implicit metaphor in ecological modernization, helping to explain its widespread appeal, is that of a tidy household. This household is concerned with maximizing its wellbeing, but at the same time realizes that minimizing waste also means meeting its needs efficiently, and that commodious surroundings contribute to the household's sense of wellbeing. In this light, it is not surprising that ecological modernization has prospered most in countries noted for the tidiness, prudence, and far-sightedness of their households.

The word "modernization," like the word "development," connotes progress, and so ecological modernization is linked quite clearly with the ever-popular notion of social progress. Again like sustainable development, ecological modernization is a discourse of reassurance, at least for residents of relatively prosperous developed societies. It assures us that no tough choices need to be made between economic growth and environmental protection, or between the present and the long-term future. Unlike sustainable development, it makes no claims that this happy coincidence of values extends to social justice, still less social justice across the rich and poor nations of the world. In fact, ecological modernization is completely silent about what might be the appropriate developmental path for Third World societies. Certainly, to get to the point where they can now choose ecological modernization, countries like the cleaner and greener five spent a lot of time in a modernization mode that was decidedly anti-ecological. If followed by the world's poor then that developmental path would surely impose intolerable stress on the world's ecosystems. Sustainable development speaks more explicitly to Third World developmental possibilities than does ecological modernization.

BOX 8.1. DISCOURSE ANALYSIS OF ECOLOGICAL MODERNIZATION

1. Basic Entities Recognized or Constructed

- Complex systems
- Nature as waste treatment plant
- Capitalist economy
- The state

2. Assumptions about Natural Relationships

- Partnership encompassing government, business, environmentalists, scientists
- Subordination of nature
- Environmental protection and economic prosperity go together

3. Agents and their Motives

- Partners; motivated by public good

4. Key Metaphors and other Rhetorical Devices

- Tidy household
- Connection to progress
- Reassurance

Radicalizing Ecological Modernization

In its most limited technical sense, ecological modernization looks like a discourse for engineers and accountants. If we left the matter there, we might question the degree of attention now being paid to the idea (at least in the more environmentally enlightened nations), and some of the more extravagant claims made on its behalf. This attention and these claims become understandable if ecological modernization is treated instead as a restructuring of political and economic life, rather than a mere re-tooling of industry. In the previous chapter, we saw that the discourse of sustainable development was home to a potentially bewildering number and variety of meanings of that term. The situation for ecological modernization is a bit simpler, for really there are only two meanings—or, at least, the various possibilities can be arrayed on a spectrum between two extremes, each of which has a clear meaning.

At one extreme we find ecological modernization for engineers and accountants. Hajer (1995) refers in this context to "techno-corporatist" ecological modernization, which treats the issues in technical terms, and seeks a managerial structure for their implementation. The management structure in question is supplied by the existing administrative organization of the corporatist state, which would, though, have to open itself more considerably to the findings and recommendations of environmental scientists and engineers. Relatedly, but in a bit more detail, Christoff (1996) refers to "weak" ecological modernization, characterized by:

- An emphasis on technological solutions to environmental problems;
- A technocratic/corporatist style of policy making monopolized by scientific, economic, and political elites working in close cooperation with each other;
- Restriction of the analysis to privileged developed nations, who can use ecological modernization to consolidate their economic advantages and so distance themselves still further from the miserable economic and environmental conditions of the poorer nations of the world;
- An attempt to impose a single, closed-ended framework on political and economic development in these privileged countries.

Christoff's "strong" ecological modernization would feature in contrast:

- Consideration of broad-ranging changes to society's institutional structure and economic system, with a view to making them more responsive to ecological concerns;

- Open, democratic decision making maximizing not only participatory opportunities for citizens, but also authentic and competent communication about environmental affairs among a broad variety of participants;
- Concern with the international dimensions of environment and development;
- Conceptualizing political-economic-ecological development in diverse and open ended terms, such that there is no single correct view of what ecological modernization must entail, but rather multiple possibilities to which ecological modernization provides an orientation.

Consistent with Christoff's "strong" viewpoint, Hajer (1995) speaks of the possibility of "reflexive" ecological modernization. By reflexive, Hajer means processes of political and economic development that proceed on the basis of a critical self-awareness. Modernization was for long treated in non-reflexive terms in just about all countries. It was just a matter of hitching a ride on the ineluctable progress from "traditional" to "modern" society which the term modernization connoted. Reflexive modernization still recognizes that the ride must in the end be taken, but introduces a host of anxieties about the quality and trajectory of the ride which must be subject to continued monitoring and control. No longer can experts and governments be trusted to know best for the rest of us; no longer should we regard economic growth of whatever composition as automatically a good thing; no longer should we place economic affairs and the organization of the economic system as off-limits to public scrutiny and democratic control.[4] Instead, society's development would make the experts and élites justify themselves and their policies in front of the citizens, in a language comprehensible to the laity, and with no recourse to the privilege of rank or expertise. Reflexive ecological modernization is for everybody.

Clearly it matters a great deal to which of these two versions of ecological modernization a society commits itself. Weak or techno-corporatist ecological modernization might, as Hajer (1995: 32–4) recognizes, involve little more than a rhetorical rescue operation for a capitalist economy confounded by ecological crises. This would defuse the radical potential of environmentalism and deflect the energies of green activists without really changing the political-economic system to make it more ecologically sustainable and socially convivial.

[4] However, Christoff (1996) criticizes Hajer for failing to recognize the true radical potential of the ecological critique of industrial society, and failing to incorporate the key lessons of that critique into the self-conscious redesign of social institutions. Christoff has a point; at one point Hajer (1995: 283) refers to the need "put an end to mediocre naturalist environmentalism" in favor of an environmentalism that would confront the need to make real choices about where society should go.

Much more is at stake in the strong version of ecological modernization, which points quite precisely to the exit from industrial society. The German sociologist Ulrich Beck (1992) has argued that issues of environmental risk, especially risk related to chemical pollution, toxic wastes, nuclear energy, and biotechnology, call into question the very foundations of industrial society. In industrial society, Beck argues, we happily put issues of economic organization and technological change off-limits to conscious and collective human control. For this reason, Beck believes that industrial society was only "semi-modern," in that it only partially fulfilled modernity's promise of rational social development. Beck's emerging "risk society," in contrast, puts these issues firmly on the agenda. To Beck, the politics of industrial society was mostly about conflict between social classes, and redistributive issues reflecting this conflict between capitalists and workers. In contrast, the politics of the emerging risk society is organized around the environmental risks which industrial society has generated, but with which it has shown itself incapable of dealing. Nobody is immune from these risks; unlike industrial society's main hazard of poverty, the rich have no immunity from the hazards of risk society. As Beck (1992: 36) puts it, "smog is democratic."

The prospects for strong or reflexive ecological modernization are improved to the extent that environmental affairs can be coupled to the kind of risk drama portrayed by Beck. But so long as these affairs are treated in more mundane terms of pollution control and management of material flows, weak or techno-corporatist ecological modernization will prevail. Mol (1996: 317) believes this mundane character is inescapable, and so excludes ecological modernization from any contribution to a reflexive modernity.

In the weak or techno-corporatist version of ecological modernization, the state, corporate capitalism, and the scientific establishment oversee and manage the transition to a more environmentally sensitive economic system. But in Beck's risk society, these same three institutions share only public disgust for their complicity in the production of risks. Beck sees scientists as risk apologists, their work for sale to the highest bidder, the latter being likely to demand studies showing there is no cause for alarm from the pollutant or hazard in question. Thus the dominant institutions of industrial society lose their legitimacy in the eyes of the public. Risk society is in fact conducive to the insurgency of a whole new set of interlinked democratic institutions, which would try to seize power from discredited states, corporations, and scientific establishments. Experts would lose their privilege, and authority in general would be reconstituted in networks which would cross over the traditional boundaries of the state, economy, and society.

These networks would be the institutions of a reflexive modernity (see also Beck, Giddens, and Lash, 1994).

Quite what these institutions might look like Beck does not specify. Indeed, he says only that they are "new, as yet unforeseeable" (Beck, 1992: 231–2). Beck's writings are rather abstract and ungrounded. Beck's colleague Hajer (1995: 288–92) gives some concrete indication, pointing to the idea of "societal inquiries." Hajer's societal inquiry is a kind of public inquiry with very broad terms of reference, unconstrained by legalistic rules of evidence and inquiry, and concerned with the participatory generation of a developmental strategy for an issue, a region, or a group of people. His main example is the famous Berger Inquiry, conducted in the mid-1970s into proposed construction of pipelines to transport oil and gas from the Canadian Arctic to Southern markets. As I observed in Chapter 5, democratic pragmatists also claim Berger as their own, as can more radical democrats. In good reflexive fashion, Berger broadened the mandate of his inquiry to consider alternative developmental strategies for the Canadian North, and the part his inquiry could play in bringing about different futures. He conducted hearings in settlements throughout the region, providing indigenous peoples in particular with a congenial forum and access to finance and expertise, such that they could contemplate, debate, and make their cases. Synthesizing the process, Berger recommended that no pipelines be built until the renewable-resource-based economy of the region were put on a sound and sustainable footing, providing a basis for a reinvigorated culture to replace the existing culture of dependence.[5] Berger's inquiry pre-dates the emergence of ecological modernization, and can also be interpreted as democratic pragmatism pushing over the boundary toward green radicalism, as I argued in Chapter 5.

Ecological Modernization in the Balance

If ecological modernization does prevail, which kind will it be? Will we get environmentally sensitive management of technological change? Or will we see instead wholesale transformation of the capitalist political economy, the doorway to a reflexive ecological modernity in which the latent human potential for full control of our destiny comes into view for the first time in

---

[5] Aside from societal inquiries, Hajer (1995: 292–4) also mentions "discursive law." Discursive law is constitutional legislation that specifies broad normative principles, presumably incorporating ecological values, which would act as the basis for subsequent policy deliberations. But Hajer gives no illustration of how this would work in practice.

history? The jury is still out. When it comes to the prospects for this strong version of ecological modernization, Beck overstates his case that the transition from industrial society to risk society has occurred. Politics is still mostly about the distribution of material rewards rather than about the production, allocation, amelioration, and distribution of risks. Moreover, if and when risk society does arrive, it will not necessarily be as conducive to broad-ranging democratization as Beck hopes. For risks can be distributed along class lines, as the environmental justice movement in the United States emphasizes. This movement begins from the recognition that toxic waste dumps and other noxious facilities are normally located in the vicinity of the poor and ethnic minorities. In this light, it becomes evident that Christoff's "weak" ecological modernization in the wealthy countries could easily be bought by transferring risks to poor countries—for example, by locating polluting industries in these countries, or exporting wastes to them, or exploiting their resources in unsustainable fashion. It is not hard to find examples of the cleanest and greenest countries engaging in such actions. For example, Japanese companies are heavily involved in the destruction of tropical forests in South-East Asia (and the conversion of Pacific Islands into golf courses).

I argued at the end of the previous chapter that sustainable development fits uneasily in a world seemingly committed to free trade and the deregulation of markets. On the face of it, ecological modernization might seem to have problems here too, given its commitment to conscious collective control of the political economy in the ecological restructuring of capitalism. However, states which operate along these lines might find that they can in fact obtain a competitive edge in the emerging world economic order, if indeed there is money to be made in environmental conservation.

Ecological modernization requires a consensual and interventionist policy style consistent with corporatism, and it is worth noting that corporatist countries have done quite well in terms of standard measures of economic growth in the recent past. Corporatism's consensual and interventionist policy style is however anathema to governments under the sway of market liberal doctrines, which helps explain why ecological modernization has made few inroads in the English-speaking industrialized nations. One of the few exceptions here is United States Vice-President Al Gore's book, *Earth in the Balance* (Gore, 1992), whose proposals are essentially consistent with ecological modernization (though he never uses the term). But Gore the Vice-President proved a pale shadow of Gore the author, and none of the book's prescriptions found any place in policy making. The disillusioned environmentalists who greeted his public appearances with a chant of "Read your book!" had a point. If the ecological modernizers are right, the United

States, along with Canada, Great Britain, Australia, and New Zealand are going to be left standing in the transition to a new green capitalist era. (For an insightful comparison of Germany's embrace of ecological modernization with British obduracy, see Weale, 1992: 79–88.)

The idea that capitalism's future might be green and corporatist is ridiculed by Prometheans. They regard ecological modernization's precautionary principle as tantamount to lunacy (see, for example, Wildavsky, 1995: 427–33), as guaranteeing only that the wealth which is the real key to environmental health will be further dissipated by excessive and costly regulations. Economic rationalists see in corporatism only opportunities for special interests to conspire against the public good. However, policy instruments developed by economic rationalists, notably quasi-market incentive mechanisms (as discussed in Chapter 6), do occasionally find favor among ecological modernizers.

Green radicals are uneasy with ecological modernization because it threatens to deflect their critiques of industrial society. Arguably the strong version of ecological modernization combined with notions of reflexive modernity could be stretched to encompass green radical views, though of course some of the more romantic green notions would have to be jettisoned in order to fit with this very rationalistic discourse. However far it is stretched, ecological modernization does not easily admit the idea that nature might have intrinsic value beyond its material uses, or green desires for living simply upon the earth in convivial fashion. Human life on earth for ecological modernizers of whatever stripe is always going to be a complicated affair, and will never be for living simply.

Ecological modernization is not yet for everyone. Survivalists, Prometheans, economic rationalists, and green romantics are probably never going to accommodate themselves to it. Governments which have always resisted consensual and corporatist policy making will probably also continue to resist ecological modernization. The discourse at the moment has little or nothing to offer Third World societies in terms of developmental alternatives. And it is therefore largely silent on what to do at the global level.

Still, in its weak and techno-corporatist senses, ecological modernization has already proved itself in the cleanest and greenest developed nations. Strong ecological modernization linked to a reflexive modernity is both more intriguing and more speculative. Alone among the discourses surveyed here, it offers a plausible strategy for transforming industrial society into a radically different and more environmentally defensible (but still capitalist) alternative.

Part V
Green Radicalism

As befits its imaginative and radical leanings, the world of green discourse is a diverse and lively place, home to a wide variety of ideologies, parties, movements, groups, and thinkers. Found here are Green parties and their factions, animal liberationists, bioregionalists, ecofeminists, deep ecologists, social ecologists, eco-Marxists, eco-socialists, eco-anarchists, eco-communalists, ecological Christians, Buddhists, Taoists, and pagans, environmental justice advocates, green economists, critical theorists, post-modernists, and many others. This sheer variety notwithstanding, I believe green radicalism can be usefully divided into just two major categories: one romantic, and one rationalistic. I shall devote one chapter to each of these.

The key difference between the two main strands of green radicalism has a very deep history, rooted in different reactions to the Enlightenment. Enlightenment is the name for the eighteenth-century movement which renounced religion, myth, and traditional social order in the name of reason. Reason in turn meant liberal politics and human rights of the sort established in the English, American, and French Revolutions of 1689, 1776, and 1789 respectively. Reason also meant that modern science became the route to secure knowledge, which enabled in turn the growth of modern technology. The defining feature of modern society is that it embodies the principles of the Enlightenment.

Just like the romantics of the eighteenth and nineteenth centuries, green romanticism rejects core Enlightenment principles. Green romanticism seeks to change and save the world by changing the way individuals approach and experience the world, in particular through cultivation of more empathetic and less manipulative orientations toward nature and other people. It is heir to the older romantic rejection of the Enlightenment's emphasis on rationality and progress.

Green rationalism, in contrast, embraces rather than rejects key aspects of Enlightenment. This embrace of Enlightenment and modernity is rarely if ever wholehearted. Green rationalists recognize that some aspects of Enlightenment are indeed complicit in the destruction of nature and the production of injustice. They agree with romantics that modern science and technology wielded in human arrogance have meant massive environmental destruction, along with profound human costs. But Enlightenment also means equality, rights, open dialogue, and critical questioning of established practices. Green rationalism builds upon this more attractive side of Enlightenment and modernity.

Green radicals generally recognize themselves as green and radical; very few would use the terms romantic or rationalist to describe themselves. Some might protest that I am committing the sin of dualism by proposing untenable dichotomies between reason and emotion, rationality and spirituality, categories that are themselves the product of Enlightenment thinking. All I would say in my defence here is that if this protest is to be tenable then romantics need to do a better job in explaining exactly how these dichotomies are to be overcome, rather than just saying that they should be overcome. I believe these two categories do in fact capture the main line of division in radical green politics, providing a useful perspective on many debates and disputes. I will also try to show that this categorization generates insights into alternative futures for green politics, and environmental affairs more generally.

9

Save the World through New Consciousness: Green Romanticism

Romantics do not concern themselves with improved policies or institutions that might be achieved in some foreseeable future. Instead, their main concern is with the nurturing and development of different kinds of subjectivity, or ways that individuals can experience the world. For romantics, politics is not about devising strategies to achieve tangible goals; rather, it is an arena in which different kinds of experiences can be sought and developed. Historically, the term romanticism was attached to an intellectual movement in the eighteenth and nineteenth centuries that opposed the rise of modern science and liberal political doctrines, favoring instead an artistic and aesthetic orientation to life and politics. To romantic poets such as Coleridge, Wordsworth, and Shelley, nature and humanity belonged in an organic relationship best understood and developed through feeling and insight. They rejected the idea that nature could be best understood through scientific knowledge, and manipulated on the basis of that knowledge.

This rejection of science, embrace of empathy and insight, and cultivation of radically different ways of experiencing one's self and nature is shared by contemporary green romantics. The kinds of subjectivity sought are in some cases radically new, in some cases radically old, looking back to primal human society before the rise of agriculture. One Earth First! slogan declares "Back to the Pleistocene!" Sometimes the radically new and radically old are combined in creative fashion. Green romantics do want to change the world, but they believe that the route to change lies through individuals. They want increasing numbers of people to experience the world in terms of a new ecological sensibility.

The Varieties of Green Romanticism

DEEP ECOLOGY

Perhaps the best-known variety of green romanticism is deep ecology. Sometimes the term deep ecology is used to describe radical environmentalism in its entirety. More accurately, the term captures one variety of green radicalism. To complicate matters a little, some adherents of a "deep" viewpoint do not use the term deep ecology, but rather refer to themselves as deep greens, and are not necessarily committed to all the tenets of prominent deep ecology philosophers. Deep ecology as a movement and a label is most prevalent in the United States, though its origins are Norwegian, and it has adherents in Canada, Australia, and New Zealand. Deep ecology was given its name and its initial content by the Norwegian philosopher Arne Naess (1973), who drew a contrast with the "shallow" ecology movement that only wanted to reform some of the practices of industrial society. Subsequent development occurred largely in the United States, especially the Western states (see especially Devall and Sessions, 1985), where it became associated with the radical wilderness defense group Earth First!, and with nature writers such as Edward Abbey and Barry Lopez. My discussion refers mainly to US deep ecology. Naess himself is actually something of a rationalist (Naess, 1989).

What exactly is deep ecology? According to Devall and Sessions (1985: 67) its two basic principles are self-realization and biocentric equality. Self-realization means identification with a larger organic "Self" beyond the individual person; or "self-in-Self," as they put it. The idea is to cultivate a deep consciousness and awareness of organic unity, of the holistic nature of the ecological webs in which every individual is enmeshed. Along these lines, Warwick Fox (1990) describes a "transpersonal ecology," a psychological condition of identification and care for other beings, ecosystems, and nature in its entirety. Deep ecologists value species, populations, and ecosystems, not just individual creatures. Clearly this transpersonal aspect of deep ecology resonates with eighteenth and nineteenth century romantic concepts of how people should experience the world. Biocentric equality means that no species, including the human species, is regarded as more valuable or in any sense higher than any other species. The effective opposite of biocentric equality is anthropocentric arrogance.

Devall and Sessions (1985: 70) elaborate on these two basic principles to argue that nature and its diversity have intrinsic value irrespective of human uses and interests.[1] Given current levels of excessive stress imposed by

---

[1] For a discussion of autopoietic intrinsic value theory, see Eckersley, 1992: 60–1. Autopoiesis is the attribute of entities capable of regenerating themselves, such as species and ecosystems.

humans, respect for nature and its diversity require a reduction in human populations. Unlike some other deep ecologists, Devall and Sessions are not misanthropic, and indeed allow that nature's diversity can be legitimately depleted in order to satisfy "vital" human needs. Though Devall and Sessions do not say exactly which needs are vital and which are not, it is probably fair to say that their conception of vital human needs does not extend to recreational vehicles, speedboats, vacation homes, or home entertainment systems.

More misanthropic deep ecologists, most notoriously the pseudonymous columnist in the Earth First! Journal, Miss Ann Thropy, deny the legitimacy of special human interests.[2] In a 1987 article Miss Ann Thropy welcomed famine and disease (such as AIDS) as useful checks on human numbers. The splinter group VEHEMENT, the Voluntary Human Extinction Movement, is by definition about as misanthropic as you can get. Given that it seeks cultivation of no long-term human experience, it perhaps also seeks to extinguish green romanticism.

These extreme forms of misanthropy are not at all representative of deep ecology in its entirety, and many take pains to distance themselves from the misanthropes. All deep ecologists seek a major reduction in human arrogance when it comes to dealing with the natural world. Most of them would probably agree with Eckersley (1992: 46), who in defining ecocentrism (roughly synonymous with biocentrism) specifies that it "recognises the full range of human interests in the nonhuman world" as well as "the interests of the nonhuman community."

The question of how to balance human and nonhuman interests is perhaps more easily answered in particular cases rather than at the level of philosophical abstraction. Philosophical dispute about the relative worth of human beings and the smallpox virus does not get in the way of the recognized need to protect the remnant ancient forests of California, Oregon, Washington, and British Columbia against logging; to prevent the hydro-industrialization of the Tasmanian wilderness (threatened by the construction of large dams); and to return the Colorado River to its free-flowing state

Deep ecologists are quite clear on what to do when it comes to wilderness: preserve and protect it. They have much less to say on other environmental issues, such as air and water pollution in urban areas. Urban agglomerations are by definition outside the bounds of defensible human–nature interactions, and thus of no concern at all to deep ecologists. In Edward Abbey's wonderful deep ecological novel *The Monkey Wrench Gang*, one of the heroes, Hayduke, measures road distances in terms of six-packs of beer the

---

[2] Miss Ann Thropy is actually Christopher Manes, whose own account of radical environmentalism can be found in Manes (1990).

driver needs to consume. Hayduke throws the empty cans out of the window: if the environment has already been trashed by a road, a few beer cans make no essential difference.

Cultural Ecofeminism

Ecofeminism is a deep philosophy in the sense that it seeks radical changes in ecological consciousness, though it is generally quite hostile to deep ecology. Ecofeminists attack deep ecologists for consorting with macho mountain men such as the fictional Hayduke and the real-world Dave Foreman, co-founder of Earth First! In this light, deep ecology is a doctrine for redneck male adventurers. Worse, its basic diagnosis is wrong. The root of all environmental problems, according to ecofeminists, is not anthropocentrism (human domination of nature), but rather androcentrism (male domination of everything). According to ecofeminists, things begin to go drastically wrong in the way humans treat each other and the natural world with the rise of patriarchy, which dominates women and nature alike. Thus the liberation of women is tied up with liberation of nature; both depend upon the abolition of patriarchy (see Diamond and Orenstein, 1990; Plant, 1989). Patriarchy is seen as cultural rather than natural, and ecofeminists look back to egalitarian and matriarchal societies, some complete with goddesses, prior to the rise of cities, kingdoms, and empires.

Ecofeminism differs further from deep ecology in its sympathy with the animal liberation movement (for example, Kheel, 1990). Deep ecologists, in contrast, show no concern for animals once they are out of nature—for example, in factory farms or laboratories. Even animals in nature are seen as (literally) fair game for deep ecologists, to be hunted and eaten as an expression of the proper human place in ecosystems. For it is only organic wholes such as ecosystems that are to be preserved, not individual creatures. Another point of divergence is on population control. Deep ecologists see a reduction in human population as essential. Ecofeminists believe such a reduction is likely to be accomplished only by further repression and control of women's fertility by the male power structure and its technology (Diamond, 1994).

For all their differences, deep ecologists and ecofeminists alike believe in the cultivation of radically different human sensibilities, involving a non-instrumental and non-dominating, more empathetic and intuitive relationship to nature. Both camps are also home to those who advocate a nature-based spirituality, with divinity located in this world, rather than in (male) figures located off the planet (for deep ecology, see Devall and

Sessions, 1985: 8, 90–1, 100–1, and Fox, 1984: 203–4, but note that Foreman, 1991: 46 is an atheist; for ecofeminism, see Christ, 1990). Spiritual ecofeminists often look to pagan religions, and are (unsurprisingly) attracted to goddess imagery (for ecofeminist witchcraft, see Starhawk, 1987).

Ecofeminism began in France in 1972 with the formation of Ecologie-Féminisme by Françoise d'Eaubonne, and flourished in the United States in the 1980s. Its Third World dimension is well represented by arguably the world's most prominent ecofeminist, Vandana Shiva, who writes from India. The root of most contemporary social and ecological evils is, according to Shiva, the Enlightenment commitment to science and economic growth, which together destroy life's diversity and sanctity (Shiva, 1989). Thus Enlightenment rationality has taken the world to the edge of destruction. Shiva is especially concerned by the degree to which imported agricultural and industrial technologies further disadvantage Third World women (for example, by denigrating their traditional knowledge of the land and its workings). And she can point to the leading role played by women in Third World environmental movements, notably her own Chipko tree-protection movement in India.

Ecofeminists believe that the kind of sensibility they advocate is not going to be easy for men to adopt. Women are seen as closer to nature by the fact of their biological essence: the ability to give birth and nurture children. It is the female virtues related to care, empathy, intuition, connection, and cooperation which are crucial. As Plumwood (1993: 9) puts it, many ecofeminists cultivate the myth of a female "angel in the ecosystem" (Plumwood herself renounces this myth). While one's biology does not necessarily determine one's destiny, it is going to be an uphill struggle for men. Men might be able to reason their way toward ecofeminism, but they could never *feel* it. And reason, as any ecofeminist will tell you, is never enough, for it is a one-sided emphasis on reason that helped get humanity into such ecological trouble in the first place, by making men so arrogant as to think they could use reason to control nature.

Cultural feminism is a romantic doctrine because its political program begins with condemnation of a particular kind of human sensibility and ends with advocacy of another. But as we shall see in the next chapter, other ecofeminists reject the biological essentialism of cultural ecofeminism. These social ecofeminists pay closer attention to the social structural causes of the domination of nature and of women, beyond a blanket condemnation of patriarchy, and to how society might be organized differently (for an account of the contrast between cultural and social ecofeminism, together with an attempted reconciliation, see Carlassare, 1994).

BIOREGIONALISM AS A SENSE OF PLACE

Bioregionalism straddles green romanticism and green rationalism. As a rationalistic doctrine, it is concerned with the redrawing of political boundaries and development of political structures to coincide with ecosystem boundaries, and I will deal with this aspect in the next chapter. Bioregions can be defined in different ways: by watershed, or by predominant vegetation type. Examples of bioregions would be Pacific Cascadia, covering the coastal forests west of the Cascade Crest from southern British Columbia to northern California; and the Murray–Darling River Basin in Australia. As a movement, bioregionalism is predominantly North American (Sale, 1985).

Bioregionalism's romantic aspect comes in the form of cultivation of a sense of place. People who live in a bioregion need to adopt it as their true home, to be respected and sustained so that the region in turn can sustain human life. Many bioregional writers and activists concern themselves almost exclusively with this dimension, ignoring more rationalistic concerns. People need to become aware of the kind of ecosystem they inhabit, and regard themselves as a part of it, rather than identify with ethnic groups or nations or other human groupings that transcend ecological boundaries. At issue here is a kind of ecological citizenship, in which individuals learn to become respectful citizens of an ecological place, rather than transforming the place to suit themselves. Such citizenship involves awareness of how the ecosystem supports life, and of life's vulnerabilities. It involves meeting one's material as well as spiritual needs from the resources available locally. Bioregional consciousness is, then, very different from the kind of consciousness inculcated by the capitalist economy and the mass media, which are destroying regional identity of any kind. Both deep ecological consciousness and ecofeminist consciousness can fit quite easily into a bioregional setting.

LIFESTYLE GREENS

For some in the movement, the essence of being green is not adherence to any deep-seated philosophical analysis of the sort favored by deep ecologists and ecofeminists, still less any kind of collective action, political or otherwise. Instead, being green is a matter of leading a green lifestyle. Gatherings of the US Greens, in particular, feature many people quite hostile to the idea that the Greens constitute a political movement, still less a political party. Green lifestyles can have many different aspects. To some, it is mostly a matter of green consumerism: buying cosmetics whose constituent chemicals are not tested on animals, eating vegetables grown organically, buying biodegradable cleaning products, using toilet paper made from recycled fibres. The green lifestyle is often vegetarian, for the vegetarian's caloric intake imposes much less stress on agricultural land than does flesh-eating. Recycling, composting, and bicycling as opposed to driving a car all play their parts.

Such decisions can be instrumentally good for the environment, and may even make good economic sense. So local councils throughout the world have adopted recycling for good environmental and economic reasons. Yet lifestyle greens are concerned with much more than the immediate piece-meal effects of such decisions. It is not just a matter of doing green things, it is a matter of being green in doing them, of using these actions to cultivate a post-industrial way of experiencing and relating to the world (see, for example, Elgin, 1982).

Eco-Theology

I have already noted that deep ecologists and ecofeminists alike are often attracted by some kind of nature-based spirituality (see also Spretnack, 1986; La Chapelle, 1978). However, these two movements do not exhaust the range of eco-theology (for a comprehensive catalogue, see Gottleib, 1996). Eco-theologians diagnose the root of environmental problems in spiritual terms, and if the root of the problem is spiritual, then so must be the cure. The classic argument here is that of the historian Lynn White (1967), who argues that environmental crisis is the product of Judeo-Christian religious tradition, which places god outside of and above nature, and then proclaims that man is made in god's image. This placement provides justification for unlimited human manipulation and abuse of nature for purely human ends. White does see in the Judeo-Christian tradition an alternative possibility, associated most prominently with St Francis of Assisi, who White proposes as the patron saint of ecology.

Other eco-theologists are more inclined to give up on Judaism and Christianity in favor of Eastern religions such as Taoism, Buddhism, and Hinduism, all of which cast humanity in far more humble terms, adopting a contemplative and reverential attitude toward nature. E. F. Schumacher's (1973) "Buddhist economics" specifies individuals who seek to maximize wellbeing at a minimum level of consumption. Critics point out that the societies in which these religions flourish are no less prone to ecological destruction than Western societies. Moreover, they also seem to go hand-in-hand with mass political passivity, which might severely hinder any attempt to reorient society in a more environmentally sound direction through grassroots action.

Eco-theology can also creep into the analyses and prescriptions of movements and thinkers who would not otherwise be characterized as green romantics. In 1991, the First National People of Color Environmental Leadership Summit in the United States declared that "environmental justice affirms the sacredness of Mother Earth." Two of the prominent survivalists discussed in Chapter 2, Robert Heilbroner and William Ophuls, both argue that the wholesale political transformations they advocate must be accompanied by some kind of spiritual transformation. So Heilbroner (1991: 176–7) speaks of governments of the future that will be "monastic" in their form, combining "religious orientation with a military discipline." Ophuls (1977: 243) for his part believes in the necessity of "metanoia . . . tantamount to religious conversion." For Heilbroner, religion's main value is instrumental rather than intrinsic: it is just a way of keeping people in line, to stop them abusing the environment. For Ophuls, it is helpful in making the transition to a different kind of political economy more palatable to the population at large. Along these lines, the leading British Green Jonathan Porritt argues that movement to a sustainable society is unlikely "without some huge groundswell of spiritual concern" (Porritt, 1986: 210).

Eco-Communalism[3]

Many green romantics are quite individualistic, seeing the development of new forms of experience as primarily a matter for each person to explore. This is especially true of deep ecologists, who can be radically individualistic when it comes to human relationships with each other, however much they seek interconnectedness in human relationships with nature. Other green romantics believe that new ecological experience can only be cultivated by individuals acting together, in green communities. Given that existing human communities are generally anything but green, the imperative then becomes to establish communities to a significant degree cut off from the rest of human society.

The historical model adduced by many eco-communalists is the monastery, especially as it existed in the European Dark Ages to keep the flame of learning and civilization alive in a hostile and barbaric world (see, for example, Nisbet, 1974; Bahro, 1986; Roszak, 1979). Obviously Christian monasteries did not have an avowedly ecological mission, though the

---

[3] This category of green thinking is identified and clarified by Eckersley (1992: 160–7), whose terminology and characterization I follow here.

Benedictine order managed to create some remarkable sustainable agro-ecosystems in the vicinity of their monasteries. Later, the Franciscans would follow some of the environmental teachings of their founder, St Francis of Assisi. Contemporary eco-communalists are not necessarily Christians. But they share the monastic idea that within the monastery's walls a particular kind of ethical social life can flourish, and culture and spirit can be regenerated. Rudolf Bahro, a prominent renegade German Green, speaks of the creation of "liberated zones" where people could repair for renewal, away from the irrationality of industrial society. Eco-communalists seek in such zones places where people could live and work in harmony with one another and with the local ecosystem.

Discourse Analysis of Green Romanticism

The essential green romantic story line is that industrial society involves and induces a warped conception of persons and their place in the world. Required to remedy this situation are new kinds of human sensibilities, ones that are less destructive to nature. While the precise content of the required sensibilities can be a matter of some dispute, green romantics would all agree that they involve a less manipulative and more humble and reverential human attitude to the natural world. Digging a little deeper, green romanticism is constructed from the following elements.

1. BASIC ENTITIES WHOSE EXISTENCE IS RECOGNIZED OR CONSTRUCTED

Lurking in the background of green romanticism are global ecological limits of the sort that energize survivalists: the existence and proximity of these limits give green romantics a sense of urgency. Green romantics would not, however, go any further than this down the survivalist path toward the sorts of authoritarian political prescriptions favored by survivalists. Green romanticism would remain coherent and defensible (though less urgent) in the absence of limits.

The basic entity whose existence is recognized and constructed, and which forms the real foundation for the discourse, is nature. Both inner nature (that is, of the mind, body, and spirit) and outer nature are at issue here. Green romantics do of course want to bring these two into closer harmony by operating on inner nature. Such harmony is the essence of deep ecological notions of "self-in-Self," and of cultural ecofeminist principles concerning a more intuitive and empathetic human orientation to the natural world—and to other humans. Opposed to these conceptions of nature and the natural are notions of the unnatural. Included here would be the core practices and—still more important—the core sensibilities which industrial society has inculcated in people. Such unnatural acts and orientations would include the anthropocentric arrogance of Private Prometheans, the relentless quest for more and better consumer goods, and an excessive belief in the powers of human reason. Ecofeminists would add patriarchy to this list.

Green romantics are generally uninterested in the social structures and institutions of industrial society, or indeed its alternatives. Thus they have little to say about governments, markets, and policies. This lack of interest can be justified by green romantics on the grounds that social structures, institutions, and policies have no life of their own, but are ultimately reducible to the underlying sensibilities of the members of society. Thus do green romantics fall squarely in the philosophical tradition of idealism (as opposed to materialism, which stresses the causal influence of economic forces in shaping society). It is ideas, not material forces, that move history: so the key to changing the world is to change ideas.

2. ASSUMPTIONS ABOUT NATURAL RELATIONSHIPS

The natural relationships stressed by green romantics are, quite simply, natural relationships. The images of nature and the kinds of relationships it contains may vary in their details. For example, deep ecologists are often quite happy with a nature "red in tooth and claw," to use an expression favored by some followers of Charles Darwin, and celebrate predation and hunting as parts of the natural order. Cultural ecofeminists are more likely to see in the natural world harmony between creatures and species. At any rate, all green romantics believe that there does exist a natural order. Whatever its balance of competition and cooperation, this order is an egalitarian one (the deep ecologists' biocentric equality), in which there is no hierarchy, and certainly not a hierarchy which puts humans on top of everything else. They also believe that this order has been violated by humankind, be it through anthropocentric arrogance, patriarchy, or industrialist indifference.

Such violation often comes in the name of rationality. The dominant form of rationality in today's world is instrumental rationality: the capacity to devise, select, and effect good means to clarified and consistent ends. Instrumental rationality, on the romantic account, calls up a dichotomy between subject and object. Only the human mind is subject. Everything else, including the natural world, consists of objects to be manipulated and dominated for the sake of whatever the mind desires. Thus instrumental rationality estranges us from nature, with all kinds of disastrous consequences for both nature and ourselves. Nature takes its revenge for our arrogance by inflicting environmental crises upon us.

3. AGENTS AND THEIR MOTIVES

There is no shortage of agents in green romanticism. If this discourse is about the cultivation of alternative kinds of ecological subjectivity, then every person can be an agent, with the capacity to craft his or her own relationships to the natural and human world. Green romanticism is, then, well populated by human subjects. More important, it contains only subjects. People are subject to themselves in that it is up to all of them to create an appropriate orientation to life; nobody else can do it for them. Collective actors such as governments, corporations, and other organizations are largely ignored, as are élites who might have the power to impose their will on other people. However, the discourse does allow for some human subjects to be more enlightened than others, and so show the way.

The ascription of agency does not stop with human beings. In a rejection of the weight of several hundred years of natural science, and of dominant notions of instrumental rationality, agency is seen as existing in (external) nature too. Nature is not blind, unthinking, and unfeeling; instead, it is truly alive with meaning and purpose. This applies to individual creatures, to species, to ecosystems, and perhaps even to the planet as a whole. James Lovelock's (1979) Gaia hypothesis has found a sympathetic reception among many green romantics (though he has hardly sought such a reception). This hypothesis states that the biosphere in its totality acts collectively to maintain the conditions for life on Earth. In this light, the biosphere is a self-regulating entity which can correct for threats to its capacity to support life—threats that come, for example, through increases in the level of solar radiation, volcanic activity, or human pollution. It should be noted that acceptance of this hypothesis does not guarantee an environmentalist outlook. On one interpretation, Gaia may be quite able to correct for any abuses that we humans can dream up, be it pollution from burning fossil fuels or nuclear holocaust. We may wipe ourselves out, but Gaia will persist, just as it has outlasted the extinction of millions of species. Green romantics are far more likely to regard Gaia as both vulnerable and worthy of reverence (see, for example, Porritt, 1986: 206–9), as a "she" rather than an "it."

4. KEY METAPHORS AND OTHER RHETORICAL DEVICES

Green romanticism makes use of an eclectic range of biological and organic metaphors. Given the focus on the cultivation of human subjectivity, many of these metaphors are incorporated into exhortations about how to experience the world. For example, according to Robert Aitken, "Deep ecology . . . requires openness to the black bear, becoming truly intimate with the black bear, so that honey dribbles down your fur coat as you catch the bus to work" (quoted in Dobson, 1990: 61). To Karen Davis (1995), the key to a feminist understanding of animal liberation is "thinking like a chicken." To use a popular expression in deep ecology, the key is instead "thinking like a mountain." Dave Foreman, deep ecological founder of Earth First!, used to conclude his standard stump speech by getting his audience to howl like wolves.

Green romantics want to change the world by changing people, more precisely the way people experience the world. At one level this can be done through argument; and there are indeed many detailed arguments, some of considerable philosophical sophistication, on behalf of the various green romantic positions. But ultimately argument is not enough: green romantics look to experience beyond reason, and so reasoned argument can only take us so far along the road. The rest of the path must be indicated by rhetorical strategies that reach beyond reason to passion. If the point is to convince listeners of the desirability of an intuitive and empathetic orientation to nature, then that has to be done by reaching the listener through the sensibility in question. This can be done by relating personal stories, analogous to accounts of religious conversion and how it changed the life of the teller of the story. So, for example, the ecofeminist Julia Russell (1990: 224) relates how she came to the realization that the Earth is a living being through contemplation of her compost pile, which showed her that "The Earth turns everything given to it into itself." Appeals can be and are made to intuitions and emotions. Poetry, art, religious and quasi-religious ceremonies, the telling and re-telling of myths of primitive Edens and creation stories all play their parts in the tapestry of green romanticism.

The Impact of Green Romanticism

For most of the discourses surveyed in earlier chapters, it makes sense to look for real-world impacts in terms of the policies of governments and international bodies, and in the reconstruction of social, economic, and political

---

Box 9.1. **DISCOURSE ANALYSIS OF GREEN ROMANTICISM**

1. **Basic Entities Recognized or Constructed**
   - Global limits
   - Inner nature
   - Nature
   - Unnatural practices
   - Ideas

2. **Assumptions about Natural Relationships**
   - Natural relationships between humans and nature which have been violated
   - Equality across people and nature

3. **Agents and their Motives**
   - Human subjects, some more ecologically conscious than others
   - Agency exists in nature too

4. **Key Metaphors and other Rhetorical Devices**
   - Wide range of biological and organic metaphors
   - Passion
   - Appeals to emotions, intuitions

---

institutions and practices. But to assess green romanticism in similar terms would be to miss its central point. For green romantics want *people* to be different; and when they are, then everything else is expected to fall into place. Many social movements do in fact take effect largely through the changes in culture, ethics, and so peoples' behavior which the movement induces (Tesh, 1993). Feminism, for example, has successfully altered relationships of power between the sexes within the family, and in society more generally. Some of these changes have been confirmed by legislation such as family law and equal opportunity measures, but many of them have not been so compelled. Similarly, a large part of the impact of the last thirty years of environmentalism comes in the form of the way people have come to think about their everyday behavior: in recycling wastes, in insulating their houses, in paying attention to the environmental friendliness of products they purchase, in what they tell their children about the world.

Thus it is in this cultural realm that we should seek the real impact of green romanticism. This possibility helps to legitimate the romantic emphasis on changing the world through changing subjectivity and the way people experience the world. The cultivation of new ways of being is done not just for the benefit of the individual so enlightened, but for the good of society, and ultimately the good of the planet.

In these terms, it is a bit ironic that green romanticism's main impact so far is probably at the level of changing consumer behavior, such that of the varieties of romanticism it is the lifestyle greens who have had the most effect. In industrial societies at least, many people do happily sort and recycle their garbage, read labels of products on the supermarket shelves, shun ozone-depleting chemicals, compost food scraps and garden waste, force companies like McDonalds to stop using Styrofoam packaging, and improve the energy-efficiency of their lifestyles. Here, green romanticism provides useful and perhaps unexpected support for ecological modernization, which requires consumers to behave in exactly this fashion.

What people have not done, except in very small numbers, is adopt any kind of ecological consciousness of the kind sought by deep ecologists, ecofeminists, eco-communalists, and eco-theologians. The relevant groups and networks are often quite small, and not especially visible to a larger public. Within the United States, one of the largest collections of green romantics is associated with the US Greens. This romantic emphasis may help to explain the greater political successes of European green parties, which are less beholden to romanticism, and so less circumspect about acting politically.

The most noteworthy green romantic group is probably Earth First!, founded in the United States in 1980. Earth First! is perhaps known less for its deep ecological philosophy that for the exploits of its members. These exploits include lying down in front of bulldozers, gatecrashing the anniversary celebrations of Lake Powell reservoir on the Colorado River, occupying the tops of trees in old growth forests scheduled for clear-cutting, putting a "crack" on the face of the Glen Canyon Dam, and so forth. Earth First! is also associated with monkeywrenching or ecotage: that is, sabotage of environmentally damaging activities. Monkeywrenching figures large in the rhetoric of Earth First! supporters and opponents alike (for a field guide, see Foreman, 1985). The possibilities include pouring emery powder into the crank-cases of earth-moving machines, pouring syrup into fuel tanks, hammering spikes into trees to make it dangerous to cut them, pulling up survey stakes, and destroying logging roads.

Sadly, the number of real-world cases of monkeywrenching do not match up to the rhetoric (of both sides). Monkeywrenching in fiction is far more thoroughgoing: the best accounts remain those of the deep ecological nature writer and novelist Edward Abbey (1975, 1990). The rhetoric and fiction have obviously influenced the United States Federal Bureau of Investigation, which devoted a great deal of effort to infiltrating Earth First! and entrapping some of its members, including Dave Foreman, in a 1989 plot to blow up power lines. The FBI has been far less diligent in seeking out the perpetrators of the real violence surrounding deep ecology, which comes almost entirely from the anti-ecological side. For example, when a bomb in her car injured Earth First! activist Judi Bari, the authorities initially described it as a case of the activists being blown up by their own bomb; when that account was discredited, no real effort was made to catch the real bombers.

Romantic green sensibilities do exist beyond these groups. Many of the individuals who share them do not belong to any group. Many belong to more conventional environmental interest groups. Green romanticism may provide the real impetus for the environmental activism of some group members and even leaders—even as they may be forced to suppress articulation of these sensibilities when they enter the arena of conventional politics. David Brower has been perhaps the most visible, militant, and influential figure in conventional environmentalism in the United States since the 1950s, leading the Sierra Club, founding the League of Conservation Voters, Friends of the Earth, and the Earth Island Institute. Green romanticism is quite explicit in his speeches and writings. Not for nothing is he known as the Archdruid (McPhee, 1970).

Can Green Romanticism Save the Earth?

Green romantics certainly believe the world needs saving, and most of them want to help save it. But is green romanticism up to the task? There are several reasons why it may fall short.

The first problem is the practical one of convincing large numbers of people to change the way they experience the world. How exactly is the green vanguard to convince everyone else? The normal answer comes down to the vanguard educating everyone else in how to think and act in ecologically defensible fashion. We have seen that a variety of alternative subjectivities is on offer, ranging from Franciscan Christianity to deep ecological consciousness to ecofeminist empathy. This variety does not necessarily lead to paralysis (though sometimes the debates can be interminable), for on most practical issues the various strands of green romanticism all point in the same direction. Still, on some issues, such as population control, they do not.

Even if these potential conflicts can be elided, a further problem arises in connection with the issue of complexity in ecological affairs. The biologist and environmental activist Barry Commoner noted long ago (1972) that the first law of ecology is that "everything is connected to everything else." While this is a slight overstatement, there is no denying the inherent complexity of ecological problems (see also Dryzek, 1987: 28–9). Interventions in complex systems can produce counterintuitive results, however well intentioned the intervention. Thus good intentions and empathetic sensibilities of the sort stressed by green romantics are never sufficient as secure guides to action. For example, it was long believed that the best way to protect ecosystems in the forests of the American West was to suppress fires; ecologists later realized that these ecosystems depended for their renewal on periodic burning. Loving the Earth never guarantees that you will treat it well.

Matters here are made more difficult still once one describes environmental affairs in terms of crisis, which just about all green romantics do. Crisis means that human interactions with the natural world are in severe disequilibrium. Now, green romantic sensibilities might be sufficient to maintain an equilibrium in which people lived in harmony with nature, but they cannot tell us how to get from our current severe disequilibrium to this harmonious state. There is no theory of the transition, which surely requires some political program, and some kind of action at the collective level, about which romanticism is silent.

This silence in turn stems from green romanticism's neglect of social, political, and economic structure. Such structure is not just a reflection of the attitudes of society's masses or élites, and so changed sensibilities will not necessarily lead to structural change.

Why does social structure matter? The main reason is that macro consequences (in terms of policies, institutions, and events such as revolutions) are rarely if ever a simple extrapolation of micro causes. In Buddhist, Taoist, and Hindu societies, pervasive environmentally sensitive sentiments can coexist with despotic and anti-environmental social, political, and economic systems. There are major issues involved in the aggregation of individual-level preferences, attitudes, and sensibilities into macro-level results (see Coleman, 1986). Speaking as a social scientist, I note that social science only exists because societal and social-structural phenomena are not reducible to individual psychology. So even if there were large-scale conversion of individuals along the lines sought by green romantics, it is quite possible that nothing at all would change at the macro level. If there is no structural setting which facilitates the articulation of frustration with the old order, the construction of solidarity against that order, and action based on that solidarity, then the old order will survive. Mass psychological and cultural changes can have macro-level consequences, but they are never a simple reflection of micro-level transformations. Psychological changes can be frustrated by a host of factors: electoral systems that discriminate against new parties, market systems that reward and reinforce materialistic and egoistic behavior, social structures that isolate individuals and privatize their concerns, employment structures that make it hard to meet and organize, family structures that either keep women in the home or reinforce privatization by making both male and female income-earners too exhausted to have time for political action.

The most important such structural constraint exists in connection with a global liberal capitalist political economy that is more secure and powerful than ever before. This political economy conditions not just structures and institutions, but also identities, subjectivities, and discourses. As Lindblom (1982) notes, the market imprisons government policy: there are certain things governments simply must do as a first priority, notably maintain the confidence of capitalist investors. He adds that the market also imprisons the way most people think: if there is a conflict between market imperatives and other values (including environmental ones), it is generally taken for granted that these other values must give way.

Thus the challenge to green romantics is: how will your proposed alternative subjectivities fare in a world currently structured to guarantee their frustration, and moving in a direction that reinforces such frustration? Here, green romantics must be pushed to answer questions which really belong outside their discourse, and with which they are profoundly uncomfortable. What aspects of the world are conducive to alternative green subjectivities? What aspects get in the way? What is the relative strength of these enabling and constraining forces? How might political and economic structures be changed so as to change the balance of these forces? Who or what would resist such changes?

It is exactly such questions that green rationalists try to answer.

10 Save the World through New Politics: Green Rationalism

Green rationalism may be defined in terms of its selective and ecologically guided radicalization of Enlightenment values. Enlightenment is still seen as having a dark side, in the form of instrumental reason in the service of anthropocentric arrogance, underwriting uncontrolled economic growth, oblivious to the constraints imposed by the natural world, and to the damage done to conviviality in the social world. Modern science and technology enable the perfection of instrumental reason. The brighter side of Enlightenment involves hostility to unquestioned hierarchy, commitment to equality (at least among humans), basic human rights, and the possibility of free dialogue as the essence of rational social relationships. For Enlightenment rationality is not just a matter of manipulating the world on behalf of the mind's desires, as green romantics would have it. Rationality is also a matter of open-ended and critical questioning of values, principles, and ways of life—which opens the door to critical ecological questioning. Thus green rationalism is defined by its selective embrace of Enlightenment values, which it then tries to push in an environmentally defensible direction. As Plumwood (1993: 4) puts it, "critiquing the dominant forms of reason which embody the master identity and oppose themselves to the sphere of nature does not imply abandoning all forms of reason, science, and individuality. Rather, it involves their redefinition or reconstruction in less oppositional and hierarchical ways." Green rationalists themselves do not necessarily dwell on post-Enlightenment history and their place in it, but their principles can still be located quite precisely in this context (for a rare explicit statement, see Hayward, 1995).

This selective acceptance of Enlightenment values leads directly to a second important difference with green romanticism. Recall that romantics are uninterested in questions of social, economic, and political structure, believing that if individuals' consciousness changes then everything else will fall into place. Rationalists, in contrast, recognize that structure itself can make a difference. It is in the spirit of Enlightenment that society's institutional arrangements be subject to rational scrutiny and, if necessary, redesign—just like all other realms of life. Contrary to what green romantics think, it does then make a difference whether individuals are joined in markets, bureaucracies, cooperatives, or democracies of various sorts. Thus green rationalists are led to contemplate the social dimensions of ecological issues which green romantics normally ignore. Green rationalists are necessarily humanists as well as environmentalists.

The Varieties of Green Rationalism

Green rationalism is perhaps best classified as an emergent discourse, in that it is still under construction as a comprehensive view of environmental affairs. It would probably benefit from the linking of several strands from different parts of the world, some of which are at present only dimly aware of one another. The component strands include the following ones.

EUROPEAN GREENS

There are of course romantics to be found in the European green movement, and a number of them put in appearances in the preceding chapter. Yet it is probably fair to say that the mainstream of European green parties reflects rationalism rather than romanticism, and in this these parties stand in direct contrast to the US Greens. In part this is due to the central position of the German Greens, *Die Grünen*, and their national context. The German Green Party was not the world's first—the claimants for that title include the United Tasmania Group in Australia and New Zealand's Values Party, both formed in 1972. But the German Greens have long been regarded as the world's most significant, for reasons relating to their size and success as both a movement and a party. *Die Grünen* were founded in 1980 and entered the federal *Bundestag* in 1983 with 5.6 per cent of the national vote. Their electoral high point came with 8.3 per cent of the vote in 1987. In 1990 their share fell below the 5 per cent threshold required for parliamentary representation,[1] but they made a comeback in 1994.

[1] In these years there was still Green representation in the *Bundestag*, as under a transitional arrangement parties scoring more than 5% in the former East Germany were allowed representation. The East German Greens did manage to achieve this threshold.

The national history with which the German Greens have had to cope is one in which romanticism looms large. The romantic reaction against modernity in the eighteenth and nineteenth centuries was stronger in Germany than elsewhere, and bound up with reactionary German nationalism. Later, this combination would gain an environmental edge in a strand within the Nazi Party, which idealized the Nordic natural environment (the Rhine, Black Forest, Alps, etc.) as well as the Nordic race, proposing a mystical connection between race and environment. As that scourge of the greens Anna Bramwell (1989) reminds us, the history of European green politics in the first half of the twentieth century is located on the fascist right rather than the progressive left. Mindful of this history, the German Greens are wary of romanticism, and especially suspicious of green spirituality (see Capra and Spretnack, 1984: 53–6).

The German Green Party was long divided into two main factions, the *Realos* and the *Fundis* (the Greens' most well-known figure from the early days, Petra Kelly, was eventually reviled by both factions, which renounced her as soon as she became a media star). *Realos* believe in action through the system, especially through parliamentary politics, accepting the need for a "long march through the institutions" if green aims are to be furthered (Goodin, 1992; Wiesenthal, 1993). They attend closely to vote-maximizing strategies, party organization, and parliamentary tactics, and are open to coalition with other progressive forces, notably the Social Democratic Party. Such coalitions have governed at the city and Land (state) levels in Germany, though not yet at the federal level (where the green ascendancy has coincided with a long period of conservative rule). *Fundis*, in contrast, believe that the Greens are properly a social movement rather than a political party, and that it is the green task to confront an irrational political system rather than work within it. The most well-known *Fundi*, Rudolf Bahro, left the party noisily in 1985 in protest against the party's refusal to issue a blanket condemnation of animal experimentation. The bitter and heated debate between the two factions was largely resolved with the victory of the *Realos* in the early 1990s, under the leadership of Joschka Fischer. It was perhaps unsurprising that the *Realos* should eventually gain the upper hand, given the degree of organizational permanence available to them but scorned by the *Fundis*. But even in his ascendancy Fischer admitted publicly that his main problem was that most members of his party thought he was a jerk.

Clearly Green *Realos* are not romantics: they want to change the world through influence on public policy, not through individual consciousness. But neither are the *Fundis* romantics. Claus Offe's (1990) analysis of the German Greens in their entirety, which resonates with Green self-conceptions, treats them as a paradigm case of a new social movement. Offe believes that such movements take on historical significance as the third major wave of protest in modern societies. The first wave was liberal capitalist protest against the rigidities of a feudal society governed by aristocracy and monarchy. The second wave involved socialist protest against the victorious liberal capitalist system. And the third is that of the new social movements, encompassing not just greens but also feminists, peace activists, and various urban protests. Such movements are not interested in any romantic return to a pre-modern past. Instead, they are committed to what Offe (1985: 853) calls a "selective radicalization of modern values," notably freedom, equality, and democracy. Thus they can be located squarely within the Enlightenment emphasis on social progress. Obviously the Greens regard much of what has transpired in the name of modernity—the destruction of nature, the depletion of resources, the bureaucratization of social relationships—as undesirable. But the solution is not to be found merely in changed individual sensibilities, in any return to a preindustrial Eden, or in postmodern playfulness. Rather, it is to be found in hardheaded analysis of social, political, and economic practice and structure. This analysis in turn can best be developed and put into effect through discursive and democratic interaction within the movement, be it the formalized party organization of the *Realos* or the more fluid and informal groupings favored by the *Fundis*.

SOCIAL ECOLOGY

Social ecology is deep ecology's main ecophilosophical rival in United States green circles. It is associated with the veteran eco-anarchist Murray Bookchin, and explicated in fine detail in his numerous writings (for example, Bookchin, 1982, 1990). As its name implies, social ecology emphasizes the "social" dimension missing in much, if not most, green romanticism (though as we will see shortly, social ecology itself has a romantic aspect). To Bookchin, the root of all evil, in human society no less than in human relationships with nature, is hierarchy. Hierarchy has arisen only in the last six thousand years or so of human civilization. Whether manifested in the domination of peasants by lords, of women by men, of the countryside by the city, of the young by the old, of workers by capitalists, of society by the state, of nature by people, or of the body by the mind, hierarchy is a profoundly undesirable and unnatural phenomenon. For Bookchin sees no hierarchy in the nonhuman world. Relationships which humans perceive as competitive or dominating in fact are subtle examples of mutual benefit. For example, herbivores benefit from predation by carnivores because it keeps their populations in check, eliminating frail and diseased members. Nature is not the violent struggle for survival of the fittest which apologists for war and capitalism portray. Instead, nature properly understood is a cooperative place, indeed a model for harmonious human society, the place where freedom originates.

At first glance this might look like a recipe for yet another romantic return to a primal Eden. What saves social ecology from this fate is Bookchin's stipulation of a special place for humanity in the natural scheme of things. Humans are not set above nature, as they are in the crude anthropocentrism of Prometheans and economic rationalists. However, they are treated as the only bit of nature that has yet achieved self-consciousness: we are nature become aware of itself. We should not deny this aspect of *our* nature in the name of biocentric egalitarianism. Human social evolution now occurs in what Bookchin calls "second nature," an environment that is cultural rather than biological. Thus we should embrace the idea that there is such a thing as progress in human sensibilities. Here social ecology comes to terms with Enlightenment. In this light, Bookchin (1986: 75) argues that "we cannot avoid the use of conventional reason, present-day modes of science, and modern technology." Certainly Enlightenment has meant that the long-standing human propensity to hierarchy has been able to take new and more insidious forms. The state has been able to perfect its domination over society with the development of bureaucratic rationality, and capitalists have been able to deploy science and technology to dominate workers and further subdue nature. But Enlightenment also brings increased ability for humans to question hierarchy, and to contemplate more open and egalitarian interchanges with each other—and with the nonhuman world.

Social ecology's place in the modern world (as opposed to the anti-modern or post-modern world) is further secured by Bookchin's socialist credentials: he is a veteran leftist as well as a veteran ecologist. Thus social ecology cares deeply about injustice within human society, and concerns itself with the analysis of the institutions and practices which perpetuate injustice—notably, hierarchy and competition associated with modern state structures and capitalism. Bookchin's anarchist solution of small-scale, mostly self-sufficient local communities existing in harmony with their neighbors and with their local environment may be utopian; but it does at least rest on a political-economic analysis, and proposes a political-economic strategy (in direct contrast to green romanticism). Bookchin in his later work and his followers in New England have developed ideas about "radical municipalism," which involves the renewal of political institutions from the ground up, starting at the local level.

One other side of social ecology which owes much to Bookchin's background on the radical left is sectarianism. Bookchin reserves his most bitter invective not for oil companies, chemical corporations, or their servants in government, but for other environmentalists. His most frequent target in the 1980s was deep ecology, which he denounced as an ugly wart on the face of the ecology movement, propounded by reactionaries guilty of racism and eco-brutalism. For deep ecology, Edward Abbey responded in kind: the late 1980s saw these two sweet old men laying into one another. Abbey at one point threatened to take a quirt (horsewhip) to Bookchin if he ever showed up in Arizona; though Abbey later relented, saying that a fat old woman like Bookchin had nothing to fear from him. Come the 1990s reconciliation was in the air: Abbey was dead, and Bookchin and Foreman (1991) showed in amicable debate just how much common ground could be found between deep and social ecology.

It is no accident that in an American context Bookchin's ideals are most at home in the pastoral landscape of Vermont, where an image of humanity and nature in productive harmony is readily envisaged, but where there is no wilderness. In the American West, in contrast, the clash between humanity and nature appears violent and intractable. Some of the wilderness remains, but human economic activity takes the form of clear-cut forests, ravaged grazing land, mining scars upon the desert that do not heal, huge dams that destroy riverine ecosystems. Deep ecology has both its most fervent supporters and its most bitter opponents in the West, which is also home to hard-line anti-environmentalism in the John Wayne tradition, for which nature exists only as a challenge to be conquered.

ENVIRONMENTAL JUSTICE

The birth of the environmental justice movement in the United States can be dated quite precisely to 1978, when the Love Canal Homeowners Association was organized by residents whose houses turned out to be on top of an abandoned toxic waste dump once operated by the Hooker Chemical Corporation in Buffalo. After dragging its feet, the federal Environmental Protection Agency eventually agreed that this situation was unhealthy and dangerous, and the federal government bought out the residents' homes. Love Canal catapulted Lois Gibbs to stardom; previously an unpolitical working-class housewife, she went on to organize and head the national Citizens' Clearinghouse on Hazardous Waste.

The environmental justice movement is concerned with the degree to which the environmental risks generated by industrial society fall most heavily on the poor and ethnic minorities (Szasz, 1994). Issues of class and race, traditionally ignored by a mainstream US environmental movement composed mostly of middle-class whites, are highlighted. The risks in question related initially to toxic waste dumps, but concern soon broadened to encompass nuclear facilities, waste incinerators, air and water pollution, mining operations as they threatened the health of rural people (especially Native Americans), and pesticide use as it threatened the health of migrant farm workers. The movement grew out of thousands of groups organized locally to fight particular environmental threats. Derided by their opponents as having only a NIMBY (Not In My Back Yard) orientation, local groups soon got in touch with each other in conscious pursuit of a goal of NIABY (Not In Anybody's Back Yard). As Lois Gibbs puts it, the idea is to "plug the toilet" on toxic wastes, and force industry to stop producing them in the first place (Dowie, 1995: 126).

The distinctive organizational form of the movement is the network (Schlosberg, 1996). Local groups relate to each other without any national leadership or bureaucratic structure. This form is very different from that of the mainstream environmental groups, such as the National Wildlife Federation, Sierra Club, and Environmental Defense Fund, with their plush offices in Washington DC, highly paid chief executives, and easy access to the corridors of power.

The contrast with the mainstream groups is dramatic enough for environmental justice to be styled an alternative environmental movement. The networks of this second movement can bring together otherwise very different kinds of people: for example, white suburban housewives, inner city blacks, and Native Americans on reservations, united in opposition to a particular polluter or an interconnected set of environmental threats. When it comes to tactics, the movement is eclectic. Like the mainstream it engages in litigation and lobbying, but it is also more comfortable with confrontational tactics involving demonstrations, blockades, sit-ins, and boycotts.

Not surprisingly, the relationship between the first and second environmental movements has proven uneasy. Environmental justice activists resent the fact that mainstream groups have come late to toxics issues, especially as they relate to race and class, but now seek foundation funding for efforts in these areas. In some cases mainstream groups have combined late entry with negotiated deals with polluters that fall far short of "plugging the toilet." Lois Gibbs, for one, does not even like being called an environmentalist. As she puts it, environmentalists are people who eat yoghurt, while her people drink Budweiser and smoke (Dowie, 1995: 171).

In raising the distributional aspect of environmental issues, environmental justice is heir to the egalitarian ideals established by Enlightenment and modernity. Its modernist credentials here are confirmed by its discursive and democratic characteristics, though arguably it also allows a post-modern politics of identity, in which groups with very different social characteristics reach out across their differences and negotiate their place with respect to one another and to the established industrial order (see Schlosberg, 1996). With its conversion from NIMBY to NIABY strategies, environmental justice eventually raises the structural issue which is one of the hallmarks of green rationalism. The implication of "plugging the toilet" is a transformed political economy, one in which hazardous wastes are no longer conceptualized as byproducts to be dealt with as an afterthought. Rather, these wastes are evidence of fundamental irrationality in the system, demanding cure in the form of production planning to eliminate the generation of wastes. Some clear parallels with ecological modernization can be discerned here. The main difference is that ecological modernizers believe capitalist enterprises themselves might lead the charge to efficiency through waste minimization, whereas the environmental justice movement believes that such changes can only be forced upon reluctant corporations through radical political action.

The only question that remains when it comes to placing environmental justice under the green rationalist umbrella concerns its weakly ecological dimension: that is, there is little appreciation of the role played by complex ecosystems in sustaining life on earth. Yet this lack of appreciation is a merely contingent feature stemming from the movement's origins in existing community groups faced with some immediate local health hazards. The movement could probably only benefit from an appreciation of the ecosystemic nature of things, as this would provide further justification for the network form of social and political organization, and further support for the need radically to overhaul the industrial political economy.

SOCIAL ECOFEMINISM

Ecofeminism is a diverse movement. As seen in the previous chapter, it is home to romantics who believe the key to environmental and social harmony is the replacement of dominant masculinist sensibilities with a feminine attitude which is intrinsically more attuned to the nonhuman world. Such biological essentialism, based on an inversion of the traditional dualism which put reason above nature, men above women, is rejected by other ecofeminists (for a critique, see Biehl, 1991). "Social Ecofeminism" is sometimes used narrowly to describe a program to link Bookchin's social ecology with ecofeminism. But the term can also be used more broadly to characterize ecofeminists who reject biological essentialism and its culturalist trappings, thus encompassing authors such as Carolyn Merchant, Chaia Heller, Val Plumwood, Janet Biehl, and Ynestra King.

Social ecofeminism shares cultural feminism's critique of patriarchy, but is more inclined to see patriarchy as one among a number of oppressions (also covering race and class), rather than the root of all oppression. Moreover, there is little that is determined by the biology of sex in either the oppression itself or resistance to it. Thus ecofeminist activism should contemplate the causes of the domination of both women and nature that lie in the structure of states, economies, and social systems. In this light, oppression should be countered not just through heightened feminist consciousness, but also through collective political action and new social institutions.

A good example of this kind of analysis can be found in Plumwood's (1995) scrutiny of alternative models of democracy. Plumwood argues democratic systems have not served environmental values well, because so long as it remains under the sway of liberalism, democracy can never extend itself in a truly ecological direction. She points out that inherent in liberalism are assumptions about the degree to which individuals are properly isolated from one another, rational in a narrowly instrumental and egoistic sense, and unequal in both material wealth and the capacity to exercise power and reason. The consequences are both socially unjust and environmentally destructive. Plumwood's proposed ecofeminist model of democracy would involve alternative notions of social and ecological citizenship more attuned to an ethic of care and responsibility, together with a more egalitarian political order extending to equality across the boundary between humanity and nature.

Bioregionalism as a Political Program

Bioregionalists concern themselves with the re-inhabitation of existing places of settlement by human societies. As seen in the last chapter, much if not most bioregional thinking is romantic, contemplating the kinds of sensibilities people should adopt in relation to the particular places and ecosystems where they live. But bioregionalism also has a rationalistic aspect, inasmuch as it concerns itself with how political and economic structures might be designed to better fit with ecosystem boundaries. Bioregionalism in this sense does not even have to be particularly radical. Some of the resource-management agencies of the United States government have contemplated reorganizing their field operations under offices defined by bioregion, rather than by state, county, or national forest boundaries. Intergovernmental authorities have been created to deal with (if rarely actually to govern) bioregions defined as river basins. For example, in the United States the Northwest Planning Power Council is now responsible for the Columbia Basin. In Australia, the Murray–Darling River Basin Commission is responsible for environmental management and restoration of a ravaged watershed central to the country's agro-economy. At this level, bioregionalism is really just another element in a discourse of environmental problem solving, of the sort analyzed in Part III, fitting quite nicely with administrative rationalism.

More radical bioregionalists want to replace local, state, and national governments by governments organized along bioregional lines. This is manifested in European green proposals for a "Europe of the regions" which would dissolve existing national boundaries. In North America, Pacific Cascadia might govern what is now Western British Columbia, Oregon, and Washington, and a portion of Northwestern California. The authorities so created would govern not just environmental policy and natural resource management, but all issue areas—though of course ecological concerns would be by definition at the forefront of the agenda of such governments, addressed across all policy areas.

Just how such bioregional governments might be structured once the boundaries have been redrawn is a matter which has yet to be treated with much sophistication by bioregionalists. Gestures in the direction of more general radical green ideas about community self-control and grassroots democracy are frequent. But bioregionalists also argue that cultural and ecological variation may need to matched by variation in governmental forms. The leading bioregionalist Kirkpatrick Sale (1985: 108) allows that authoritarianism may prove appropriate in some localities.

The main non-romantic argument for bioregionalism is that governments whose focus is provided by the ecosystems which they inhabit, and upon which their populations must rely for their sustenance, will have to care for those ecosystems much more carefully than do existing governments. This assumes that trade across bioregions will be limited, though quite how to regulate such trade in the absence of governmental arrangements that transcend such boundaries remains a tricky issue. Also unresolved is the basic question of how exactly to draw such boundaries in the first place, and how large bioregions should be. In terms of size, bioregions may be nested within one another. In terms of where to draw boundaries, vegetation type, terrain, human culture, and watersheds may give different answers, and compromises may be necessary across these principles. For example, Pacific Cascadia is a bioregion defined by temperate Douglas Fir forests. But parts of this bioregion fall within the Columbia River Basin— which also contains mid-continent deserts.

LEFT GREENS

One of the German Green slogans is "Neither left nor right, but in front." Not all greens agree, least of all in Germany, where there used to be a sizeable Marxist faction within the greens. Of course, there is much more to the left than Marxism, and so much more to left green thinking than eco-Marxism.

In the early years of environmental resurgence in the 1970s, Marxists typically denounced environmentalism as bourgeois and concerned only with life's pleasures, at best only a distraction from the real stuff of class struggle. Marx himself was a Promethean, who cared about nature mostly for the sake of its conquest, the best efforts of some contemporary Marxists to rehabilitate his environmental reputation notwithstanding. Matters have now changed, and many if not most intelligent Marxists are now eco-Marxists. With capitalism's own dynamics having failed to culminate in socialist revolution as Marxists once predicted, they can now look to ecological crisis as a harbinger of a general crisis of capitalism. On this account, capitalism destroys the ecological base upon which all human economic activity rests. Eco-Marxism departs from most other varieties of green radicalism in believing that this destructiveness is contingent upon capitalism, such that a more rational economic system would not be subject to ecological limits.

Eco-Marxists see ecological issues as laying bare many of the contradictions of capitalism, and ultimately contributing to its demise, though they are a bit coy on exactly how and when this will happen. They are still less forthcoming on whether or not that demise may come in the form of socialist revolution, still less on what kind of political-economic system might replace capitalism. Any alternative system would of course have to avoid the gross environmental failings of the countries of the former Soviet bloc—failings which provide plenty of ammunition to anti-Marxists (for example, Lewis, 1992: 163–6).

Eco-Marxists devote their energies not just to the critique of capitalism, but also to criticism of green thinking that involves blanket condemnation of anthropocentrism or modernity. Eco-Marxists believe that the real explanation for ecological crisis revolves around material economic factors. Human consciousness is relevant only to the extent it can be tied to these forces. Thus they scorn the romantic proposals of deep ecologists and cultural ecofeminists (Faber and O'Connor, 1989). Eco-Marxism is a lively intellectual community. Its leading light is the US sociologist James O'Connor (1988), founder of the red-green journal *Capitalism, Nature, Socialism*.[2]

---

[2] Whose pages I have also graced (see Dryzek, 1992*c*).

Eco-socialists who are not eco-Marxists are often proponents of the need for government planning to cure the ecological irrationalities of capitalism (see, for example, Stretton, 1976; Ryle, 1988). There is no suggestion that capitalism needs to be superseded, merely that it needs to be tamed so that it uses resources less wastefully and involves less wanton environmental destruction. The distinction between eco-socialism and administrative rationalism as discussed in Chapter 4 is sometimes hard to sustain. Certainly eco-socialists would happily use the same range of policy instruments as administrative rationalists, though their goals might include a broader range of social justice concerns. This emphasis on state planning might distress *Fundis* whose version of green politics would oppose the state rather than use it. Social ecologists, bioregionalists and other greens believing in economic and political decentralization would likewise be skeptical about eco-socialism. Yet neither centralization nor decentralization is a litmus test for green radicalism. Even eco-anarchists recognize the need for some kind of authority above the local level, though they prefer loose confederations of communities rather than states. The debate about centralization versus decentralization is internal to green rationalist discourse.

ANIMAL LIBERATION

One of the defining features of the Enlightenment was the establishment of the principle of rights. In the wake of the Enlightenment, we have seen a gradual expansion in the range of human beings deemed worthy of a full range of rights: the poor, women, non-whites, children, disabled people, gays and lesbians. Animal liberations ask: why stop there? Why not extend the same rights to animals as well (see, for example, Regan, 1983)? It is in this sense that animal liberation is a continuation of the Enlightenment project, and so belongs under the heading of green rationalism. The rights in question would involve rights against being killed for pleasure, against being used as food, against being imprisoned, against being experimented upon— even when such activities yield clear benefits to humans (for example, the medical benefits of animal experimentation).

The key question is, are animals morally considerable to the extent that they deserve rights? Do we give rights only to entities capable of asserting those rights? Animal liberationists reply that we do not hesitate to grant rights to people (the mentally incompetent, very young children) who are incapable of asserting them. The leading animal liberationist Peter Singer (1975) argues that the criterion of sentience should be our guide (and not just for the gastronomic reason that it allows him to eat oysters). Here, Singer follows the Enlightenment rationalist philosopher Jeremy Bentham, who almost two hundred years ago argued for the moral worth of animals because, just like humans, they had the capacity to experience pain and pleasure.

Animal liberation is a movement as well as a philosophy (see Garner, 1993). Some of its more radical actions have involved the freeing of animals from factory farms, the destruction of animal experimentation laboratories, and firebombing of shops selling animal products. Britain's Animal Liberation Front is especially active. But animal liberationists are also active in more conventional pressure group and party politics, in part by trying to radicalize long-established animal welfare organizations such as Britain's Royal Society for the Prevention of Cruelty to Animals. Peter Singer himself was a Green Party candidate for the Australian Senate in 1996.

Singer's candidacy notwithstanding, animal liberation sometimes fits uneasily in green discourse because it is weakly ecological, some would say anti-ecological. For in its concern with individual creatures, it can lose sight of larger ecological connections. Does not the wellbeing of the ecosystem sometimes require the deaths of individual creatures (for example, the elimination of exotic species such as cats and foxes, which in Australia are wiping out native species)? What are we to say about predation in the natural world? Should predators be forced to become vegetarian, on the grounds of their violation of the right to life of their prey? Are not humans, as many deep ecologists insist, "naturally" hunters? Despite these objections, animal liberation can lead directly into green concerns because a commitment to the rights of wild animals means a commitment to preservation of their habitat. Moreover, an end to the exploitation of animals for human purposes in the end raises all kinds of structural political-economic questions. It would mean a thorough reorientation of agriculture and agribusiness, and in power relationships more generally—the power of humans to use land and other species for their own benefit (Benton, 1993).

Discourse Analysis of Green Rationalism

The story line of green rationalism points to multi-faceted social and ecological crises which can only be resolved through radical political action and structural change. A change of heart is all very well, and alternative subjectivities (even romantic ones) may be welcome as part of this project, but both the causes of crisis and the required approaches to solution involve a lot more than consciousness. Complex social relations are at issue too, and action needs to take place both within and upon these relationships.

1. Basic Entities whose Existence is Recognized or Constructed

Green rationalism's urgency in the face of crisis is backed by recognition of ecological limits (though in eco-Marxism such limits are treated as applying only to capitalism, and in environmental justice limits receive little explicit attention).

Nature is recognized in the form of complex ecosystems whose wellbeing requires that humans change their ways. But the necessary change is not any romantic return to nature. For green rationalism also recognizes that we humans are indeed different from the rest of nature, and perhaps even special, most notably in terms of a capacity to reason and reflect. It is important to recognize, however, that this capacity does not mean that humans have to be *homo economicus* individuals, concerned only with calculation of what is in their own immediate material interest. Nor is there any license for humans to exploit and dominate nature. Human horizons can and should be much wider. In further contrast to romanticism, social, political, and economic structures are recognized as having important influence that cannot be reduced to the sensibilities of the individuals inhabiting them.

2. Assumptions about Natural Relationships

As heirs to the Enlightenment legacy, green rationalists assume a natural relationship of equality across individuals, at least in terms of the capacity to engage in reasoned debate about collective ends. As selective appropriators of that legacy, they recognize and condemn the existence of hierarchy that both pre-dates and is reinforced by Enlightenment and modernity. Unlike green romantics, green rationalists can explain hierarchy as well as condemn it. The most elaborate such explanation comes in social ecology, whose political philosophy is rooted in a demonstration of the unnaturalness of hierarchy of all kinds.

Despite its core egalitarianism, green rationalism also allows compromise with other kinds of relationships, such as competitive ones, especially in its contemplation of economic systems. Such competitive relationships should, however, be kept in check by more egalitarian political structures. The precise character of desirable political structures is disputed among green rationalists. There is a substantial gap between the quasi-anarchism of social ecology and the statism of Realo greens and eco-socialists.

When it comes to specifying appropriate relationships linking human systems and natural systems, there is a strong conception of complex ecological connections. Unlike green romanticism, this does not reduce to any simple biocentric egalitarianism. For green rationalism, humans are set apart from nature by virtue of their reasoning capacities, but this does not warrant hierarchy and domination of nature. A stewardship relationship is more likely to be posited.

3. AGENTS AND THEIR MOTIVES

Political agency is granted to a variety of actors, both individual and collective, and so encompasses movements, parties, and states as well as persons. The possibility that their might be agency in nature is generally downplayed, except in social ecology and social ecofeminism (see also Dryzek, 1990a). Green rationalists are likely to treat the essence of human motivation as multi-dimensional, at once competitive and cooperative, violent and peaceful, instrumental and communicative, selfish and public-spirited. Political life is mainly about promoting the institutional structure and political action such as to evoke the more benign motivation in each of these pairs, and control the more nefarious one.

4. KEY METAPHORS AND OTHER RHETORICAL DEVICES

Any self-respecting rationalistic discourse should probably try to avoid too much in the way of metaphor, and those metaphors present in green rationalism are perhaps less vivid and colorful than those featured in green romanticism. Yet green rationalism is still green, and so is home to organic metaphors. Over the last few hundred years, the modern world has of course been constructed in terms of mechanistic images of both human social systems and natural systems (as we have seen in earlier discussions of Promethean discourse and economic rationalism). Thus in stressing the organic, green rationalism shows that its appropriation of Enlightenment values is indeed very selective. Green rationalism walks a fine metaphorical line between the green and the rational. As a green discourse, it must see the world in terms of organic balance, where wholes cannot be understood by reduction to their component parts, and living things interact in ways that can never be understood fully. As a rational discourse, it must ascribe elements of the rationality of individual humans to collectivities such as political and economic systems, especially in their interaction with natural systems. Human systems may be irrational at present (committed, for example, to blind pursuit of material riches, or the generation of toxic wastes with nowhere to put them), but they are capable of a greater rationality. Moreover, we rational humans can apply standards of ecological rationality to the analysis and redesign of these systems. Social systems, like individuals, must be treated as capable of learning.

Green rationalists are inclined to offer argument, rather than appeal to the emotions. The accompanying rhetoric is likely to appeal to ideals of progress beyond an irrational industrial order, rather than promise return to some primal Eden. Like sustainable development and ecological modernization, a belief in progress is grounded in a model of individual human development.

Box 10.1. **DISCOURSE ANALYSIS OF GREEN RATIONALISM**

1. **Basic Entities Recognized or Constructed**
   - Global limits
   - Nature as complex ecosystems
   - Rational humans
   - Social, economic, and political structures

2. **Assumptions about Natural Relationships**
   - Equality among people
   - Complex interconnections between humans and nature

3. **Agents and their Motives**
   - Many individual and collective actors, multi-dimensional motivation
   - Agency in nature downplayed, though not necessarily denied

4. **Key Metaphors and other Rhetorical Devices**
   - Organic metaphors
   - Appeals to reason, and potential rationality of social structures
   - Link to progress

Green Rationalism in Political Practice

Green rationalism is at the heart of a social movement which has sought to change institutions, practices, and policies, though the discourse also extends beyond the movement. Thus the impact of the discourse should be sought not just in the tangible achievements of particular parties, networks, or other green organizations, but also in the degree to which green discourse has permeated political-economic life more generally.

Green parties have been represented in the parliaments of an increasing number of countries since 1981, when the Francophone Ecolo and Flemish

Agalev parties won seats in the Belgian parliament. The highest vote achieved by any green party in a national election was achieved in 1989 by the British Greens in elections to the European Parliament. But their 15 per cent of the vote won them a grand total of zero seats, and they have yet to come anywhere close to winning a seat in the Westminster parliament, though in 1992 Cynog Dafis, of the Welsh nationalist party Plaid Cymru, was elected with Green backing. By 1996 the British Greens were debating at their annual conference whether it was even worth their while contesting the next general election. Their electoral difficulties illustrate the degree to which the success of green parties in winning seats depends crucially on the kind of electoral system in operation. Proportional representation is far more conducive to green electoral success than is the first-past-the-post or simple plurality system (which is the norm in the English-speaking world, except for the Irish Republic and, from 1996, New Zealand). Proportional representation does of course advantage all small and emerging parties, not just green ones.

Green parliamentary representation has reached a high point in the German *Bundestag*, though *Die Grünen* have not yet participated in a national governing coalition, or been in a position to influence the composition of any such coalition. As I mentioned earlier, their presence in the *Bundestag* has coincided with a long period of secure conservative majorities.

The trajectory of green votes and green seats reveals slow spread in the number of countries with electorally significant green parties, but no take-off in the strength of any one party beyond single percentage points in terms of votes or seats. Given the degree to which voters in post-industrial societies should in principle be sympathetic to many of the values that green parties stand for (see Inglehart, 1990), this leads some observers to write off the greens as having missed their opportunity, and destined for electoral oblivion (see, for example, Bramwell, 1994).

But the real impact of green parties may be in the degree to which they have forced more established "grey" parties, and the political system as a whole, to craft responses to the green electoral threat. The development of the discourse of ecological modernization detailed in Chapter 8 can be interpreted as an attempt by the prevailing political order to head off the green challenge. Ecological modernization has developed in the European heartland of green party politics, and has appropriated more than a few ideas originally developed by the greens. Certainly, ecological modernization lacks the radical edge of green rationalism (and green romanticism). Yet it still posits a structural transformation of capitalism. The irony is that if this transformation succeeds it will deprive green radicalism of its bite by showing that transition to a totally different political economy is unnecessary. The historical analogy here is with the rise of socialism, which in the early to mid twentieth century forced the capitalist political economy to develop welfare states and full employment practices, thus blunting the radical edge of the socialist critique of capitalism. The difference is that socialist parties participated in parliamentary majorities, and sometimes formed governments by themselves.

Green parties have however participated in governing coalitions in city and state governments in several European countries, normally alongside parties of the social democratic left. In the Italian national election of 1996 the Greens formed part of the victorious Olive Tree alliance. As a rough generalization, governments containing greens have not enacted policies radically different from social democratic governments that do not contain greens; certainly no program of wholesale political-economic transformation is in view. Yet to focus on this seeming lack of policy impact would be to miss the crucial role of green rationalist discourse in transforming the terms of political debate, and requiring other parties to adjust their positions on green issues. The German Greens have a name for this: *themenklau*, the stealing of green ideas by grey parties.

As I observed earlier, not everyone within the green movement believes that electoral politics is the proper focus of green energies. Political life is not just party politics. It can also cover discussions in bars and coffee shops, community organizing, educational efforts, self-help groups, boycotts, demonstrations, strikes, blockades, ecotage, sit-ins, and various kinds of media events. (Greenpeace specializes in media events—for example, inserting a plug into the end of a pipeline discharging radioactive waste into the Irish Sea from the British Nuclear Fuels Ltd. installation at Sellafield.) Shunning the state in favor of movement politics might seem to some an abdication of ambition, even of responsibility, leading to voluntary exile in a political wasteland. But such a perception is in error. Political pressure can be exerted at a distance upon the state. Here, social movements have at their disposal a number of instruments. They include the rhetorical ability to change the terms of policy debate; creation of fear of political instability; the production of ideas; and the embarrassment of governments.

When it comes to changing public ideas and attitudes, it is hard to disentangle the relative influence of more mainstream environmentalism and green radicalism, but at least in Europe the established mainstream environmental groups (such as the Council for the Protection of Rural England, the World Wildlife Fund, and *Deutsch Naturschutzring*) have been rather staid and unimaginative. They were around long before the 1970s upsurge in green politics, with very little to show in terms of value change in society at large. It is the green radicals who have made the running in instigating change in ideas and attitudes, which extends to those who do not vote for green parties, still less join more radical green actions. Aspects of this change include (dim) awareness of ecological limits, sensitivity to the risks generated by industrial society in terms of chemical, nuclear, and biotechnological hazards, and of the possibilities for a more convivial way of life than the aggressively individualistic materialism of contemporary market society. Green rationalism has had less success in achieving broad cultural acceptance of its core values relating to grassroots democracy and structural change.

Green politics itself helps to constitute a parallel political society where at least some individuals can lead their social and political lives, an alternative to the grey mainstream of party politics (see Dryzek, 1996a: 46–53). For green rationalists, unlike their romantic counterparts, this parallel polity can be oriented to the public policy debates of the day, even as a critical distance from mainstream politics is maintained.

Green politics can also involve action oriented to the solution of particular well-defined problems in a fashion that attempts to reclaim political authority from the state. For example, in 1995 Greenpeace activists occupied the Brent Spar, an oil storage platform whose working life in the North Sea had come to an end. The Shell corporation intended to dispose of the platform by towing it into deeper water in the North Atlantic and sinking it. The publicity generated by Greenpeace, which also organized a consumer boycott of Shell throughout Europe, forced the company to change its plans and dispose of the platform on land. Shell's decision angered the British government, which was prepared to use force to evict the Greenpeace protestors. In this case at least, green activists possessed more political authority in relation to Shell than did the British government.

Another case of such reclamation of political authority arises with the practice of "popular epidemiology," or community-based research on risk assessment. The paradigm case occurred in the community of Woburn in Massachusetts, where citizens angered by government denial that any problem existed organized a group called FACE (For a Clean Environment) which then conducted its own survey of the incidence of leukemia and birth defects which its members believed were linked to toxic waste sites. State and federal government agencies rejected this effort, arguing that the citizen risk investigators had no proper training in risk assessment, such that their findings were unreliable. Yet the results assembled by FACE were used as evidence in a lawsuit which was eventually settled out of court by one of the companies which had dumped toxics (see Brown and Mikkelsen, 1990).

In the United States, green rationalism's more tangible impacts are largely associated with the environmental justice movement (under which the Woburn action can also be classified). Unlike green parties, this movement has developed without contemplation of any kind of political or social theory, and without any debate over the appropriate degree of engagement with conventional political action and the state (though debate has occurred over how to relate to established mainstream environmental groups). Instead, the movement has moved radically but pragmatically on a variety of fronts, involving conventional litigation and lobbying as well as demonstrations, blockades, and boycotts. In the negative, the movement has achieved many victories, blocking plans for noxious facilities and forcing corporations and governments to compensate victims. No significant toxic waste disposal facility has been constructed in the United States since 1980. The toilet is well and truly plugged. As yet this plugging has not led to any real movement toward a greener economy. However, the simple presence of environmental justice and its network form of organization is itself a significant political development, pointing to a kind of politics that is more authentically democratic and more green (in terms of green rationalism) than its mainstream alternative. As discourse, environmental justice has permeated the highest levels of policy making, forcing at least a symbolic response from President Clinton in signing an executive order in 1993, declaring that federal environmental agencies must henceforth take principles of environmental justice into account in their decision making.

If environmental justice represents achievement in practice without much in the way of theoretical reflection, social ecology, social ecofeminism, and eco-socialism represent intellectual achievements without much obvious accompanying political or economic practice, beyond the parallel polity that greens help to constitute.

Being Green in Capitalist Times

In the last two decades or so green radicalism has come from nowhere to develop a comprehensive critique of the environmental, social, political, and economic shortcomings of industrial society. As such, it represents perhaps the most significant ideological development of the late twentieth century. Yet there remains a great deal of uncertainty about the best way to practise green politics in the face of a seemingly recalcitrant and secure liberal capitalist political economy. That political economy is reinforced by several of the discourses analyzed in earlier chapters. Private of course have nothing but scorn for green critiques, and when they do address green thinking completely trivialize it. The three problem-solving discourses see no need for the kind of wholesale structural change green rationalists seek. Sustainable development and ecological modernization are more likely to take these concerns seriously, but believe a structural response can be crafted that does not involve abandoning the basic parameters of liberal capitalism.

So just what kind of alternative political economy do green rationalists want? Is capitalism to be overthrown, transcended, or transformed? Certainly capitalism as it currently stands is regarded as unacceptable, but most greens remain uncertain about exactly what to do with it. Even eco-Marxists and eco-socialists are a bit coy about whether they envisage capitalism being overthrown in favor of some socialist alternative, or even gradually transformed into such an alternative. These viewpoints perhaps make more sense as critical devices, in which socialism is raised mainly as a way of highlighting the flaws of capitalism, the real-world prospects for any kind of socialism (be it reformist or revolutionary) having receded rather dramatically in recent years.

But to demand a blueprint for an alternative society may be asking too much of green rationalism. If the twentieth century holds one political lesson, it is that we should beware of anyone peddling such blueprints, be they socialist paradises, fascist Reichs to last a thousand years, or free-market utopias popularized in the Anglo-American world in the 1980s and exported in the form of "shock therapy" to several East European countries after 1989. Whatever the leanings of their advocates and supporters, such blueprints inevitably go wrong when confronted with the complexities of the real world, and bring at best only the kind of state centralization and authoritarianism introduced in Britain by Margaret Thatcher (ironically alongside a rhetoric of freedom and choice). At worst, they bring totalitarianism and a police state. The explanation is simple: as soon as real world surprises come along, proponents of the blueprint feel they have to save it via increasingly coercive measures. The notion that the blueprint itself may be flawed never crosses their minds (for more detail on this general argument, see Popper, 1966; 1972; for an application to free-market utopias in Eastern Europe, see Pickel, 1993).

In this light, the fact that green rationalists do not have any well-defined blueprint for a new society twinned with a coordinated strategy for achieving it is actually a point in their favor. What green rationalists do have in abundance are ideas that can be pressed into a decentered approach to the achievement of a greener society, where there is room for a variety of experiments whose general orientation is given by green discourse, but whose specifics can vary quite substantially. Bioregional projects, networks of community activists, oppositional political fora, experiments in local grassroots democracy, social ecology's radical municipalism, and attempts to radical-ize democratic pragmatist initiatives of the sort discussed in Chapter 5 can all fit in here. There are plenty of green theorists around to provide reflections upon, and further ideas for, such experiments and initiatives.

Such a decentralized approach fits quite nicely with green ideas about local initiative and community self-control. However, it means that green rationalism may in the end have little more success than green romanticism in confronting entrenched political-economic systems. For can such a loosely coordinated set of responses ever be adequate in the face of a liberal capitalist political economy which is more secure and more entrenched than ever before in history? This system is increasingly geared to free trade, economic growth, and the mobility of investment capital across national boundaries. It is this system which is the dominant political reality of our times. All national, regional and local governments now see it as their first task to accommodate themselves to the imperatives of this system, to keep investors happy by promoting a positive climate for business. A decentered program of green initiatives might appear just a minor set of irritants to this monolithic, global, transnational capitalist political economy. If green politics is to be nothing more than theatre, then green romanticism is more attractive than green rationalism, because it is always true that romantics have more fun.

If on the other hand green politics is to be more than theatre then perhaps it has something to learn from other discourses of environmental concern. Some possibilities along these lines are addressed in the concluding chapter.

PART VI
CONCLUSION

11   Ecological Democracy

What can be said by way of conclusion about how the various discourses have survived the questions asked of them here, and their comparison with other discourses? First, the discourses are not always and inevitably competitors. There are some complementarities. For example, a "weak" form of ecological modernization is quite compatible with administrative rationalism and economic rationalism. And green radicalism is happy to subscribe to many of the ideas about global limits developed by survivalists—though not to survivalists' political analysis and prescription. Equally clearly, there can be plenty of tension between discourses. Survivalists have core disagreements with Prometheans, sustainable development, and ecological modernization. Economic rationalists are never going to agree with administrative rationalists, democratic pragmatists, or green radicals about the best way of ordering environmental affairs.

One way of easing the tensions somewhat is to note that different discourses may be applicable to different kinds of problems. In essence, survivalism and Promethean discourse are about global issues. Whatever position one reaches in the dispute between them, it would be possible to follow any one of the three problem-solving discourses at the local level (though Prometheans might say that even such local efforts are often unnecessary). Other compatibilities might be found: for example, one might be a green romantic when it comes to lifestyle, but a democratic pragmatist when it comes to policy.

Such potential compatibilities notwithstanding, it remains the case that most of the discourses analyzed offer a comprehensive account of and orientation to environmental affairs at all levels, from the global to the local, and across different issue areas (pollution, resource depletion, wilderness protection, and so forth). This comprehensiveness certainly applies to Promethean discourse, administrative rationalism, democratic pragmatism, economic rationalism, sustainable development, green romanticism, and green radicalism. It is less applicable to survivalism, which concerns itself only with global affairs, and ecological modernization, which has so far addressed only how industrial economies might be restructured, with little application to non-industrial societies or global analysis.

With these competing comprehensive visions and the need to identify productive compatibilities in mind, I would argue by way of approaching a conclusion that an intelligent approach to environmental issues demands two things. The first is a dynamic, structural-level analysis of the liberal capitalist political economy, where it might be headed, and what realistically can be done to alter this trajectory to more ecologically benign ends. For a confident and globally organized liberal capitalism mostly insensitive to environmental concerns is the dominant political fact of our times. Without such an analysis, we are reduced to wishful thinking about how things might be different. Of the discourses surveyed, ungrounded wishful thinking about a different world characterizes survivalism, economic rationalism, and green romanticism—though of course they wish for very different things! Only two of the discourses provide a coherent analysis of the kind needed: Promethean discourse and ecological modernization.

Prometheans believe that the current trajectory of liberal capitalism is unproblematical, and that all we need do is leave it alone to provide abundance for humanity, in the future as in the past. Ecological modernizers, in contrast, recognize that *laissez-faire* liberal capitalism is environmentally destructive. Thus they seek an ecological restructuring of capitalism that respects the constraints imposed by this economic system on political action, and which is consistent with the basic imperatives of the system. If one accepts the Promethean viewpoint, then the matter ends. On the other hand, if one rejects that viewpoint—and I argued in Chapter 3 that there are good reasons to do so—then the second quality demanded by an intelligent approach to environmental affairs comes into play.

This second quality is the capacity to facilitate and engage in social learning in an ecological context. Environmental issues feature high degrees of uncertainty and complexity, which are magnified as ecological systems interact with social, economic, and political systems. Thus we need institutions and discourses which are capable of learning—not least about their own shortcomings. Survivalism, Promethean discourse, administrative rationalism, economic rationalism, and green romanticism provide few such resources, and exhibit little or no awareness of their own limits. In contrast, resources for this learning project are provided by democratic pragmatism, sustainable development, ecological modernization, and green rationalism. In each case, though, our appropriation from the discourse must be selective.

From democratic pragmatism come discursive procedures for the resolution of disputes through cooperative problem solving. Such procedures, including policy dialogue, environmental mediation, regulatory negotiation, and societal dialogues, are often limited in their scope and constrained by the structural context in which they operate. Critics of them rightly note that they can involve co-optation and neutralization of troublemakers by powerful state and corporate officials. The key, then, is try to break these shackles, moving such experiments in the direction of what I have described elsewhere as discursive designs, which arguably transgress the boundaries of democratic pragmatism by pointing to a more radical participatory democracy. Discursive designs involve collective decision making through authentic democratic discussion, open to all interests, under which political power, money, and strategizing do not determine outcomes (see Dryzek, 1990b: 29–56). That such radicalization is possible is shown by the rightly celebrated Berger Inquiry, discussed in Chapters 5 and 8. That such radicalization is problematical is shown by the frequency of Berger's celebration in the literature as an exemplary case. But a careful search would reveal an ever-growing number of cases, some of which I have mentioned under democratic pragmatism and green rationalism.

From sustainable development comes the possibility of a decentered approach to the pursuit of sustainability. While at first glance the sheer variety of available definitions of sustainable development seems like a defect of this discourse, from the perspective of social learning it is a distinct advantage, for it does not rule out a variety of experiments in what sustainability can mean in different contexts, including the global context. A decentered approach to sustainability meshes quite nicely with discursive designs, which could find roles as the steering institutions and reflective components of experiments in sustainability (as Torgerson, 1994; 1995 also recognizes).

From ecological modernization comes the possibility of a "strong" or "reflexive" version of the discourse, the essence of which goes beyond the re-tooling of the economy with waste reduction and profitability in mind. Ecological modernization so radicalized can involve institutional change in the direction of democratic experimentation, and open-ended exploration of what ecological modernization itself might mean. The very idea of reflexive development is that it is self-monitoring and critically aware of itself, thus conducive to social learning. Again, this fits quite nicely with a decentered approach to sustainability and discursive designs.

From green rationalism come the reasons why democratic pragmatism, sustainable development, and ecological modernization need to be radicalized to begin with. Green rationalism can bring to them a sense of urgency which survivalism shares but finds more difficult to disseminate, given that survivalism's imagery of certainty leaves little space for search and experimentation. Moreover, survivalism's flirtation with authoritarianism alienates democratic pragmatists, sustainable developers, and ecological modernizers alike. Green romanticism for its part is not easily connected with radicalized versions of these three discourses, given that its adherents are uninterested in institutions, or institutional experimentation. Green rationalism can also remind us that oppositional politics in social movements can play a key role in social learning, which does not have to be tied to conventional politics (and may indeed proceed more readily outside the realm of conventional politics). Green rationalists can further bring to bear plenty of ideas about how political and economic institutions might look in an ecological future beyond industrial society. Linking these ideas to the other three discourses is a way of grounding such ideas in a more realistic analysis of how the future can actually unfold, as opposed to wishful thinking about how it should unfold.

The common thread that can be developed here is a renewed democratic politics, an ecological democracy.[1] But would such a politics indeed promote ecological values? One affirmative answer comes from democratic pragmatism: the kinds of values that can survive authentic democratic debate are those oriented to the interests of the community as a whole, rather than selfish interests within the community (or outside it). Foremost among such community interests is the integrity of the ecological base upon which the community depends. From green rationalism comes a reminder to democratic pragmatism that existing liberal democracies typically frustrate such processes: the influence of power, money, and strategy need to be unmasked and countered, as does the degree to which human communities have lost any sense of their ecological foundations.

For democracy, if it is about anything, is about authentic communication. Overcoming the impediments that distort such communication is crucial. One such impediment, ignored in the history of democratic theory but now exposed by the rise of green thinking, concerns communication with the non-human world. It would be absurd to think of that world as having preferences, or able to "vote," which is why most models of democracy are of limited applicability in a green context. But the nonhuman world can communicate, and human decision processes can be structured so as to listen to its communications more or less well. Large bureaucracies operating according to standard procedures insensitive to local ecological contexts fail

[1] More extensive discussion of ecological democracy may be found in some of my other writings (Dryzek, 1987; 1990*a*; 1992*c*; 1996*c*; 1996*d*).

this test; bioregional authorities governed by citizens with a thorough know-ledge of local circumstances are likely to do much better.

Ecological democracy blurs the boundary between human social systems and natural systems. There is an additional sense in which ecological democ-racy is democracy without boundaries. Ecological problems and issues tran-scend established governmental jurisdictions, such that democratic exercises may need to be constituted in order to fit the size and scope of par-ticular issues. When established authority in governmental jurisdictions is recalcitrant, then such fora may need to be constituted as oppositional democratic spheres. The impact of non-governmental organizations in international politics (highlighted in the discussion of sustainable develop-ment) can be understood in these terms. When it comes to politics above local action, the appropriate organizational form may often be the network, as developed by the environmental justice movement discussed in Chapter 10.

This sort of democracy without boundaries is clearly very different from the institutions established by and in industrial society which still dominate today's world. Yet discourses, including environmental ones, help to consti-tute and re-constitute the world just as surely as do formal institutions or material economic forces. And in this discursive realm, as we have seen, the beginnings of ecological democracy are already present. Environmentalism already flourishes in opposition to industrialism; but much remains to be done if industrial society is ever to give way to ecological society.

References

Abbey, Edward (1975), *The Monkey Wrench Gang*. Philadelphia, Pa.: J. B. Lippincott.

—— (1990), *Hayduke Lives!* Boston, Mass.: Little Brown.

Ackerman, Bruce A. and Hassler, William T. (1981), *Clean Coal, Dirty Air: or How the Clean Air Act became a Multibillion-Dollar Bail-Out for High-Sulfur Coal Producers and What Should Be Done About It*. New Haven, Conn.: Yale University Press.

Alexander, Christopher (1964), *Notes on the Synthesis of Form*. Cambridge, Mass.: Harvard University Press.

Amy, Douglas J. (1987), *The Politics of Environmental Mediation*. New York: Columbia University Press.

—— (1990), "Decision Techniques for Environmental Policy: A Critique," pp. 59–79 in Robert Paehlke and Douglas Torgerson (eds.), *Managing Leviathan: Environmental Politics and the Administrative State*. Peterborough, Ontario: Broadview.

Andersen, Mikael Skou (1994), *Governance by Green Taxes: Making Pollution Prevention Pay*. Manchester: Manchester University Press.

Anderson, Charles W. (1990), *Pragmatic Liberalism*. Chicago, Ill.: University of Chicago Press.

Anderson, Frederick L., Kneese, Allen V., Reed, P. D., Stevenson, R. B., and Taylor, S. (1977), *Environmental Improvement Through Economic Incentives*. Baltimore, Md.: Johns Hopkins University Press for Resources for the Future.

Anderson, Terry L. and Leal, Donald R. (1991), *Free Market Environmentalism*. Boulder, Colo.: Westview.

Arrow, K., Costanza, R., Dasgupta, P., Folke, C., Holling, C. S., Jansson, B. E., Levin, S., Maler, K.-G., Perrings, C., and Pimental, D. (1995), "Economic Growth, Carrying Capacity and the Environment," *Science*, 268: 520–1.

Bahro, Rudolf (1986), *Building the Green Movement*. London: Heretic Books.

Barnet, Richard J. (1980), *The Lean Years: Politics in the Age of Scarcity*. New York: Simon and Schuster.

Barnett, Harold J. and Morse, Chandler (1963), *Scarcity and Growth: The Economics of Natural Resource Availability*. Baltimore: Johns Hopkins University Press for Resources for the Future.

Bartlett, Robert V. (1990), "Ecological Reason in Administration: Environmental Impact Assessment and Administrative Theory," pp. 81–96 in Robert Paehlke and Douglas Torgerson (eds.), *Managing Leviathan: Environmental Politics and the Administrative State*. Peterborough, Ontario: Broadview.

Beck, Ulrich (1992), *Risk Society: Towards a New Modernity*. London: Sage.

—— Giddens, Anthony, and Lash, Scott (1994), *Reflexive Modernization: Politics, Tradition and Aesthetics in the Modern Social Order*. Cambridge: Polity.

Beckerman, Wilfred (1974), *In Defence of Economic Growth*. London: Cape.

—— (1995), *Small is Stupid: Blowing the Whistle on the Greens*. London: Duckworth.

Bennett, Jane and Chaloupka, William (eds.) (1993), *In the Nature of Things: Language, Politics, and the Environment*. Minneapolis, Minn.: University of Minnesota Press.

Benton, Ted (1993), *Natural Relations: Ecology, Animal Rights, and Social Justice*. London: Verso.

Berejikian, Jeffrey (1995), *The Gains Debate: Framing State Choice*. Unpublished Ph.D. dissertation, University of Oregon.

Berger, Thomas (1977), *Northern Frontier, Northern Homeland: Report of the MacKenzie Valley Pipeline Inquiry*. Toronto: James Lorimer.

Biehl, Janet (1991), *Rethinking Ecofeminist Politics*. Boston, Mass.: South End Press.

Bobrow, Davis B. and Dryzek, John S. (1987), *Policy Analysis by Design*. Pittsburgh, Pa.: University of Pittsburgh Press.

Bookchin, Murray (1982), *The Ecology of Freedom: The Emergence and Dissolution of Hierarchy*. Palo Alto, Calif.: Cheshire.

—— (1986), *The Modern Crisis*. Philadelphia, Pa.: New Society.

—— (1990), *Remaking Society: Pathways to a Green Future*. Boston, Mass.: South End Press.

—— and Foreman, Dave (1991), *Defending the Earth*. Boston, Mass.: South End Press.

Boulding, Kenneth R. (1966), "The Economics of the Coming Spaceship Earth," in Henry Jarrett (ed.), *Environmental Quality in a Growing Economy*. Baltimore, Md.: Johns Hopkins University Press.

Bramwell, Anna (1989), *Ecology in the Twentieth Century: A History*. Cambridge: Cambridge University Press.

—— (1994), *The Fading of the Greens: The Decline of Environmental Politics in the West*. New Haven, Conn.: Yale University Press.

Brooks, D. B. (1992), "The Challenge of Sustainability: Is Integrating Environment and Economy Enough?," *Policy Sciences*, 26: 401–8.

Brown, Lester R. (1978), *The Twenty-Ninth Day: Accommodating Human Needs and Numbers to the Earth's Resources*. New York: Norton.

—— (1981), *Building a Sustainable Society*. New York: Norton.

—— Flavin, Christopher, and Postel, Sandra (1992), *Saving the Planet: How to Shape an Environmentally Sustainable Global Economy*. London: Earthscan.

Brown, Phil and Mikkelsen, Edwin J. (1990), *No Safe Place: Toxic Waste, Leukemia, and Community Action*. Berkeley, Calif.: University of California Press.

Caldwell, Lynton K. (1978), "The Environmental Impact Statement: A Misused Tool," in Ravinder Jain and Bruce Hutchings (eds.), *Environmental Impact Analysis*. Urbana, Ill.: University of Illinois Press.

—— (1982), *Science and the National Environmental Policy Act: Redirecting Policy Through Administrative Reform*. Tuscaloosa, Ala.: University of Alabama Press.

—— (1984), "The World Environment: Reversing U.S. Policy Commitments," pp.

319–38 in Norman J. Vig and Michael E. Kraft (eds.), *Environmental Policy in the 1980s: Reagan's New Agenda*. Washington, DC: Congressional Quarterly Press.

Capra, Fritjof and Spretnack, Charlene (1984), *Green Politics: The Global Promise*. New York: E. P. Dutton.

Carlassare, Elizabeth (1994), "Essentialism in Ecofeminist Discourse," *Capitalism, Nature, Socialism*, 5 (3): 1–18.

Catton, William R. (1980), *Overshoot: The Ecological Basis of Revolutionary Change*. Urbana, Ill.: University of Illinois Press.

Chock, Phyllis Pease (1995), "Ambiguity in Policy Discourse: Congressional Talk About Immigration," *Policy Sciences*, 28: 165–84.

Christ, Carol P. (1990), "Rethinking Theology and Nature," pp. 58–69 in Irene Diamond and Gloria Feman Orenstein (eds.), *Reweaving the World: The Emergence of Ecofeminism*. San Francisco, Calif.: Sierra Club Books.

Christoff, Peter (1995), "Whatever Happened to Ecologically Sustainable Development?," *Capucchino Papers* (Australian Conservation Foundation), 1: 69–74."

Christoff, Peter (1996), "Ecological Modernisation, Ecological Modernities," *Environmental Politics*, 5.

Coase, Ronald H. (1960), "The Problem of Social Cost," *Journal of Law and Economics*, 3: 1–44.

Cohen, Bernard L. (1984), Statement of Dissent, p. 556 in Julian L. Simon and Herman Kahn (eds.), *The Resourceful Earth: A Repsonse to Global 2000*. New York: Basil Blackwell.

Coleman, James S. (1986), "Social Theory, Social Research, and a Theory of Action," *American Journal of Sociology*, 91: 1309–35.

Commoner, Barry (1972), *The Closing Circle*. New York: Bantam.

Conca, Ken (1994), "Peace, Justice, and Sustainability," *Newsletter of the Committee on the Political Economy of the Good Society*, 4 (1): 1–7.

Daly, Herman E. (1977), *Steady-State Economics*. San Francisco: W. H. Freeman.

—— (1992), "Free Market Environmentalism: Turning a Good Servant into a Bad Master," *Critical Review*, 6: 171–83.

—— (1993), "Sustainable Growth: An Impossibility Theorem," pp. 267–73 in Herman E. Daly and Kenneth E. Townsend (eds.), *Valuing the Earth: Economics, Ecology, Ethics*. Cambridge, Mass.: MIT Press.

Davis, Karen (1995), "Thinking Like a Chicken: Farm Animals and the Feminine Connection," pp. 192–212 in Carol J. Adams and Josephine Donovan (eds.), *Animals and Women: Feminist Theoretical Explorations*. Durham, NC: Duke University Press.

Department of the Environment (United Kingdom) (1988), *Our Common Future: A Perspective by the United Kingdom on the Report of the World Commission on Environment and Development*. London: HMSO.

Devall, Bill and Sessions, George (1985), *Deep Ecology: Living as if Nature Mattered*. Salt Lake City, Utah: Peregrine Smith.

Diamond, Irene (1994), *Fertile Ground: Women, Fertility, and the Living Earth*. Boston: Beacon.

—— and Feman Orenstein, Gloria (eds.) (1990), *Reweaving the World: The Emergence of Ecofeminism*. San Francisco, Calif.: Sierra Club Books.

DiZerega, Gus (1993), "Unexpected Harmonies: Self-Organization in Liberal Modernity and Ecology," *The Trumpeter*, 10: 25–32.

Dobson, Andrew (1990), *Green Political Thought: An Introduction*. London: Unwin Hyman.

Dowie, Mark (1995), *Losing Ground: American Environmentalism at the Close of the Twentieth Century*. Cambridge, Mass.: MIT Press.

Dryzek, John S. (1987), *Rational Ecology: Environment and Political Economy*. New York: Basil Blackwell.

—— (1988), "The Mismeasure of Political Man," *Journal of Politics*, 50: 705–25.

—— (1990*a*), "Green Reason: Communicative Ethics for the Biosphere," *Environmental Ethics*, 12: 195–210.

—— (1990*b*), *Discursive Democracy: Politics, Policy, and Political Science*. New York: Cambridge University Press.

—— (1992*a*), "The Good Society versus the State: Freedom and Necessity in Political Innovation," *Journal of Politics*, 54: 518–40.

—— (1992*b*), "How far is it From Virginia and Rochester to Frankfurt? Public Choice as Critical Theory," *British Journal of Political Science*, 22: 397–417.

—— (1992*c*), "Ecology and Discursive Democracy: Beyond Liberal Capitalism and the Administrative State," *Capitalism, Nature, Socialism*, 3 (2): 18–42.

—— (1995), "The Informal Logic of Institutional Design," pp. 103–25 in Robert E. Goodin (ed.), *The Theory of Institutional Design*. New York: Cambridge University Press.

—— (1996*a*), *Democracy in Capitalist Times: Ideals, Limits, and Struggles*. New York: Oxford University Press.

—— (1996*b*), "Foundations for Environmental Political Economy: The Search for Homo Ecologicus?," *New Political Economy*, 1: 27–40.

—— (1996*c*), "Political and Ecological Communication," pp. 13–30 in Freya Mathews (ed.), *Ecology and Democracy*. London: Frank Cass.

—— (1996*d*), "Strategies of Ecological Democratization," pp. 108–23 in William M. Lafferty and James Meadowcroft (eds.), *Democracy and the Environment: Problems and Prospects*. Cheltenham: Edward Elgar.

Eckersley, Robyn (1992), *Environmentalism and Political Theory: Toward an Ecocentric Approach*. Albany, NY: State University of New York Press.

—— (ed.) (1995), *Markets, the State and the Environment: Towards Integration*. Melbourne: Macmillan.

Ehrlich, Paul (1968), *The Population Bomb*. New York: Ballantine.

—— and Ehrlich, Anne H. (1974), *The End of Affluence: A Blueprint for Your Future*. New York: Ballantine.

Elgin, Duane (1982), *Voluntary Simplicity: An Ecological Lifestyle that Promotes Personal and Social Renewal*. New York: Bantam.

Faber, Daniel and O'Connor, James (1989), "The Struggle for Nature:

Environmental Crisis and the Crisis of Environmentalism in the United States," *Capitalism, Nature, Socialism*, 2: 12–39.

Fiorino, Daniel J. (1995), *Making Environmental Policy*. Berkeley, Calif.: University of California Press.

Fischer, Frank (1993), "Citizen Participation and the Democratization of Policy Expertise: From Theoretical Inquiry to Practical Cases," *Policy Sciences*, 26: 165–87.

Fischoff, Baruch, Slovic, Paul, and Lichtenstein, Sarah (1982), "Lay Fables and Expert Foibles in Judgments About Risk," *American Statistician*, 36: 240–55.

Foreman, Dave (1985), *Ecodefense: A Field Guide to Monkeywrenching*. Tucson, Ariz.: Ned Ludd Books.

—— (1991), Contribution to Murray Bookchin and Dave Foreman, *Defending the Earth: A Dialogue Between Murray Bookchin and Dave Foreman*. Boston, Mass.: South End Press.

Foucault, Michel (1980), *Power/Knowledge: Selected Interviews and Other Writings, 1972–1977*. Brighton: Harvester.

Fox, Warwick (1984), "On Guiding Stars to Deep Ecology: A Reply to Naess," *The Ecologist*, 14: 203–4.

—— (1990), *Toward a Transpersonal Ecology: Developing New Foundations for Environmentalism*. Boston, Mass.: Shambhala.

Freeman, Christopher (1973), "Malthus with a Computer," in H. S. D. Cole, C. Freeman, M. Jahoda, and K. L. R. Pravitts (eds.), *Models of Doom: A Critique of The Limits to Growth*. New York: Universe.

Fukuyama, Francis (1989), "The End of History?," *National Interest*, Summer, 3–18.

—— (1992), *The End of History and the Last Man*. New York: Free Press.

Garner, Robert (1993), *Animals, Politics and Morality*. Manchester: Manchester University Press.

Georgescu-Roegen, Nicholas (1971), *The Entropy Law and the Economic Process*. Cambridge, Mass.: Harvard University Press.

Gerth, H. H., and Wright Mills, C. (1948), *From Max Weber: Essays in Sociology*. London: Routledge and Kegan Paul.

Goodin, Robert E. (1992), *Green Political Theory*. Cambridge: Polity.

—— (1994), "Selling Environmental Indulgences," *Kyklos*, 47: 573–95.

Gordon, H. Scott (1954), "The Economic Theory of a Common-Property Resource: The Fishery," *Journal of Political Economy*, 62: 124–42.

Gore, Albert (1992), *Earth in the Balance*. Boston: Houghton Mifflin.

Gottleib, Roger S. (ed.) (1996), *This Sacred Earth: Religion, Nature, Environment*. New York: Routledge.

Gregg, Alan (1955), "A Medical Aspect of the Population Problem," *Science*, 121: 681–2.

Gundersen, Adolf (1995), *The Environmental Promise of Democratic Deliberation*. Madison, Wis.: University of Wisconsin Press.

Haas, Peter M. (1992), "Banning Chlorofluorocarbons: Efforts to Protect Stratospheric Ozone," *International Organization*, 46: 187–224.

—— Keohane, Robert O., and Levy, Marc A. (1993), *Institutions for the Earth: Sources of Effective Environmental Protection*. Cambridge, Mass.: MIT Press.

Hahn, Robert W. (1995), "Economic Prescriptions for Environmental Policy Instruments: Lessons from the United States and Continental Europe," pp. 129–56 in Robyn Eckersley (ed.), *Markets, the State, and the Environment: Towards Integration*. Melbourne: Macmillan.

Hajer, Maarten A. (1993), "Discourse Coalitions and the Institutionalization of Practice: The Case of Acid Rain in Great Britain," pp. 43–76 in Frank Fischer and John Forester (eds.), *The Argumentative Turn in Policy Analysis and Planning*. Durham, NC: Duke University Press.

—— (1995), *The Politics of Environmental Discourse: Ecological Modernization and the Policy Process*. Oxford: Oxford University Press.

Hardin, Garrett (1968), "The Tragedy of the Commons," *Science*, 162: 1243–8.

—— (1977), "Living on a Lifeboat," pp. 261–79 in Garrett Hardin and John Baden (eds.), *Managing the Commons*. San Francisco, Calif.: W. H. Freeman.

—— (1993), *Living Within Limits: Ecology, Economics, and Population Taboos*. New York: Oxford University Press.

Hayek, Friedrich A. von (1979), *Law, Legislation, and Liberty: The Political Order of a Free People*. Chicago: University of Chicago Press.

Hays, Samuel P. (1959), *Conservation and The Gospel of Efficiency: The Progressive Conservation Movement, 1890–1920*. Cambridge, Mass.: Harvard University Press.

—— (1987), *Beauty, Health, and Permanence: Environmental Politics in the United States, 1955–1985*. Cambridge: Cambridge University Press.

Hayward, Tim (1995), *Ecological Thought: An Introduction*. Cambridge: Polity.

Heilbroner, Robert (1991), *An Inquiry into the Human Prospect: Looked at Again for the 1990s*. New York: Norton.

Huber, Joseph (1982), *Die verlorene Unschuld der Okologie*. Frankfurt am Main: Fischer Verlag.

Inglehart, Ronald (1990), *Culture Shift in Advanced Industrial Society*. Princeton, NJ: Princeton University Press.

International Union for the Conservation of Nature (1980), *World Conservation Strategy*. Gland, Switzerland: International Union for the Conservation of Nature.

—— United Nations Environment Program, and World Wildlife Fund (1991), *Caring for the Earth: A Strategy for Sustainable Living*. Gland, Switzerland: International Union for the Conservation of Nature.

Jacobs, Michael (1991), *The Green Economy: Environment, Sustainable Development and the Politics of the Future*. London: Pluto.

Jacobs, Michael (1995), "Financial Incentives: The British Experience," pp. 113–28 in Robyn Eckersley (ed.), *Markets, the State, and the Environment: Towards Integration*. Melbourne: Macmillan.

Jänicke, Martin (1985), *Preventive Environmental Policy as Ecological Modernization and Structural Policy*. Berlin: Wissenschaftszentrum.

Jänicke, Martin (1992), "Conditions for Environmental Policy Success: An International Comparison," *The Environmentalist*, 12: 47–58.

—— (1996), "Democracy as a Condition for Environmental Policy Success: The Importance of Non-Institutional Factors," pp. 71–85 in William M. Lafferty and James Meadowcroft (eds.), *Democracy and the Environment: Problems and Prospects*. Cheltenham: Edward Elgar.

Jevons, W. Stanley (1865), *The Coal Question*. London: Macmillan.

Kelman, Steven (1981), *What Price Incentives? Economists and the Environment*. Boston: Auburn House.

—— (1987), *Making Public Policy: A Hopeful View of American Government*. New York: Basic Books.

Kemp, Ray (1985), "Planning, Public Hearings, and the Politics of Discourse," pp. 177–201 in John Forester (ed.), *Critical Theory and Public Life*. Cambridge, Mass.: MIT Press.

Kheel, Marti (1990), "Ecofeminism and Deep Ecology: Reflections on Identity and Difference," pp. 128–37 in Irene Diamond and Gloria Feman Orenstein (eds.), *Reweaving the World: The Emergence of Ecofeminism*. San Francisco, Calif.: Sierra Club Books.

Kneese, Allen V., and Schultze, Charles L. (1975), *Pollution, Prices, and Public Policy*. Washington, DC: Brookings.

La Chapelle, Dolores (1978), *Earth Wisdom*. San Diego, Calif.: Guild of Tudors.

Lafferty, William (1996), "The Politics of Sustainable Development," *Environmental Politics*, 5.

Lee, Kai N. (1993), *Compass and Gyroscope: Integrating Science and Politics for the Environment*. Washington, DC: Island Press.

Lehmbruch, Gerhard (1984), "Concertation and the Structure of Corporatist Networks," in John H. Goldthorpe (ed.), *Order and Conflict in Conetemporay Capitalism*.Oxford: Clarendon.

Levine, Robert A. (1972), *Public Planning: Failure and Redirection*. New York: Basic Books.

Lewis, Martin W. (1992), *Green Delusions: An Environmentalist Critique of Radical Environmentalism*. Durham, NC: Duke University Press.

Light, Andrew, and Katz, Eric (1996), *Environmental Pragmatism*. London: Routledge.

Lindblom, Charles E. (1959), "The Science of Muddling Through," *Public Administration Review*, 19: 79–88.

—— (1965), *The Intelligence of Democracy: Decision Making through Mutual Adjustment*. New York: Free Press.

—— (1977), *Politics and Markets: The World's Political-Economic Systems*. New York: Basic Books.

—— (1982), "The Market as Prison," *Journal of Politics*, 44: 324–36.

Litfin, Karen T. (1994), *Ozone Discourses: Science and Politics in Global Environmental Cooperation*. New York: Columbia University Press.

Lovelock, James E. (1979), *Gaia: A New Look at Life on Earth*. Oxford: Oxford University Press.

Ludwig, Donald, Hilborn, Ray, and Walters, Carl (1993), "Uncertainty, Resource Expolitation, and Conservation: Lessons from History," *Science*, 260.

Luke, Timothy (1995), "Ecocritics and Ecocritique: Contesting the Politics of Nature, Economy, and Culture," draft manuscript.

McFarland, Andrew (1984), "An Experiment in Regulatory Negotiation: The National Coal Policy Project," paper presented at the Annual Meeting of the Western Political Science Association.

McPhee, John (1970), *Encounters with the Archdruid*. New York: Farrar, Straus, and Giroux.

Manes, Christopher (1990), *Green Rage: Radical Environmentalism and the Unmaking of Civilization*. Boston, Mass.: Little Brown.

Meadows, Donella H. (1976), "Equity, The Free Market, and the Sustainable State," in Dennis L. Meadows (ed.), *Alternatives to Growth, I: Toward a Sustainable Future*. Cambridge, Mass.: Ballinger.

—— Meadows, Dennis L., Randers, Jorgen, and Behrens, William H. III (1972), *The Limits to Growth*. New York: Universe Books.

—— Meadows, Dennis L., and Randers, Jorgen (1992), *Beyond the Limits: Confronting Global Collapse, Envisioning a Sustainable Future*. Post Mills, Vt.: Chelsea Green.

Meiners, Roger E., and Yandle, Bruce (1993), "Taking the Environment Seriously: What Do We Mean?," pp. vii–xiv in Roger E. Meiners and Bruce Yandle (eds.), *Taking the Environment Seriously*. Lanham, Md.: Rowman and Littlefield.

Merchant, Carolyn (1992), *Radical Ecology*. London: Routledge.

Michaels, Patrick J. (1993), "Global Warming: Facts vs. The Popular Vision," 341–62 in David Boaz and Edward H. Crane (eds.), *Market Liberalism: A Paradigm for the 21st Century*. Washington, DC: Cato Institute.

Milbrath, Lester W. (1989), *Envisioning a Sustainable Society: Learning Our Way Out*. Albany, NY: State University of New York Press.

Mitchell, William C. and Simmons, Randy T. (1994), *Beyond Politics: Markets, Welfare, and the Failure of Bureaucracy*. Boulder, Colo.: Westview.

Mol, Arthur P. J. (1996), "Ecological Modernisation and Institutional Reflexivity: Environmental Reform in the Late Modern Age," *Environmental Politics*, 5: 302–23.

Moran, Alan (1995), "Tools for Environmental Policy: Market Instruments versus Command-and-Control," pp. 73–85 in Robyn Eckersley (ed.), *Markets, the State, and the Environment: Towards Integration*. Melbourne: Macmillan.

Mosher, Lawrence (1983), "Distrust of Gorsuch May Stymie EPA Attempt to Integrate Pollution Wars," *National Journal*, 15: 322–4.

Murphy, E. F. (1967), *Governing Nature*. Chicago, Ill.: Quadrangle Books.

Myers, Norman, and Simon, Julian L. (1994), *Scarcity or Abundance: A Debate on the Environment*. New York: Norton.

Naess, Arne (1973), "The Shallow and the Deep, Long-Range Ecology Movement: A Summary," *Inquiry*, 16: 95–100.

—— (1989), *Ecology, Community and Lifestyle*. Cambridge: Cambridge University Press.

Nef, John U. (1977), "An Early Energy Crisis and its Consequences," *Scientific American*, 237: 140–51.

Nelkin, Dorothy and Pollack, Michael (1981), *The Atom Besieged*. Cambridge, Mass.: MIT Pess.

Nelson, Robert H. (1993), "How Much is Enough? An Overview of the Benefits and Costs of Environmental Protection," pp. 1–23 in Roger E. Meiners and Bruce Yandle (eds.), *Taking the Environment Seriously*. Lanham, Md.: Rowman and Littlefield.

Nisbet, Robert (1974), *The Social Philosophers: Community and Conflict in Western Thought*. London: Heinemann.

O'Connor, James (1988), "Capitalism, Nature, Socialism: A Theoretical Introduction," *Capitalism, Nature, Socialism*, 1: 11–38.

Offe, Claus (1985), "New Social Movements: Challenging the Boundaries of Institutional Politics," *Social Research*, 52: 817–68

—— (1990), "Reflections on the Institutional Self-Transformation of Movement Politics: A Tentative Stage Model," pp. 232–50 in Russell J. Dalton and Manfred Kuechler (eds.), *Challenging the Political Order: New Social and Political Movements in Western Democracies*. New York: Oxford University Press.

Olson, Mancur (1965), *The Logic of Collective Action*. Cambridge, Mass.: Harvard University Press.

Ophuls, William (1977), *Ecology and the Politics of Scarcity*. San Francisco, Calif.: W. H. Freeman.

—— and Stephen Boyan, A., Jr. (1992), *Ecology and the Politics of Scarcity Revisited*. San Francisco: W. H. Freeman.

Opschoor, J. B., and Vos, H. (1988), *The Application of Economic Instruments for Environmental Protection in OECD Member Countries*. Paris: OECD.

Organization for Economic Cooperation and Development (1989), *Economic Instruments for Environmental Protection*. Paris: OECD.

—— (1991), *OECD Environmental Data 1991*. Paris: OECD.

Ostrom, Elinor (1990), *Governing the Commons*. Cambridge: Cambridge University Press.

Paehlke, Robert (1988), "Democracy, Bureaucracy, and Environmentalism," *Environmental Ethics*, 10: 291–308.

Pearce, David, Markandya, Anil, and Barbier, Edward R. (1989), *Blueprint for a Green Economy*. London: Earthscan.

Peccei, Aurelio (1981), *One Hundred Pages for the Future*. New York: Mentor.

Pickel, Andreas (1993), "Authoritarianism or Democracy? Marketization as a Political Problem," *Policy Sciences*, 26: 139–63.

Plant, Judith (ed.) (1989), *Healing the Wounds: The Promise of Ecofeminism*. Philadelphia, Pa.: New Society Publishers.

Plumwood, Val (1993), *Feminism and the Mastery of Nature*. London: Routledge.

—— (1995), "Has Democracy Failed Ecology? An Ecofeminist Perspective," *Environmental Politics*, 4 (4): 134–68.

Popper, Karl R. (1966), *The Open Society and its Enemies*. London: Routledge and Kegan Paul.

—— (1972), *The Poverty of Historicism*, revised edition. London: Routledge and Kegan Paul.

Porritt, Jonathan (1986), *Seeing Green: The Politics of Ecology Explained*. Oxford: Basil Blackwell.

Press, Daniel (1994), *Democratic Dilemmas in the Age of Ecology: Trees and Toxics in the American West*. Durham, NC: Duke University Press.

Press, F., and Atiyah, M. (1992), *Joint Statement on Biodiversity*. Washington, DC and London: National Academy of Sciences and Royal Society.

Pressman, Jeffrey and Wildavsky, Aaron (1973), *Implementation*. Berkeley, Calif.: University of California Press.

Rabe, Barry G. (1991), "Beyond the Nimby Syndrome in Hazardous Waste Facility Siting: The Albertan Breakthrough and the Prospects for Cooperation in Canada and the United States," *Governance*, 4: 184–206.

Regan, Tom (1983), *The Case for Animal Rights*. Berkeley, Calif.: University of California Press.

Reisner, Marc (1993), *Cadillac Desert: The American West and its Disappearing Water*, rev. edn. New York: Penguin.

Richardson, Dick (1994), "The Politics of Sustainable Development," paper presented to the International Conference on the Politics of Sustainable Development within the European Union, University of Crete, Greece.

Ridley, Matt (1995), *Down to Earth: A Contrarian View of Environmental Problems*. London: Institute of Economic Affairs.

Roodman, David Malin (1996), "Harnessing the Market for the Environment," pp. 168–87 in Lester R. Brown (ed.), *State of the World 1996*. New York: W. W. Norton.

Rosenbaum, Walter A. (1985), *Environmental Politics and Policy*. Washington, DC: Congressional Quarterly Press.

—— (1995), "The Bureaucracy and Environmental Policy," pp. 206–41 in James P. Lester (ed.), *Environmental Politics and Policy: Theories and Evidence*, 2nd edn. Durham, NC: Duke University Press.

Roszak, Theodore (1979), *Person/Planet: The Creative Disintegration of Industrial Society*. London: Victor Gollancz.

Rowell, Andrew (1996), *Green Backlash: Global Subversion of the Environmental Movement*. London: Routledge.

Russell, Julia Scofield (1990), "The Evolution of an Ecofeminist," pp. 223–30 in Irene Diamond and Gloria Feman Orenstein (eds.), *Reweaving the World: The Emergence of Ecofeminism*. San Francisco: Sierra Club Books.

Ryle, Martin (1988), *Ecology and Socialism*. London: Century Hutchinson.

Sagoff, Mark (1988), *The Economy of the Earth*. Cambridge: Cambridge University Press.

Sale, Kirkpatrick (1985), *Dwellers in the Land: The Bioregional Vision*. San Francisco: Sierra Club Books.

Schmidheiny, Stephan (1992), *Changing Course: A Global Business Perspective on Development and the Environment*. Cambridge, Mass.: MIT Press.

Schlosberg, David (1996), "Diversity, Action, and Participation in the U.S. Environmental Movement: The Case for a Critical Pluralism," unpublished Ph.D. diss., University of Oregon.

Schmitt, Carl (1986), *Political Romanticism*. Cambridge, Mass.: MIT Press.

Schumacher, E. F. (1973), *Small is Beautiful: Economics as if People Mattered*. New York: Harper and Row.

Shiva, Vandana (1989), *Staying Alive: Women, Ecology and Development*. London: Zed Books.

Simon, Herbert A. (1981), *The Sciences of the Artificial*, 2nd edn. Cambridge, Mass.: MIT Press.

Simon, Julian (1981), *The Ultimate Resource*. Princeton, NJ: Princeton University Press.

—— and Kahn, Herman (eds.) (1984), *The Resourceful Earth: A Response to Global 2000*. New York: Basil Blackwell.

Singer, Peter (1975), *Animal Liberation*. New York: Avon.

Smith, V. Kerry (ed.) (1979), *Scarcity and Growth Reconsidered*. Baltimore, Md.: Johns Hopkins University Press for Resources for the Future.

Spretnack, Charlene (1986), *The Spiritual Dimension of Green Politics*. Santa Fe, NMex.: Bear and Co.

Starhawk (1987), *Truth or Dare: Encounters with Power, Authority and Mystery*. San Francisco: Harper and Row.

Stretton, Hugh (1976), *Capitalism, Socialism, and the Environment*. Cambridge: Cambridge University Press.

Stroup, Richard L., and Shaw, Jane S. (1993), "Environmental Harms from Federal Government Policy," pp. 51–72 in Roger E. Meiners and Bruce Yandle (eds.), *Taking the Environment Seriously*. Lanham, Md.: Rowman and Littlefield.

Sugden, Robert, and Williams, Alan (1978), *The Principles of Practical Cost-Benefit Analysis*. Oxford: Oxford University Press.

Szasz, Andrew (1994), *Ecopopulism: Toxic Waste and the Movement for Environmental Justice*. Minneapolis, Minn.: University of Minnesota Press.

Taylor, Bob Pepperman (1992), *Our Limits Transgressed*. Lawrence, Kan.: University Press of Kansas.

Taylor, Jerry (1993), "The Growing Abundance of Natural Resources," pp. 363–78 in David Boaz and Edward H. Crane (eds.), *Market Liberalism: A Paradigm for the 21st Century*. Washington, DC: Cato Institute.

Tesh, Sylvia N. (1993), "New Social Movements and New Ideas," paper presented at the Annual Meeting of the American Political Science Association, Washington, DC, 2–5 Sept.

Thompson, Michael (1993), "The Meaning of Sustainable Development," paper presented to the Conference on Global Governability, London School of Economics.

Torgerson, Douglas (1990), "Limits of the Administrative Mind: The Problem of Defining Environmental Problems," pp. 115–61 in Robert Paehlke and Douglas Torgerson (eds.), *Managing Leviathan: Environmental Politics and the Administrative State*. Peterborough, Ontario: Broadview.

—— (1994), "Strategy and Ideology in Environmentalism: A Decentered Approach to Sustainability," *Industrial and Environmental Crisis Quarterly*, 8: 295–321.

—— (1995), "The Uncertain Quest for Sustainability: Public Discourse and the Politics of Environmentalism," pp. 3–20 in Frank Fischer and Michael Black (eds.), *Greening Environmental Policy: The Politics of a Sustainable Future*. Liverpool: Paul Chapman.

—— and Paehlke, Robert (1990), "Environmental Administration: Revising the Agenda of Inquiry and Practice," pp. 7–16 in Robert Paehlke and Douglas Torgerson (eds.), *Managing Leviathan: Environmental Politics and the Administrative State*. Peterborough, Ontario: Broadview.

Vig, Norman J., and Kraft, Michael E. (1984), *Environmental Policy in the 1980s: Reagan's New Agenda*. Washington, DC: Congressional Quarterly Press.

Vogel, David (1986), *National Styles of Regulation: Environmental Policy in Great Britain and the United States*. Ithaca, NY: Cornell University Press.

Wapner, Paul (1996), *Environmental Activism and World Civic Politics*. Albany, NY: State University of New York Press.

Weale, Albert (1992), *The New Politics of Pollution*. Manchester: Manchester University Press.

White, Lynn, Jr. (1967), "The Historical Roots of our Ecologic Crisis," *Science*, 155: 1203–7.

White, Rob (1994), "Green Politics and the Question of Population," *Journal of Australian Studies*, 40: 27–43.

Wiesenthal, Herbert (1993), *Realism in Green Politics: Social Movements and Ecological Reform in Germany*. New York: St. Martin's.

Wildavsky, Aaron (1988), *The New Politics of the Budgetary Process*. Boston: Little Brown.

—— (1995), *But Is It True? A Citizen's Guide to Environmental Health and Safety Issues*. Cambridge, Mass.: Harvard University Press.

Williams, Bruce A. and Matheny, Albert R. (1995), *Democracy, Dialogue, and Environmental Disputes: The Contested Languages of Social Regulation*. New Haven, Conn.: Yale University Press.

World Bank (1995), *Monitoring Environmental Progress*. Washington, DC: The World Bank.

World Commission on Environment and Development (1987), *Our Common Future*. Oxford: Oxford University Press.

Yandle, Bruce (1993), "Community Markets to Control Nonpoint Source Pollution," pp. 185–207 in Roger E. Meiners and Bruce Yandle (eds.), *Taking the Environment Seriously*. Lanham, Md.: Rowman and Littlefield.

Index